The Ancient

Brinkmann

Brinkmann Family - German Coat of Arms

Photo Source: Google-Panoramio-RYDOJ-Brazil.

Panoramic Destiny

There are many trees of life,
The seeds of which have little choice,
Some long lived, some short.
The fruit can be sweet, or tart.
Death can swing from its branches.
Life can begin in their dead ashes.
One thing is certain.
It all ends, when time comes calling.

Alvin Von Brinkenhausen

A History of the Brinkmann Family & Other Ancestors:

Volume One
The Long Journey

Table of Contents

Introduction

A *History of The Brinkmann Family & Other Ancestors: Volume 1, The Long Journey* presents the known written and oral history of the early European Brinkmann family and explores information obtained from documents discovered during genealogy research. I begin this book with a Brinkmann surname review, then a brief historical summary of European and German history (which includes major wars, outcomes, photographs, and a history of the glass industry in Germany). This is followed by a detailed Brinkmann Descendants List containing known Brinkmann family members (as of the date of this edition's publication). Next detailed are individual ancestors' family histories, photographs, and documents. Included are notes about the research process, life stories submitted by family members, comments from contributors, timeline historical notations, and elements of human emotions (such as stories about who we were, how we struggled, and what we became). I have included references for all known records and reported all publicly documented historical events. I ask the reader to make the final decision as to the ultimate credibility of the information contained herein. History is not always kind, nor is it always accurate. I have done my best to be truthful, and to separate what I know to be the official record from written and oral family history elements.

Family is more than appreciating the loved ones we presently know. We are all a product of our ancestors and our very existence is dependent upon the success and courageous efforts of all those who walked this earth before us. Respect for one's family history is an important part of our human evolution. Writing this book has been a great adventure for me, as I found my way back into our family's history and can now celebrate the richness of our unique cultures, our distinct diversities, and our precious family life stories.

This book is the culmination of several years of research that have been joyful, arduous, and epic in its reach over many family generations. It is my sincere hope that everyone will find a way to add his or her own important and personal life stories to this family history collection.

Acknowledgments

In many ways, this book could not have been written without the previous family genealogy records originally gathered and compiled by Elsie Louise (Brinkman) Mertig and the generous help and assistance of the following:

Alvin Carl Herman Brinkman
Tiger Nicholas Young
Natalie (Weiss) Frese
Irene Mae (Parson) Brinkman
Doris (Brinkman) Taylor
Clara (Klein) Behr
Lynda (Klein) Kehrein
Donna (Behrens) Kuhls
Virginia Ruth (Brinkman) Conrad
Janet (Gorsline) Brinkman
Rose (Frese) Brinkman
Marilyn Ruth Ann (Boevers) Brinkman
Martin J. Kehrein
Mildred (Klein) Becker
Ann Hermine (Brinkman) Wolfram
Robert Adolph Brinkman
Margaret Rose (Brinkman) Eannelli
Diane Joy (Brinkman) Zimmerman
Renee (Brinkman) Kealey
Ruth (Benson) Hefty
Lois (Case) Macke
Patricia (Hahn) Bugalski
Jens Thomas Kaufmann
Rodney W. Frese
Richard D. Brinkman
Laura Marie (Brinkman) Roehl
Beverly Vaillancourt
June (Thompson) Ambro
Millie (Behr) Becker
Joanne (Behr) Stucky
-and-
Everyone else who has contributed to this family history

Chapter One

Brinkmann Surname History
Early Russian History
Early German History
German Kings & Kingdoms
Modern German History
World War I
World War II
The Reorganization of Germany

Brinkmann Surname History

Origin of the Brinkmann Surname

The Brinkmann surname derived from the Middle German word *Brink,* meaning "meadow" or "pasture." The word Brink in North German, and in the Dutch, Danish, and Swedish languages, means "lived by a pasture, or green place." In Middle Low German, Brink and Brinkmann mean "edge," slope, grazing land," and especially a "raised meadow in low-lying marshland." In Swedish, Brink is a "waterside slope," and in Danish it means "where the water runs deep." The original German Brinkmann surname is from the Rhineland region of Germany where the rivers are vast, supporting productive fertile croplands and providing major water transportation routes that helped make the German Rhineland a dominant force in European history.

Use of "von," or "Von," in a surname

Originally, many German family surnames were preceded by "von" which had nothing to do with nobility, but rather was part of the original name-creation process. When these original surnames were developing, some were based solely on the family's place of origin and "von" meant "from." Someone could have been "von Essen" (meaning the person came originally from Essen, Germany). These name variations are common in genealogy research regarding German surnames. However,"Von" was also used as a title to indicate that a certain status was associated with a family's surname. Titles of nobility (such as Von and Baron) in Germany could not be sold legally but could be transferred from one family to another under special circumstances.

Brinkmann Surname Spelling Variations

Research regarding the history of any family's surnames reveals that they often undergo major changes over time. German names frequently have elements added to their stem to tell something of the person's place of origin, character, or religious beliefs. Because few ordinary people could read, spell, or write, church scribes often recorded the spelling of names based on how they sounded. Hence the spelling would often vary from region to region. It was not until around 1950 that different spellings were commonly interchanged for some German given names (first names) and surnames (last names). The capital letter "K," for example, was introduced late in the 19th century in many given names (such as Carl or Karl and Catherine or Katherine). The same principle applies to the use of the letters "d," "dt," "nn," or "n," at the end of surnames (such as Hildebrand or Hildebrandt and Brinkmann or Brinkman).

Note: Some of the many historical variations of the Brinkmann surname include Brink, Brinker, Brinck, Brincke, Brinkman, Brinckmann, Brinckman, Brinckemann, and Brinckeman. Unless otherwise specified herein, the known surname Brinkmann will be used in this reference book.

Ancient Brinkmann Surname History

The Rhineland region is where the surname Brinkmann has its most ancient origin and is referred to as the "birthplace of Germany's recorded history." The romantic Rhine River has been immortalized in songs such as "Die Lorelei" and the medieval epic "Song of the Nibelungen." The word Rhine means "big river" in the Celtic language, and the river is often referred to as the "Father Rhine." It was once the centerpiece of the European transportation network. The region has long been the site of struggles between many European nations (each hoping to gain control over this rich industrial and agricultural territory). In early German history, domination of the Rhineland initially alternated between the Franks and the Alemanni tribes. The Romans, under Caesar Augustus, occupied all the territories west of the Rhine River and south of the Danube River. In 1500 B.C. Caesar Augustus founded Germany's oldest city, Trier. It was named after the Germanic tribe of the Treverer. This city became the capital of Western Rome in the third and fourth centuries.

The surname Brinkmann first appeared in the Rhineland region of Germany during the Middle Ages (5th-15th centuries). The family became a prominent contributor to the area's development. Always notable in social affairs, the Brinkmann surname became an integral part of this turbulent region and later emerged to form alliances with other families within the feudal system and the Germanic Nations.

After the fall of the Eastern Roman Empire, tribes (who had invaded and occupied the lower Rhine in the third century) conquered the Rhineland and continued their expansion into Gaul (now known as France). Charlemagne (the Holy Roman Emperor) chose the city of Aachen as his capital; he was later buried there. The cities of the Rhine (be they founded by the Catholic Church or feudal dynasties) were recognized for their steadfast desire for independence, although they associated with the economically advantageous Hanseatic League. The Rhine region was then the center of the Holy Roman Empire. After the division of Charlemagne's empire, in 870, the Rhineland became (by treaty) part of the Eastern Frankish kingdom (under Louis the German). However, access and control of the Rhine had long been the objective of the West Frankish tribes of France, and it is not surprising that numerous battles were fought for control of the territory.

The current surname spelling of Brinkmann (or Brinkman) are mostly a northern German name. Some very early surname spellings were Brinkeman (around 1334), Bringke (around 1421), and then Brinkmann (around 1428). Later, bearers of the surname Brinkmann moved to the Rhine region, which is currently one of the most common locations of the Brinkmann family name. The Brinkmann name has flourished for several centuries throughout the early Middle Ages. Later (around the middle of the 16th century), the Brinkmann family surname began migrating to other parts of Europe (such as East Prussia and the Grand Duchy of Posen) as Brinkmann family members pursued their interests in the military, the church, or politics. Planned marriages at this time were socially and economically advantageous, and very common; for example, the Brinkmanns intermarried with the von Motz and von der Osten-Sacken families. Later, around 1835, the Brinkmann surname of some family lines achieved the distinction of being elevated to the rank of Baron.

Note: Please keep this Brinkmann surname nobility legend in mind when you consider some of the recorded Brinkmann written family history within this book. The written Brinkmann family history has several references to the name Von Brinkenhausen as being part of the heritage. It would be great if this were easy to verify. However, as of 2014, no Brinkmann family ancestors in this Brinkmann family line have been documented as nobility, and the surname Von Brinkenhausen has not been documented in any search of any historical records in Germany (as far back as the 1700s).

Elsie Louise Brinkman's Family History & Stories of German Nobility
Elsie Louise (Brinkman) Mertig (1912-1980) was the Brinkmann family historian of her generation. Elsie noted in her written Brinkmann family history that Karl Von Brinkenhausen was "once a wealthy man with a large estate, many farm servants, and the German title of nobility represented by the "Von" in front of his family surname 'Von Brinkenhausen.' Elsie also noted that Karl Von Brinkenhausen transferred his nobility title to a German Army officer (around 1837) so that he could feed his family and farm laborers. A period of famine came to Germany after several wars that weakened the German economy and seriously diminished the Von Brinkenhausen family fortune. This nobility claim is cited in this book not only because it is part of the written Brinkmann family history record, but also because it has a story to tell that makes for good conversation. As of 2014, no evidence has been discovered to support this claim of nobility.

Note: It is fairly common for immigrants of European descent to make unsupported claims of nobility within their written family histories and oral stories. Elsie is said to have gathered old family papers and saved them for her records, and she provided the main foundation for all future written Brinkmann family history records. Elsie's written Brinkmann family history listed all known ascending Brinkmann family surname members, their spouses, and their children. The majority of this original written Brinkmann family history information turned out to be very accurate. New genealogy research (in Germany and America) has revealed many new Brinkmann ancestors and has also refined the genealogy data of known existing Brinkmann family surname members. This book contains the revised Brinkmann family history to date, which reflects all newly discovered information documented by original German or American vital records and other citations as described herein.

Name Changes in America
The idea that made America unique was the opportunity for people to live in a state of nature (a society of farmers whose perception of "truth" is unfettered by ancient social and political convention) which lies at the base of Jeffersonian Democratic Theory. The "New World" became a place for humanity to begin again. A place where every man and woman could be reborn and re-create themselves. In such circumstances the adoption of a new given and surname is not surprising. It was also not unusual in the cases of immigrants who came to America after having abandoned their spouses and families in their homeland, or for those who immigrated to escape conscription in a European army. There were many reasons, both political and practical, to take a new name.

A newspaper in California once ran a story of a Vietnamese immigrant with a long Vietnamese name. This young man came to America to work and study. He began every day by stopping at a convenience store to buy a Bonus Pack of chewing gum. Chewing all those sticks of gum got him through long days of working several jobs and studying English at night. When he was finally naturalized as a U.S. citizen he requested his name be changed to "Don Bonus," the surname taken from the Bonus Pack. Following his name change he essentially became a "new man." This newspaper story helps one understand the name change process in America during this period of immigration. Mr. Bonus's naturalization papers would simply, and without further legal requirements, record the name change, but not the reasons behind it. If Mr. Bonus had not changed his name then his family descendants, generations later, would not be at a loss as to explain why they cannot find their family name in historic records.

Note: Surname evolutions can be a big problem in genealogy research. If your surname is known, and traceable in history, you should be grateful that your surname is not a "Bonus" (a situation where the name is lost in time and not easily trace to its ancestors). In a broader sense the term Anglicized is often used to characterize a name change from one language into a more understandable English form. This process is defined as "to make English, as to customs, culture, pronunciation, spelling, or style." This surname phenomenon is also called Americanization and was most common during the eighteenth and nineteenth centuries as many European immigrants were coming to America (especially if the immigration was occurring during, or soon after, times of war in Europe). There are may given and surname changes noted in this Brinkmann family history.

The European and North American Continents in the 19th Century
The 19th century was an important time of massive global population shifts that led to an evolutionary change in global thinking. The invention of the steam ship was followed by massive rates of immigrations by people with minimal resources but plenty of desire. Countries like the United States and Canada opened their doors and made it possible for Europeans to find a new home for expressing their religious views, and gave them a place to stake their own claim and own their own land. The idea that land could be owned for the price of hard work was appealing all over the world, and when the gates opened, they were flooded with believers from all nations.

German Civil Registry and Vital Records
The German Civil Registry (official agencies charged with the responsibility of keeping all vital records in Germany) first began (geographically speaking) in what was known as Prussia in the late 1870s when the old hand written birth record (now called a birth certificate) was introduced. Before that time, church birth or baptismal records were commonly the only documents that recorded one's birth and name. This handwritten recording process was the sole responsibility of the many independent Protestant and Catholic church parishes (who kept all of these records in their church buildings, usually in basement safe rooms or vaults). One might think that the majority of these records would have been damaged or destroyed given the constant Germanic wars and World Wars

that racked a havoc on Germany. However, this is, for the most part, not true. Most of Germany's original church records are in good physical condition, and many have been microfilmed (stored on microfiche) and are kept in central church archive locations (with public and highly regulated library access).

Note: The real deterrent to finding genealogy records in Germany is that the older records (before 1870) are readily accessible only if you know the area church parish name where the record originated. If one doesn't know the parish name where a relative once lived, then finding the location of those records is very difficult. Surprisingly, many German municipal archives and church archives personnel only speak (and read) German, which is a huge hurdle if one only speaks English. Creating accurate German translations of German records into English is a major problem for American researchers who do not speak German. Having a reliable German-speaking translator in Germany is an excellent resource. Some small church parish archives will send you various small record copies for free. However, that is the exception to the rule. Most German archives require payment in advance before they will do anything regarding your search request. I must say that the Germans have always been polite and considerate if you communicate with them in German. For the most part Germans speak and write in an old Victorian style manner, unlike English-speaking German Americans who tend to be rough around the edges. Free, internet-based translation tools (like Google's) are not always dependable, and can often yield offensive results if used to construct a written German language letter or response. Although not intentional, this is mainly due to language software translation deficiencies. I recommend that one uses multiple translation websites to compare their accuracy and that you keep a copy in your files for reference should there be a problem in your translated request.

High German and Low German
High German is the official written German language one would learn today in any German language course. Low German is derived from the Old Saxon dialect (which is also the origin of the English and Dutch languages). German soldiers were once part of the British Imperial Army fighting all over the world (including against the "rebels" in North America). It is unfortunate that World War I and World War II destroyed this once cordial and brotherly relationship between England and Germany.

Maiden Names & Married Surnames
Women's maiden names are often set apart by use of née (Meaning "born," in French) preceding their family surname. This book replaces née with (parentheses) to designate a woman's recorded maiden name, which is followed by the surname of her husband.

- End of Section -

Early Russian History

Early Surnames & Geographic Locations

As of 2014, the Brinkmann surname of this author's Brinkman family line has been traced mainly to various areas in Germany but have not been traced to any regions of Russia, Poland, or the Ukraine. However, several other previously unrelated surname ancestors (who later married into this author's[1] Brinkman family) have been traced to countries deep in Eastern Europe, to what was the Russian Empire. Some of these early Eastern European Germanic ancestors had surnames such as Weiss, Klein, and Frese. Many were German-born, who migrated as settlers to the Russian frontier during the early 1800s (now known as Ukraine). Many of these ancestors immigrated to America and married into this author's extended Brinkmann family.

Early Western European Geographic Town Name Searches

In 2013, an inquiry was made by this author at the Max Kade Institute for German-American Studies [2] requesting assistance in finding the European locations of towns listed in the written Brinkmann family history and the histories of other related ancestors. This search was forwarded to the Germans From Russia Heritage Collection at North Dakota State University library [3] where the results were inconclusive. This search was then referred to the Society of German Genealogy in Eastern Europe [4] (SGGEE), which specializes in old maps and town names in Eastern Europe. Thanks to the help provided by the SGGEE, we now know where the Weiss, Klein and Frese ancestors lived (around 1800) before their immigration to America (between 1909 to 1912).

History of the Volhynian Principality of Ukraine

Medieval Europe (5th to 15th centuries), was home to a very civilized and advanced state known as the Volhynian Principality (located in what is now the most northwestern region of the Ukraine, near the Polish and Belarusian borders). The geographic and ethnic history of this region is beyond the scope of this book's work, but efforts have been made herein to concentrate on the known towns where extended ancestors lived in Eastern Europe. During the early modern Russian period (1500 to 1800), this geographic area of the world was part of Imperial Russia's southwestern border. There are many current provinces within Ukraine. Of importance to this book are the Volyn and Rivne Provinces. These provinces are the historic homes of the Weiss, Klein and Frese families.

In the 18th & 19th century the Russian Empire (1721-1917) emerged to become one of the most powerful nations in the world. By 1897, it was home to the third largest population in the world (125.6 million people) and stretched from Eastern Europe across Asia and into North America and Hawaii. Tsar Peter I "The Great" (1672-1725) was largely responsible for transforming Russia during this early modern period. His immediate successors were inconsequential until the reign of Catherine II, "Catherine the Great" (1762-1796). She was the longest-ruling leader in Russia and was renowned for making many reforms that included offering of free land in Russia's Ukraine provinces to foreign immigrants, and a 1775 decree that any "Surf" (indentured farm slave) who were freed could not be forced into serfdom again. In 1861, Alexander II freed all Russian surf's. Another significant figure in Russia was Nicholas II (1894-1917), who was assassinated in the midst of World War I (1914-1918). The Russian Revolutions (1905 and 1917) resulted, in part, from strains exacerbated by Russia's participation in World War I. In response to the Russian revolutionaries' mandates, the Russian monarchy was dissolved, and the Duma Empire (puppet electorate of the wealthy) was created as the Lower House of the Russian Parliament.

Religious worship in this mostly rural empire was dominated by the Russian Orthodox Church. However, the Tsars also allowed most other faiths to worship freely (except for restrictions on the Jews). In 1918, the Russian Civil War (1918-1922) broke out and the Red Army, led by the Bolsheviks, took on the task of fighting insurgents (including wars with the Ukrainian National Army). In 1921, the Great Ukrainian Famine ensued claiming the lives of ten million people. In

1932, more than 33 million Russians died from starvation during the Great Russian Famine. In 1939, World War II erupted when Nazi Germany invaded Poland, the Ukraine, and then Russia. At first, the Germans were welcomed into some Ukrainian towns near Poland because of the cruel treatment Ukrainians had received from the Russian Red Army. Then, the Nazis began a genocide campaign slaughtering thousands of Jews, Poles, and ethnic Ukrainian civilians alike. It was an extremely intense time of suffering, exterminations, mass graves, and forced relocations to labor camps (from which many were never heard from again). The towns of Rozhyshche, Kovel, and Lutsk in eastern Ukraine were among the most deadly kill zones, with bodies lining the sides of roads and corpses dumped in mass graves. It was not until World War II ended, in 1945, that a sense of order was gradually restored to this region. Then, the Western Allied forces approved mandatory relocation reprisal campaigns against all German populations. Relative peace finally came around 1946. However, by then the Ukraine was a part of the Soviet Union. In 1991, the Soviet Union dissolved, and Ukraine became an independent state. In 2013, a great national controversy arose in Ukraine over the merits of joining the Eurozone or remaining allied with Russia. This controversy led to great civil unrest. For a detailed history of the Volhynia region, please visit Donald N. Miller's website [5] for a comprehensive review of Volhynia's place in history (and a list of books Miller has written).

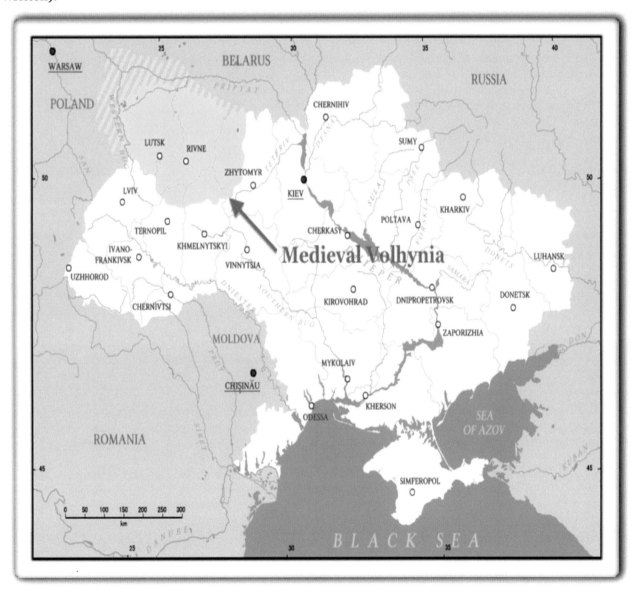

Map of medieval Volhynia, in Russia-Ukraine, c. 5th-15th century.
Source: Wikipedia

Influences on Ukrainian city & town names, as recorded in written family histories
It is often very difficult for genealogists to look at a family's written history and translate the old geographic place names to current ones. Many written family histories spell place names in what are called "variations of language." Variations are simply the spellings in an ancestor's given language (at a specific time) compared to the spellings of the nation or state in which they now exist. An example might be the German spelling of the town name for a Russian place, or one's surname that does not show up in a database of known names. Therefore, searches for such names and places in databases need to be neutral, and not specific. If one is looking for Mr. Frese, it is best to know all the other possible spellings of the Frese surname (or town name) in a given region, and then enter all variables in each search in any database. In Germany, it is most advantageous to genealogists if they have first isolated a town name, parish, or region place name before searching. However, blind searches are not uncommon even though they can produce unpredictable outcomes.

Current Ukrainian Town Names
In 2014, an extensive Russian and Eastern European search were conducted in an attempt to track down the historical, geographic locations of extended Brinkmann family ancestors noted in various family documents. This search revealed several current place names that fit the place names listed in the written Brinkmann family history records. Each of these towns, cities and provinces contains extended histories that span hundreds of years. The following are some geographic place names in various Eastern European locations once occupied by ancestors of this extended Brinkmann family. Many of these place names have changed since family members lived at these locations. There are several reasons why these place names have changed including modifications from Polish and German names to Russian and Ukrainian spellings. Such name changes can make searches difficult and finding a source that can help you make the name transitions is essential. It is also helpful to use website posting boards where one can leave questions about name conversions. There are also several books that list old and new geographic names in various languages.

Alexandrowka is now Aleksandrowka/Oleksandrivka. Google name: *Oleksandrivka, Volyn, Ukraine.* Cited as the birthplace of Conrad Weiss and Emile Weiss, and the birthplace of the children born to Daniel Weiss and Wilhelmine (Friedrich) Weiss, in 1871 & 1873.

Klewan is now Klewan/Klevan. Google name: *Klevan, Rivne, Ukraine.* Cited as the location where Ferdinand August Frese lived in Russia around 1908.

Kowell is now Kowel/Kovel. Google name: *Kovel, Volyn, Ukraine.* Cited as the largest city near ancestors' towns in the Volyn Province, Ukraine.

Ludsk-Lutzk is now Luck/Lutsk. Google name: *Lutsk, Volyn, Ukraine.* Cited as the main town near the original birth place of Daniel Weiss, in 1848, and Wilhelmine (Friedrich) Weiss, in 1851. Death place of Daniel Weiss's parents, Katherina (Friedrich) Weiss, in 1894, and her husband Konrad Weiss, in 1872.

Porsk-Kowell is now Porsk, Kowell. Google name: *Malyi Pors'k, Volyn, Ukraine.* Cited as the birthplace for Ferdinand Klein, on July 16, 1888, and thought to be the location of the Klein family farm in Russia in the 1800s and 1900s.

Rozyszcze is now Rozyszcze/Rozhyshche. Google name: *Rozhyshche, Volyn, Ukraine.* Cited as the birthplace of Natalie (Weiss) Frese, in 1892, and the place where the Weiss family lived in Russia.

Walynia is now Volhynia/Valhynia. Google name: *Volhynia (Volyn), Ukraine.* Cited as the province where the Weiss, Klein, and Frese families lived in Russia.

Walarianowka is now Walerianowka/Valerianivka. Google name: *Valer'Yanivka, Volyn, Ukraine.* Cited as the birthplace of Daniel Weiss, in 1848, and his wife, Wilhelmine (Friedrich) Weiss, in 1851.

Current Provinces in Ukraine

As of 2014, there were 24 separate oblasts (provinces) in the Ukraine. Two of these (Volyn and Rivne) are of special interest to this author because it appears that all known Eastern European extended Brinkman family members were born in (and immigrated from) cities and towns in this region. In February of 2014, the Ukrainian Revolution ousted President Viktor Yanukovych and appointed a new Ukrainian government. The Russians argued that Yanukovych was illegally removed and impeached, and Russia began to mass its military along the northern Ukrainian border with Russia. In late February of 2014, the Russians began to take control of Ukrainian military bases in Crimea, Ukraine. Then, the Crimean Parliament declared Crimea independent from Ukraine, and the Crimean electorate voted to declare itself a state of Russia (withdrawing from the Ukrainian Federation). This turmoil caused immediate reactions from governments around the globe and as of 2014, remained a significant international concern.

Ukraine's 24 provinces
Crimea, southeastern province in lower right
Volyn and Rivne, northwestern provinces in upper left, c. 2014
Source: Wikimedia Commons

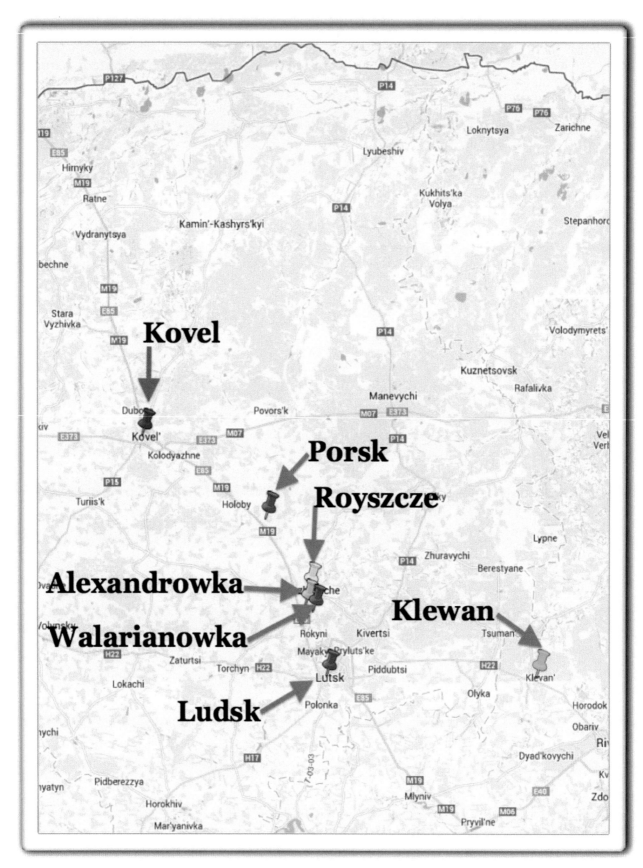

Map of variation names of European ancestors' locations in Russia, c. 1910
Volyn and Rivne, Ukraine, c. 2014
Source: Wikimedia Commons

Map of Eastern Europe, c. 2013
Source: About.com by Terry Kubilius

Map of the German Reich, c. 1871-1918
Source: Wikimedia Commons

The Thirty Years' War among Religious Rivals in Europe

The Thirty Years' War (1618-1648) broke out after the Peace of Augsburg (1555), signed by Charles V. T., Holy Roman Emperor," and began between German Lutherans and German Catholics. Eventually, this war included most of the countries of Europe. It was one of the most deadly and continuous conflicts in modern European history. Initially, religion was the main motivation, as Protestant and Catholic states battled each other, even though they were each part of the Holy Roman Empire. Changing the balance of power was at issue. The war then developed into a more general conflict involving most of the greatest powers in Europe and became less religious, and more about the rivalry between empires and political domination. The worst consequence of the Thirty Years' War was the destruction of entire towns, stripped of all food and wealth by the foraging armies. Famine and disease devastated the populations in many countries, including Germany, Bohemia, Netherlands, France, and Italy. Discipline eroded quickly when armies discovered that they were largely self-funding (leading to looting and the exacting of bribes from settlements where they operated). This lawlessness imposed severe hardships on the civilian populations. The Thirty Years' War ended in 1648, after the treaties of Osnabrück and Münster. Some of the quarrels that provoked this war went unresolved for a much longer time.

German Migration to Russia

Germans had been demoralized by years of religious, political, and economic strife. Then, in 1762 the Germans received an enticing offer from the new Russian Tsar Catherine II "Catherine the Great," a former German princess. Russia had just won a series of campaigns against the Turks during the second half of the 18th century and the Russian crown had acquired large areas of land along the Volga River and the Black Sea. Catherine the Great issued manifestos inviting foreign immigrants (especially Germans) to settle this rural Russian territory. German settlers (colonists) were offered freedom of religion, no taxation for 10 years, 160 acres of free land, and exemption from Russian military service. This land offer by the Russians sounded good to Germans who suffered from too little land, and upheaval in Germany. Many German families headed east to Russia and settled in small villages. Religion was practiced freely, including Reformed-Lutheran, Mennonite, and Catholic faiths. Village members elected village officers, and spoke in German. Taming the land, cutting timber, and draining swamps was hard labor for these immigrant farmers, but little by little they built churches and schools. Choirs were formed, and pipe organs were imported around the end of the 19th century. Traditional folk music flourished and songs were performed on many different occasions. Single men even sung on street corners in the evening to serenade prospective brides. It seemed as though this was going to be their permanent home, but history tells a much different story.

Catherine the Great believed these highly skilled German farmers and tradesmen would promote progress and lead to a more modern Russia. Many Germans colonized in the Volga region of Russia and became known as the "Volga Germans." In 1804, Germans also colonized the southern Ukraine and were known as the "Black Sea Germans." Around 1812, more Germans emigrated from Württemberg (a former German State in southwestern Germany) and Prussia to areas in the Ukraine and were known as the "Bessarabian Germans." Then, Russia experienced a devastating defeat by Turkey in the Crimean War (1853-1856), which had been caused by Russian aggression against Turkey. Turkey was aided by her European allies: Great Britain, France, and Sardinia. Turkey and it's European allies destroyed the Russian Navy in the Black Sea in 1854, and in 1855, the allies continued on to capture the Russian fortress city of Sebastopol (a huge fortress and naval base in the Ukraine). After the Crimean War, Russia realized that its outdated military and system of government must be modernized. This led first to the 1861 freeing of the serfs (an agricultural labor force bound under the feudal system). Three years later (in 1864), the Russians instituted the Great Reforms (Russification efforts) under Alexander III, which reorganized and democratized local government and reformed the court systems. In 1874, Russia established universal military service. The privileges previously enjoyed by the German colonists (including those allowing them to run their own affairs and not be required to serve in the Russian military) were revoked. Russian officials now regarded Germans as inconsistent with their new reforms. In addition, the Germans' rights seemed unfair to the newly freed Russian serfs who now competed with the German colonists as equal subjects. Thus, the rights once afforded to the Germans were removed in the hope that they would now participate directly in Russian public affairs. The result was that the hard working German colonists resented Russian control, and many began preparations for emigration from Russia. The Germans who made the decision to leave Russia were the fortunate ones. Those who stayed behind were devastated by the effects of World War II, and many disappeared never to be seen or heard from again.

Treasuring their own identity, and culture, many of these German immigrants decided to leave Russia and the Ukraine. Many of these immigrants settled in Canada and the United States and journeyed across the Great Plains from Saskatchewan to Texas. The American Homestead Act of 1862, offered 160 acres of land to any man in exchange for a nominal homestead fee. The Canadian Dominion Land Act of 1872, offered 160 acres to any male over the age of 21 for a ten dollar registration fee. The world was open for the taking and the "old way of doing business" was over. Wherever they settled worldwide the Germans preserved their distinctive identity, rich culture, and heritage. It was not until the World Wars that many German immigrants began to Americanize and lose their German ethnic identity.

History of the Rhineland in Germany
The German Rhineland was eventually divided into several principalities, including Prince-Bishoprics of Trier, Cologne, Rhenish Hesse, Palatinate, and the Duchy of Cleves. After the Reformation of the Catholic Church, the majority of the Rhineland remained Catholic (except for the Duchy of Cleves). The Thirty Years War brought devastation to this entire region. Post war French influence attempted to exert their power over the Rhine but eventually Rhine was united by Prussia under the name "Rhine Province," after the Congress of Vienna in 1815.

History of Prussia - Germany
Prussia was a German kingdom and historic state originating from the Duchy of Prussia and the Margraviate of Brandenburg (Holy Roman Empire) periods of early German history. For centuries, the royal house of Hohenzollern ruled Prussia successfully, expanding its size by way of an unusually well-organized and effective army. Prussia shaped the early history of Germany and in 1451, Prussia located its capital in Berlin. The name Prussia is derived from the term "Old Prussians," those who were conquered by German crusaders (around 1308). This formerly Polish region of Europe was mostly Germanized through immigration from Central and Western Germany. After 1466, Prussia was split into Western Royal Prussia (a province of Poland) and the eastern region called the "Duchy of Prussia." The union (marriage) of the Brandenburg and Duchy of Prussia in 1618, led to the proclamation of the Kingdom of Prussia in 1701, led by King Frederick William I (1714-1740). After 1810, Prussia dominated Germany (politically, economically, and in population) and was the core of the unified North German Confederation which was formed in 1867, and became part of the German Empire in 1871 (when the smaller German states merged with Prussia). In November 1918, (after Germany was defeated in World War I) the Prussian royalty abdicated the throne, and the Prussian nobility lost most of its political power. Prussia was effectively abolished by 1932, and officially abolished in 1947. Kaiser William I, named Otto von Bismarck as his Chancellor. Bismarck helped to unite the German States into the German Empire of Lesser Germany.

Flags and Insignias
The Holy Roman Empire (known as the Holy Roman Empire of the German Nation after 1512) did not have a national flag, but black and gold were used as colors of the Holy Roman Emperor and featured in the imperial banner with a black eagle on a golden background. Germans have always been interested in decorative coat of arms, flags, and insignias. There are hundreds of German national, residential, civil, military, state, service, confederation, empire, imperial, republic, Nazi, East German, and German Republic flags. The German Empire used the colors black, red, and gold on its flag during their defeat of Napoleon's army. The Kingdom of Prussia used the black eagle on a white background with black boarders during its reign. The current German *Bundesflagge* (federal flag) contained the three solid colors of black, red, and gold and was introduced in 1949, as part of the Federal Republic of Germany's constitution.

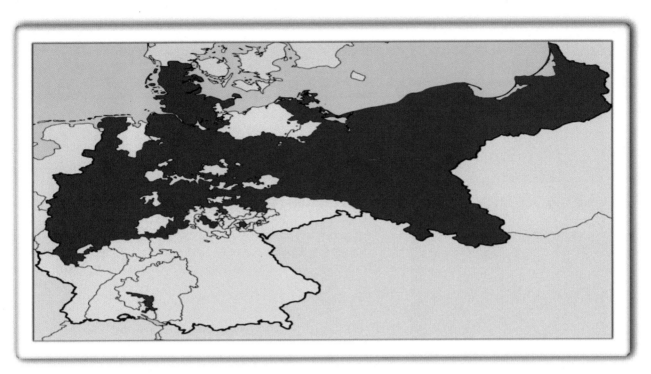

Kingdom of Prussia (dark blue), and states of the German Empire (yellow), c. 1918
Source: Wikimedia Commons

Kingdom of Prussia flag, Germany, c. 1892-1918
Source: Wikimedia Commons

- End of Section -

German Kings & Kingdoms

c. 1784

Frederick II (son of King Frederick William I of Prussia) ascended to the throne in 1740 and ruled until 1786 (46 years). Known as "Frederick The Great" for his brilliant, victorious military campaigns against the Austrian and Polish empires, Frederick II modernized Prussian bureaucracy and civil service, promoted religious tolerance, and supported music and the arts. He had no children, so the throne went to his nephew, Frederick William II of Prussia, upon his death in 1786.

Source: Wikimedia Commons

c. 1796

Frederick William II (son of Friedrich II of Prussia) ascended to the throne in 1786 and ruled until 1797 (11 years). He was known as easy-going, pleasure-loving, averse to sustained efforts of any kind, and sexual by nature (having two spouses and a mistress). He reformed tax collecting, lifted the ban on the German language in the Prussian Academy, encouraged trade by reducing customs duties, and constructed roads and canals. Although popular with the masses, he had many critics who called him "the fat bastard" for his lack of foreign policy leadership, which left Prussia morally isolated in Europe. Upon his death in 1797, at the age 53, Prussia was in a state of bankruptcy and confusion. The Prussian Army had decayed, and the monarchy was discredited. The throne went to his son, Frederick William III.

Source: Wikimedia Commons

Frederick William III (son of King Friedrich Wilhelm II) came to the throne in 1797 and ruled until 1840 (43 years). He was known as a pious and honest person. He was a Prussian Army Colonel in 1790 and fought bravely in the campaigns against France between 1792 and 1794. When he became ruler in 1797, he distrusted his ministers, did not delegate authority well, and lacked the willpower to strike a consistent course. His first endeavor was to restore morality to his dynasty. He attempted a policy of neutrality in the French Napoleonic Wars, but in 1806 joined the Battle of Jena-Auerstädt (where the Prussian Army was defeated and collapsed). The Prussian royal family fled to Memel (in East Prussia) which was later conquered by the French. France eventually made peace with Prussia but kept many of Prussian territories. Later, Russia and Prussia defeated the French, and the Congress of Vienna returned a few territories to Prussia. Upon his return to Prussia, Friedrich withdrew his promise to create a constitution and died in 1840 (age 70) leaving his throne to his son Frederick William IV

Source: Wikimedia Commons

c. 1838

Frederick William IV (son of King Frederick William III) came to the throne in 1840 and ruled until 1861 (21 years). He was known as a patron of the arts, a skilled architectural draftsman, and a staunch Romanticist (devoted to the nostalgia of the Middle Ages). He was against the unification of the German states and preferred for Austria to remain the principal power in the region. He eased press censorship, was the only King of Prussia to enter the Roman Catholic church, and when the Prussian Revolution broke out in 1848, he first joined the revolution, convened a national assembly, and then dissolved it. In 1848, he promulgated a new constitution that favored the aristocrats and the monarchy. The new parliament and Prussian Constitution were more liberal than the previous regime, but the aristocracy, military, and powers of the King were retained until the dissolution of the Prussian Kingdom in 1918. In 1857, he suffered a stroke that left him paralyzed and mentally incapacitated. His brother, William, served as his regent from 1858 until his death in 1861. He had no children, and his throne was passed to his brother, who became King William I.

Source: Wikimedia Commons

c. 1860

23

William I (second son of King Frederick William III) came to the throne in 1861 and ruled until 1888 (27 years). He fought bravely in the Napoleonic Wars and was an excellent diplomat. During the German Revolution of 1848, he successfully defended his brother, Frederick William IV, with the use of cannons and infantry. He was considered politically neutral and had little desire to intervene in political affairs. He appointed Otto von Bismarck the Minister President (responsible only to the monarch) and had a hand in all domestic politics, foreign policy, and war strategy. As king, he successfully led (and directed) the Second Schleswig War, the Austro-Prussian War, and the Franco-Prussian War. He was proclaimed German Emperor of the German Empire at Versailles Palace on January 18, 1871. He implemented the Anti-Socialist Law against the Social Democratic Party and banned workers' strikes. He died in 1888 (at age 90) and was succeeded by his son, Frederick II.

Source: Wikimedia Commons

c. 1886

Frederick III (son of William I) came to the throne in 1888 and ruled until 1888 (99 days). He was known as a brave soldier in the Prussian Army and for over 27 years, during the Second Schleswig War, the Austro-Prussian War, and the Franco-Prussian War. He often stated that he hated war itself and was known for his humane conduct during a battle. As German Emperor, he was opposed to the policies of conservative Chancellor Otto von Bismarck and urged that the power of the Chancellor be restrained. Liberals in both Germany and Britain (who sought a unified Germany with a constitution that protected equal civil rights) had hoped that the Emperor would liberalize the German Empire. Unfortunately, Frederick III suffered from cancer of the larynx and died on June 15, 1888, at age 56. His oldest son, Wilhelm II, succeeded him.

Source: Wikimedia Commons

c. 1888.

c. 1890

Emperor Wilhelm II (son of Emperor Frederick III) came to the throne in 1888 and ruled until 1918 (30 years). He was the last German emperor (Kaiser) and the last monarch of Prussia. He quickly dismissed Chancellor Otto von Bismarck (known as the "Iron Chancellor"), who had achieved a fragile balance of interests with Germany, France, and Russia. When Bismarck was dismissed, the Russians expected a reversal in policy from Berlin and quickly came to treaty terms with France, isolating Germany from its European allies. Wilhelm II launched Germany into "the New Course" in foreign policy and spoke openly about supporting Austria and Hungary in the Crisis of 1914 (which led to World War I and ultimately World War II). Wilhelm II's rule was characterized as the "German ship of state going out of control" and he was known as "bombastic, impetuous and tactless." He often made policy statements without consulting his ministers. His ultimate undoing came after a disastrous interview with the London's *Daily Telegraph* that cost him most of his support and power in 1908. During World War I (1914-1918) the German Army generals dictated domestic and foreign policy with little regard for civilian or government demands. Wilhelm II soon lost support from his generals, and abdicated in November 1918, fleeing to exile in the Netherlands. This was the end of the German Empire. Soon, Germany was headed down a path of self-destruction that would forever change the landscape of the world.

Source: Wikimedia Commons

c. 1915

Modern German History

The Austro-Prussian War, 1886
The Austro-Prussian War of 1866 (also called the Three Week War) was fought between the Austrian Empire (a loose collection of Austrian German states) and the Kingdom of Prussia. During this brief war, several German provinces (such as Hanover) voted in favor of mobilizing troops against the Prussian Army on June 14, 1866. Prussia saw this as just cause for declaring war on all independent Austrian kingdoms. Prussia soon overpowered, dissolved, and annexed six Austrian German states.

Creation of the Great German Empire, 1870
On December 10, 1870, the victorious North German Confederation renamed itself the German Empire, and on January 18, 1871, it gave the title of Emperor to King Wilhelm I. Germany then became a mighty, united nation that remained in power for 47 years, until 1918 when the Federal Republic was declared.

The Franco-Prussian War, 1870-1871
On July 19, 1870, the Franco-Prussian War (also called the One Year War) began between the Empire of France and the Kingdom of Prussia. Prussia was aided by its 27 alliances with the North German Confederation, and several south German states. The war took many lives and destroyed the landscapes of Germany and France. The French Army was composed of only 400,000 regular soldiers. The Prussian Army was made up of 1.2 million conscripts (which enabled the Prussians to mass huge deployments and encircle their enemy). The Prussians also had the most sophisticated rail system in Europe. Soon, the Prussians had outwitted the French (led by Napoleon III), and even marched into France. Paris was seized and looted. Then, on September 1, 1870, a decisive military battle, the Battle of Sedan, was fought. Napoleon III, and his entire army were defeated and captured. The Franco-Prussian War ended on May 10, 1871, with the Treaty of Frankfurt, which led to the unification of the German Confederation States under King Wilhelm I.

The German Empire, through World War I, 1870-1918
The German Empire, officially named the Deutsches Reich (German Realm), lasted for 47 years until 1918 when Germany was defeated in World War I. Upon the fall of the empire, Emperor Wilhelm II abdicated his throne and went into exile.

The German Revolution, the Weimar Republic, 1918-1933
In 1918, the German Empire was stripped of its rulers and monarchs, following the Great German Revolution that ended in 1819. In 1918, Germany had lost World War I and was in a state of economic and financial ruin. The German people demanded democracy and social reforms. The Parliamentary Weimar Republic pretended to meet those changes, but secretly kept vast and sweeping powers under the control of the monarchial governments of the German States.

German Great Depression, Third German Reich, Nazi Party, 1933-1945
The German economy was devastated after World War I. The victorious European Allies (under the Treaty of Versailles) punished the German Empire by partitioning (separating) several German states and placing them under the control of allied states. This turmoil eventually led to the Great German Depression of 1930, the rise of the Third Reich (Nazi Germany), 1933-1945, and ultimately to World War II, 1935-1945.

- End of Section -

Gallery

German Warfare, 1600-1900

The Thirty Years War - Battle of Breitenfeld, Germany, c. 1631
Source: Wikimedia Commons

The Thirty Years War-The hanging of religious heretics, Germany, c. 1632
Source: Wikimedia Commons

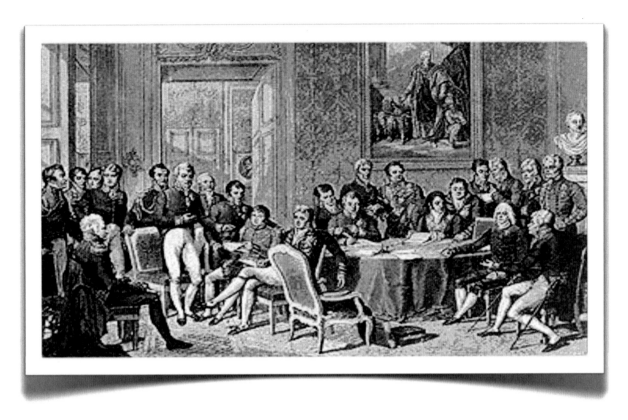

Congress of Vienna, September 1814-June 1815
Source: Wikimedia Commons

Map of Europe after the Congress of Vienna, 1815
Source: Wikimedia Commons

European infantry troops in combat, c. 1850
Source: Wikimedia Commons

Draftees in the German Imperial Army - 500,000 soldiers were conscripted, c. 1898
Source: Wikimedia Commons

World War I

World War I, 1914-1918

World War I (also known as the World War and the Great War) was a four-year-long war that began in Europe on July 28, 1914, and lasted until November 11, 1918. It was fought between the Allied Forces (the United Kingdom, France, Russia and the United States), and the Central Powers (Germany, Austria, Hungary, and Italy). Italy later left the Central Power alliance, reorganized, and fought with the Allied Forces. Eventually, more nations (including Japan) entered into the war. Seventy-million military personnel were mobilized in what was to become the sixth largest war in history, leaving more than nine million dead soldiers. By 1918, the landscape of Europe had changed forever. The Allied Forces won after the American forces entered the trenches in 1918. Soon, the Prussian Empire collapsed, and the Germans and Austrian Empires ceased to exist. World War I was a "war to end all wars." Unfortunately, history has proved that this was not to be the case. Even more horrific wars, like World War II, would follow. World War I had fewer victims than World War II, and destroyed less property, but still led to the brutal killing and displacement of millions of noncombatant civilians. The end of World War I left deep scars on the minds and maps of Europe. The "Old European World" was shattered forever and would never recover from the shock it endured during this war.

It is impossible for this author to summarize the many wars that plagued Europe for centuries. However, it is possible to try to narrow the scope to more recent times (within 100 years) and focus on the two World Wars which were the most devastating in all the global histories. Any war between national powers usually ends in tragedy and great suffering. Shifts of power during some wars create giant leaps in history. Other wars resolve and fadeaway, but some fester and grow, to become "monsters" that overwhelm the world. In 1918, after its defeat in WW I, Germany was in a state of economic and financial ruin. It had exhausted its national resources and faced a 50% unemployment rate and rampant social unrest. Germany pondered the question, "What to do now?" Adolf Hitler, born in Austria, was anxiously waiting for an opportunity to advance his Aryan propaganda and began to address the German masses. He sold the German people on his master plan to conquer the world at a time when the German population had no confidence in its old republic and was hungry for the idea of a common goal and united German nation. Hitler's propaganda was a perfect fit to fill this void, and in a matter of months Hitler was declared Chancellor. Hitler then set out to purge all resistance by killing any party members who opposed him. Soon, Hitler was named head of the Nazi Party, and he quickly appointed staff generals who were hungry for power and influence at any cost. In 1934, Hitler was declared the Führer (Guide) of Germany. There was no turning back. The world was about to be sent on a downward spiral stopped only by Germany's 1945 defeat in World War II.

Note: Throughout much of European history, second born sons were regularly conscripted (drafted) in times of war. These young men had no alternative but to take up arms and fight. By age 14 or 16, most young men were considered combat ready. European societies held their military soldiers in high regard. One's position of honor was at stake, and one was judged by his performance during combat. Many of the 18th and 19th-century civilian family portraits show men displaying their combat rifles and clothing adorned with military medals from the campaigns in which they fought. Examples can be seen in some historic Brinkmanns' portraits. Many Brinkmann ancestors lived, fought, and suffered through generations of European wars through the end of World War II. Because of the great influence of these wars it is imperative that any Brinkmann history contain a broad description of the major wars in which Brinkmann ancestors may have participated in, and what consequences these wars wrought upon them. The following Gallery photos help tell part of that story.

- End of Section -

Gallery

World War I

Imperial Eagle of the German Empire, 1889-1918
Source: Wikimedia Commons-Author: David Liuzzo-2013

Archduke Franz Ferdinand & Sophie, Duchess of Hohenberg arriving in Serbia just before their assassination in 1914, that act that sparked the beginning of WWI.
Source: Wikimedia Commons

Kaiser William II & war generals, WWI, Germany, c. 1914
Source: Wikimedia Commons

German soldier and German officer posing before deployment, WWI, c. 1913
Source: Wikimedia Commons

German SA stormtroopers invading Russia, WWI, c. 1917
Source: Wikimedia Commons

4321. Fra en fransk Fangelejr. En tysk Soldat henrettes.

French Army officer shooting a captured German soldier, WWI, c. 1913
Source: Wikimedia Commons

Winston Churchill and the British Army, WWI, c. 1916
Source: Wikimedia Commons

German mustard gas attack, WWI, c. 1917
Source: Wikimedia Commons

Russian soldiers in trenches at the Battle of Sarikamish, Turkey, WWI, 1916
Source: Wikimedia Commons

Dead French soldiers in northern France, WWI, c. 1917
Source: Wikimedia Commons

Victorious U.S. Army 64th Regiment on the day of the Armistice, November 11, 1918. 60 million soldiers were mobilized worldwide, 8 million died, 7 million were disabled, and 15 million were critically injured. Millions of civilians also died, and the war left millions of homeless refugees all over of Europe

Source: Wikimedia Commons

Decorated German Army soldier, Adolf Hitler, WWI, c. 1916
Source: Wikimedia Commons

41

Armistice celebration in New York City, November 11, 1918
Source: Wikimedia Commons

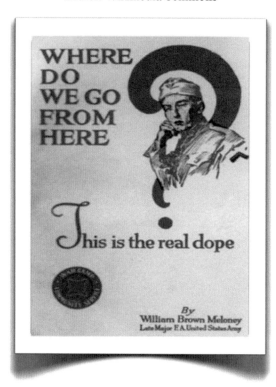

U.S. Government propaganda booklet, WWI, c. 1918
Source: Wikimedia Commons

French military cemetery with over 130,000 unknown soldiers, WWI, c. 1920
Source: Wikimedia Commons

The German Revolution began in 1918 after Germany's defeat in WWI. Germany lost 1.4 million of its men, and had an unemployment rate of over 50 percent. Phillip Scheiderman (Majority Social Party Democrat-MAPD) is speaking from the open window (marked with an X) to the German people at the Reich Chancellery Building in Berlin, 1918

Source: Wikimedia Commons

National flag of the Republic of Germany, Weimar Republic, 1919-1935
and became the national flag of the Federal Republic of Germany, 1949-Present.
Source: Wikimedia Commons-2013

Coat of Arms - German Empire, Weimar Republic, 1919-1933
Source: Wikimedia Commons-Author: David Liuzzo-2013

World War II

World War II, 1939-1945

World War II (also known as the Second World War) had the highest causality rate of any war in history. It began in September 1939 and ended in September 1945 (6 years and 1 day later). It included most of the nations in the world and was fought between the rival powers of the European Allied Forces and the Nazi-affiliated Axis Powers. The Allied Forces of World War II initially consisted of France, Poland, the United Kingdom, the British Commonwealth (Australia, New Zealand, Newfoundland, and South Africa), the Soviet Union, and later, the United States of America. These alliances changed and expanded as the war progressed. The Axis Powers included Germany, Japan, and Italy. During WWII, more than 100 million men served as combat soldiers. It was a state of "total war" and all nations participating placed their entire economic, industrial, and scientific capabilities at the service of the war effort. By the wars's end in 1945, 70 million people had died, and many went unidentified and were entombed in mass graves.

The German Army was assuredly aggressive in WWI, but in WWII the Germans appeared wholly possessed by social propaganda madness. They not only exterminated other inconvenient races that got in their way, but also tortured and killed their own fellow Germans if they showed any signs of not being in line with Adolf Hitler's vision for Nazi Germany. Some historians describe Hitler as "a man of lies," and that he was nothing more than an "idle paper pusher" during World War I, when he was assigned to a clerk's job and passed over for promotion several times because he had no military leadership skills. Others say Hitler's claim to have been wounded in WWI (for which he says he received the German Iron Cross) are nothing more than Nazi propaganda with no historical evidence to support Hitler's claims. However, Hitler did learn to master his public speaking skills and had a mesmerizing ability to take his audiences into a state similar to that of a "trance." Hitler was a natural "cult master," and this proved to be a paramount skill that he used everywhere he went.

After World War II

It is very troubling to this author that Nazi leaders were able to escape from Germany to other countries after their defeat in WWII. Many other Nazi scientists were encouraged by U.S. commanders to defect to the United States and work for the U.S. War Department designing new missiles and aerospace technologies using German war research (including the production of the Redstone Rockets). During the Cold War of the 1960s, NASA raced to get to the moon before Russia. America recruited many World War II Nazi scientists (like Dr. Von Wernher Braun, who was under suspicion for war crimes associated with Nazi prison labor camp deaths). This post-WWII Nazi recruiting was also done to escalate the capability of America's arsenal and meet America's NASA Project Apollo objectives. The result was the development of the Saturn family of rockets that supposedly landed Neil Armstrong and Buzz Aldrin on the moon in July 1969, and redefined America's intercontinental ballistic missile technology.

After WWII ended in 1945, millions of Germans living outside their native country were expelled (forced) by the Allied Forces to migrate from their homes, regardless of their ethnicity or level of participation in WWII. Many were sent back to Germany including the *Reichsdeutsche* (German nationals) and *Volksdeutsche* (ethnic Germans). It was "payback time" in postwar Europe. Expulsion areas included: Poland, Czechoslovakia, Hungary, Romania, Yugoslavia, Austria, and provinces controlled by the Soviet Union. These mandatory relocations were part of a geographic, ethnic cleansing and reconfiguration of postwar Europe that forced approximately 20 million people from their homes and resulted in 500,000 to 2 million civilian deaths.

- End of Section -

Gallery

World War II

Emblem of the German Third Reich, Nazi Germany 1933-1945.
Source: Wikimedia Commons-Author: RsVe-2013

National flag of the German Third Reich, Nazi Germany 1935-1945
Source: Wikimedia Commons-Author: Formax-2013

Chancellor of the Third Reich, the Führer of Germany, Adolf Hitler, 1934-1945.
Source: Wikimedia Commons.

Benito Mussolini (Italy) and Adolf Hitler (Germany), c. 1939
Source: Wikimedia Commons

Adolf Hitler and German generals after the occupation of Paris, France, 1942
Source: Wikimedia Commons

Hermann Göering, c1934
Nazi Party Leader, Commander of the German Air Force, & the Gestapo
Source: The History Place-USHMM Photo archives

Heinrich Himmler, c. 1933
Nazi Party leader - Commander of SS troops, oversaw the Nazi death camps
Source: Conservapedia photo archives

Joseph Goebbels, c. 1933
Nazi Party leader, Minister of Propaganda and Jewish extermination
Source: Imgur, LLC photo archives

Rudolf Walter Richard Hess, c. 1942
Nazi Party leader, Deputy Führer, & co-author of Mien Kampf
Source: The history Place-USHMM Photo archives

Adolf Hitler receiving flowers from German girl at a youth camp, c. 1935
Source: Imgur, LLC photo archives

Adolf Hitler signing his autobiography for a German boy, c. 1942
Source: Imgur, LLC photo archives

Execution of Jewish resistance fighters, Warsaw Ghetto, Poland, c. 1944
Source: Pinterest photo archives-Pin

German boy in his father's WWII German officer's uniform, c. 1942
Source: Imgur, LLC photo archives

United Kingdom Prime Minister Winston Churchill.
Swimming in the Atlantic Ocean, c. 1942
Source: Wikimedia Commons

German bombing raid over London, England and airplane dog fight, c. 1940
Source: Wikimedia Commons

Shell-shocked reindeer during German bombing of Russia, c. 1945
Source: Wikimedia Commons

Frozen dead German soldiers at Stalingrad, Russia, 1945
Source: Wikimedia Commons

Arial view of America's atomic bomb exploding over Nagasaki, Japan, 1945
Source: Wikimedia Commons

Hiroshima, Japan after the atomic bomb blast that left 80,000 dead civilians, 1945
Source: Imgur, LLC photo archives

Atomic bomb exposition at Nagasaki, Japan, 1945
Source: Wikimedia Commons.

Bombed-out business district of Berlin, Germany, c. 1945
Source: Wikimedia Commons

Bombed-out residential city section of Berlin, Germany, c. 1945
Source: Wikimedia Commons

United Kingdom's Prime Minister Winston Churchill - Victory in Europe Day, 1945
Source: Wikimedia Commons

Americans executing German, SS soldiers at the Dachau concentration camp, 1945
Source: Imgur, LLC photo archives

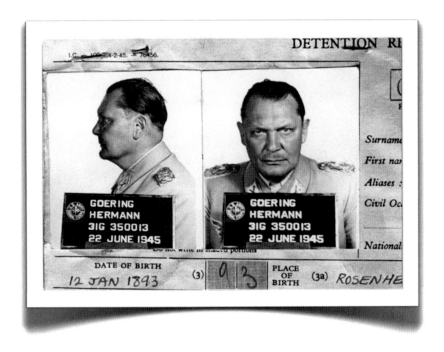

General Hermann Wilhelm Göering on trial in Nuremberg, Germany, 1945
Source: Imgur, LLC photo archives

German boy walks along road next to the corpses of murdered victims of the
Bergen-Belsen Nazi concentration camp, in Lower Saxony, Germany.
70,000 people where exterminated at this camp during WWII, Photo 1945
Source: George Rodger/Time Life Pictures-Waralbum.ru-Pinterest.com-Pin

U.S. Military members of the service arriving in New York Harbor after WWII, 1945
Source: Imgur, LLC photo archives

Adolf Hitler's nephew, William Patrick Hitler, immigrated to America, changed his name to Stuart Houston, and enlisted in the U.S. Navy in 1944. He served on a hospital ship until 1947, when he married and moved to Long Island, New York. Photo c. 1944

Dr. Von Wernher Braun, German WWII-V2 rocket scientist at the German forced labor missile camp in Peenemünde, Germany, posing (in a suit) with Nazi generals, c. 1941
Source: Wickimedia Open Source photo

Dr. Von Wernher Braun, U.S. rocket and NASA scientist, walking with President John F. Kennedy at the Redstone Missile Arsenal in Huntsville, Alabama, 1963
Source: Wickimedia Open Source photo

Captured World War II German soldiers marching to a prison camp, 1945
Source: Painting by Jim Eannelli-2013

Dead American World War II soldiers lined up in a sea of neat rows, c. 1950
Source: Wikimedia Commons

The Reorganization of Germany

The Transformation of Germany, 1946

In 1946, after the end of World War II, the British Army's military administration recreated Germany into the Land of Hanover (based on the former Kingdom of Hanover). One year later, at the instigation of German leadership, it was merged into the new Bundesland, a federation of 16 states that were partly sovereign constituents. The old German Empire was gone forever, and the old Austrian and Prussian territories were modified into what became known as the Federal Republic of Germany.

Map of the Federal Republic of Germany, 2013
Source: Wikimedia Commons

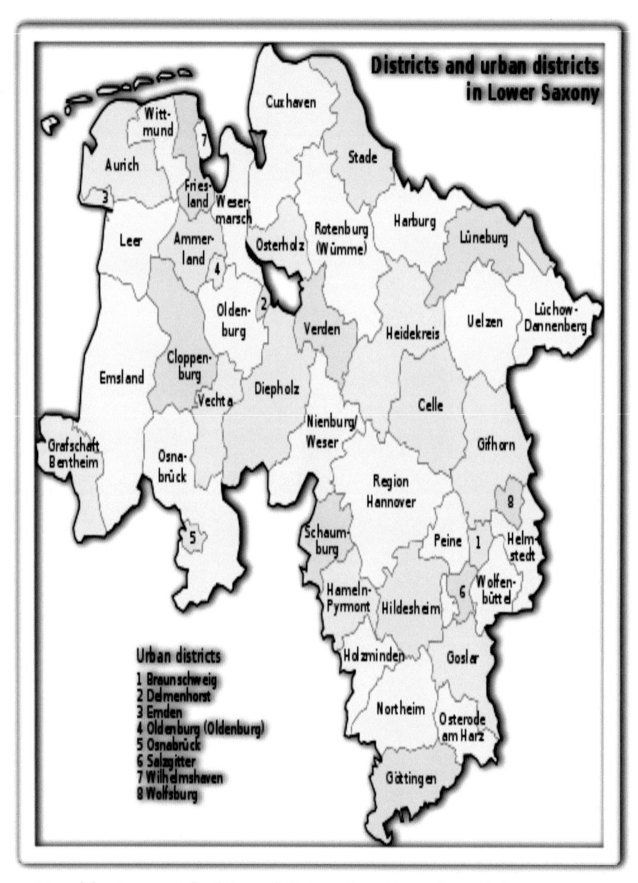

Map of the German Federal State of Niedersachsen (Lower Saxony), Germany, 2013
Source: Wikimedia Commons

Flag of the Federal Republic of Germany, 1949-2014.
This was the original German Empire flag of the Weimar Republic, 1919-1935.
Source: Wikimedia Commons

Flag of the German State of Niedersachsen (Lower Saxony), Germany, 1949-Present
Source: Wikimedia Commons

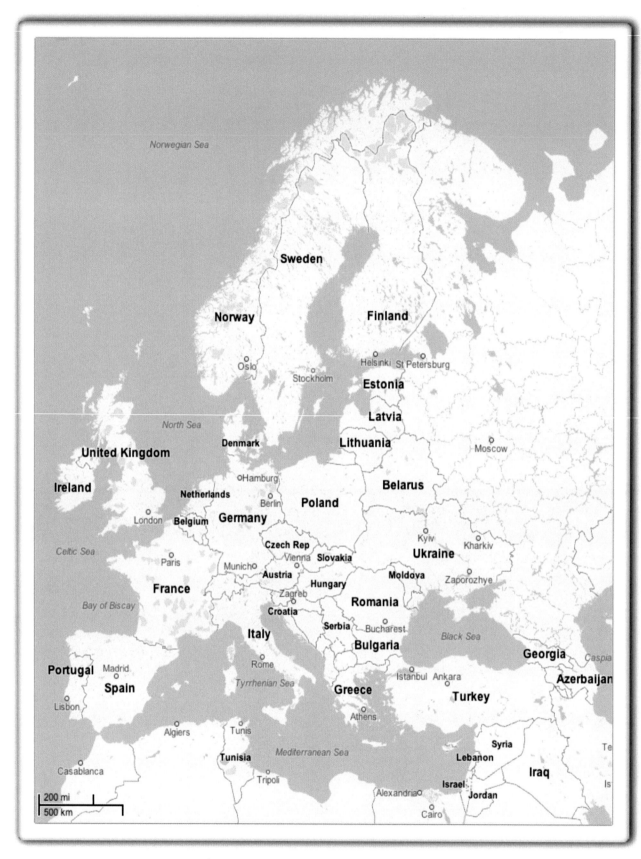

2014 map of Europe. The European political landscape has changed dramatically since the sixteenth century.

Statue of Liberty

The Statue of Liberty

In 1864, there were four million African-American slaves in America, and by 1865, the American Civil War had ended. Newly freed black Americans began to organize and begin reconstituting their families after slavery was abolished. On August 2, 1834, a child named Auguste Bartholdi was born in France. Early in his career, Bartholdi studied art, sculpture, the humanities, and architecture. From 1855 to 1856, Bartholdi embarked on what was to become a life-changing trip throughout Europe, Ethiopia, and the Middle East. Bartholdi visited the Sphinx and the Pyramids of Giza in Egypt (where he discovered a passion for large-scale public monuments, and colossal sculptures). In 1869, the Egyptian government expressed interest in designing a lighthouse at the entrance to their newly completed Suez Canal. Eager and excited, Bartholdi designed a colossal statue of a robed woman holding a torch, which he called "Progress Brings Light to Asia." However, when he attended the canal's opening, Bartholdi was informed that he would not be able to continue with his lighthouse. Although disappointed, Bartholdi would later have a second chance to design a colossal statue.

In 1865, Édouard René Lefèbvre de Laboulaye (also known as the "Father of the Statue of Liberty") proposed that a monument representing freedom and democracy be created by the French government as a gift to the United States of America. Laboulaye was a prominent and important political thinker, an abolitionist, and supporter of President Abraham Lincoln during the American Civil War. Laboulaye believed in the "common law of free peoples," and that every person born had an inalienable right to freedom. The recent Union Army victory in the American Civil War (1861-1865) served as a platform for Laboulaye to argue that honoring the United States for freeing the slaves would also help to strengthen the cause for more democracy in France. As the President of the French Antislavery Society, Laboulaye believed that the 1865 passage of the Thirteenth Amendment to the United States Constitution (abolishing slavery) proved that justice and liberty for all was possible. Ten years later, with the help of his friend and sculptor Auguste Bartholdi, De Laboulaye turned his proposal into a reality.

In September 1875, Laboulaye and Bartholdi publicly announced what was to become their colossal "Statue of Liberty Project" and organized the Franco-American Union as its fundraising arm. At this public ceremony the project was first given the name "Liberty Enlightening the World." A written proposal was then set to pen that promised the French people would finance, design, build, and then disassemble and ship the statue to America, if the American people would finance the construction of the statue in America's New York Harbor. Historians (such as those from the U.S. National Park Service) claim that Bartholdi's statue was meant to be a gift from France to America in honor of their mutual friendship. Bartholdi said the statue represented France's celebration of America's abolition of slavery. Bartholdi used his Ethiopian inspired painting described as "Woman holding the scales of justice in one hand, with one foot stepping on the American flag sitting at her feet, and her other foot stepping on a large chain representing the broken chains of past American enslavement policies" for sculpting his original model of the Statue of Liberty, later modified to its current form. Bartholdi's original design was rejected by America's aristocracy who felt that the original model was too controversial, and that America was not in the mood for a colossal statue in the image of a black woman stepping on the American flag while perched at the entrance to the New York Harbor. The current Statue of Liberty is described as having a "Masonic symbol imbedded pedestal with a robed female statue image of a European female face holding a book of the law in her left hand, and a torch in her right hand, with no American flag at her feet." What's very interesting about this story is the fact that the broken chains (referred to previously in Bartholdi's original design) remain to this day at the Statue of Liberty's feet.

In 1878, the first full-scale version of the Statue of Liberty was constructed in France. A large steel framework was built and covered with hand-hammered sheets of thin copper that created the exterior form of the statue. The steel frame engineering was first designed by the French engineer Eugene Viollet-le-Duc (who died unexpectedly in 1879). Viollet-le-Duc was replaced by the French architect and steel engineer Alexandre-Gustave Eiffel (who later designed the Eiffel Tower in Paris, France). The Statue of Liberty was completed in France at the end of 1884, disassembled, and shipped in pieces to America, where it's components were stored on land at New York Harbor.

In 1882, the Statue of Liberty faced funding problems. Wealthy Americans were reluctant to finance the statue, and articles in newspapers of the time cited the American government's failure to support the statue's construction. It was during this period that the Statue of Liberty came close to not being erected at all. American Nativists (Americans who opposed all forms of immigration) linked the proposed Statue of Liberty to immigration threats, which were most starkly expressed in political cartoons of the day depicting foreigners as threats to American liberties and values. It is ironic that the Statue of Liberty would eventually end up owing its very existence to the thousands of small financial donations from American immigrants, and from the American middle class, who finally provided the money to construct the statue.

In 1883, the construction phase of the Statue of Liberty's huge granite pedestal began on Liberty Island. Designed by architect Richard Morris Hunt, the base was 87 feet high (and said to be the largest granite structure in the world). The actual work of building the pedestal's foundation, and then the statue itself, was the responsibility of the decorated U.S. General Charles Pomeroy Stone, of the U.S. Army. Stone was a master at organizing, engineering, and executing his duties. He was referred to as the "man who built the Statue of Liberty." Unfortunately, Stone died of pneumonia after the Statue of Liberty was officially dedicated. Member of Congress William Maxwell Evarts and the industrialist Richard Butler worked very hard to engage wealthy and prominent Americans to contribute to the project. In late 1884, all the funds for the pedestal's construction had been exhausted, and no one came forward to save the project from its apparent doom. Then, in 1885, wealthy newspaper publisher Joseph Pulitzer came to the statue's rescue. Pulitzer wrote a front-page article urging the American public to donate money toward the construction of the statue. Pulitzer wrote:

We must raise the money! The New World is the people's paper, and now it appeals to the people to come forward and raise the money. The $250,000 that the making of the Statue cost was paid in by the masses of the French people-by the working men, the tradesmen, the shop girls, the artisans-by all, irrespective of class or condition. Let us respond in like manner. Let us not wait for the millionaires to give us this money. It is not a gift from the millionaires of France to the millionaires of America, but the gift of the whole people of France to the whole people of America.

By the end of August 1885, the New World had collected over $100,000 in donations (most being about $1 or less). Roughly 125,000 people contributed to the Statue of Liberty campaign (due mainly to the efforts of Pulitzer's newspaper crusade). To personally thank the contributors, the New World published the names of each person who donated (no matter the size of the donation). This money assured that the Statue of Liberty was built and go on to become a symbol known around the world. Pulitzer died 26 years later, on October 29, 1911.

In 1886, the Statue of Liberty was finally finished and dedicated. There was a huge celebration of fireworks and New York Harbor's waters that filled with boats and vessels of all sizes. All the newspapers in America ran a story about this historic moment.

In 1892, a sonnet by the American Jewish immigrant Emma Lazarus was published. It was dedicated to the Statue of Liberty and reads as follows:

The New Colossus
Not like the brazen giant of Greek fame,
With conquering limbs astride from land to land;
Here at our sea-washed, sunset gates shall stand
A mighty woman with a torch, whose flame
Is the imprisoned lightning, and her name
Mother of Exiles. From her beacon-hand
Glows worldwide welcome; her mild eyes command
The air-bridged harbor that twin cities frame.
'Keep, ancient lands, your storied pomp!' cries she
With silent lips. 'Give me your tired, your poor,
Your huddled masses yearning to breathe free,
The wretched refuse of your teeming shore.'
Send these, the homeless, tempest tossed to me,
I lift my lamp beside the golden door!

During the late 1800s, the "Black Press" began to debunk romantic notions about the Statue of Liberty and raised issues about racism and discrimination, which they claimed continued to exist in America toward African-Americans. Some scholars and activists view the Statue of Liberty not as a symbol of equal liberty for all, but rather as a symbol of a failed democracy where the rights of some minorities are not equal. Millions of new-arriving immigrants told a much different story. Most immigrants arriving at Ellis Island were in awe when they reached the entrance to New York Harbor and saw the Statue of Liberty, which most immigrants thought was placed there to welcome each of them to America and their new "land of opportunity."

It was not until 1877, that Congress passed a resolution accepting France's gift and appropriated $56,000 for its construction and maintenance. The famous poem now inscribed on a bronze plaque on the pedestal of the Statue of Liberty was not installed until 1903, 17 years after the author's death. The Statue was not declared a National Monument until 1924, 38 years after being erected. Since its dedication, the Statue of Liberty has evolved from a time when anyone could pay 50 cents at the monument to walk up the stairs inside the statue's head and peer out of the windows in the statue's crown, to today's high security requiring that all tickets be bought in advance.

- End of Section -

Gallery

The Statue of Liberty

Auguste Bartholdi's sketch of the Statue of Liberty on Bedloe's Island, N.Y., c. 1872
Source: National Park Service-Statue of Liberty-National Monument Photo Collection

Auguste Bartholdi's model of the proposed Suez Canal Lighthouse, c. 1880
Source: National Park Service-Statue of Liberty-National Monument Photo Collection

American Committee Statue of Liberty Fundraising miniature, c. 1885
Source: National Park Service-Statue of Liberty-National Monument Photo Collection

Construction of the Statue of Liberty in Paris, France, c.1 878
Source: Wikimedia Commons

Completed Statue of Liberty, Paris, France, 1885
Dismantled and shipped to America, stored on land in New York Harbor
Source: Wikimedia Commons

Pedestal construction of the Statue of Liberty on Bedloe's Island, New York Harbor, c. 1884

Edouard de Laboulaye, the "Father of the Statue of Liberty," c. 1874

Frédéric Auguste Bartholdi, sculptor and designer of the Statue of Liberty, c. 1882
Source: National Park Service-Statue of Liberty-National Monument Photo Collection

Joseph Pulitzer - Owner of the New York's New World newspaper, responsible for the
public fundraising that paid to build the Statue of Liberty, c. 1883
Source: National Park Service-Statue of Liberty-National Monument Photo Collection

Emma Lazarus, poet who wrote *The New Colossus* sonnet which was
cast in bronze and fixed on the Statue of Liberty's pedestal.

Statute of Liberty, Liberty Island, New York Harbor, erected in 1886, photo c. 2008
Source: Photo by: Daniel Schwen-Wikipedia Open Source Photo

Statue of Liberty - Left foot standing on broken, unshackled chain at her feet, photo 2008
Source: National Park Service-Statue of Liberty-National Monument Photo Collection

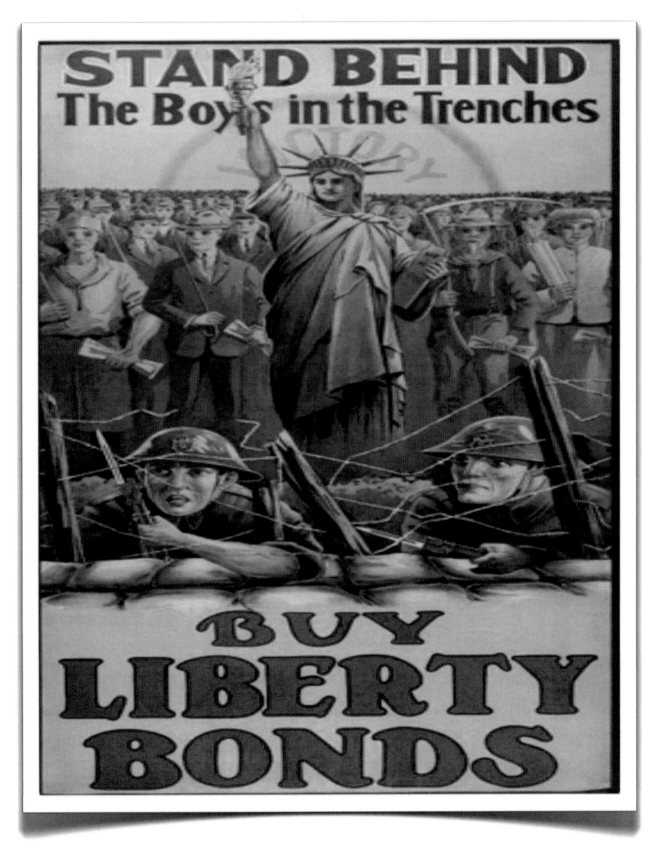

World War I poster to promote the sale of American Liberty War Bonds, c. 1915
Source: National Park Service-Statue of Liberty-National Monument Photo Collection

World War II poster to promote the sale of American War Bonds, c. 1942
Source: National Park Service-Statue of Liberty-National Monument Photo Collection

Chapter Two

Immigration to America

Immigration to America

Early German Immigration to America

More than eight million Germans are estimated to have immigrated to America between 1680 and 2000. In 1890, German immigrants outnumbered all other immigrants who had come to America. Between 1683 and 1700, the most modern American immigration port of entry was the coastline port in the state of Pennsylvania. By 1800, the most famous American port of entry was New York Harbor; followed by Baltimore, Maryland; New Orleans, Louisiana; and Galveston, Texas. The most popular European ports of departure for emigration to America were Bremen and Hamburg, Germany. By 1900, the "go to" immigration port of entry in America was the Ellis Island Immigration Station, in the New York Harbor. On April 17, 1907, workers in the Great Hall of the Immigration Center at Ellis Island processed 11,747 immigrants in one day. This enumeration captured the diversity of this "golden era of American immigration." The 1910 Federal Census showed a population of 92,228,496 people in 46 states. German immigrant settlements grew and prospered in many locations including Pennsylvania, New York, and Wisconsin. It was not until 1920 that the Federal Census began recording immigration information, including what language each person spoke, and his or her country of origin. The number of German immigrants declined sharply between 1948 and 1950. By the year 2000, over forty-three percent of Wisconsin residents claimed to have German ancestors.

There are many historical photographs depicting images of immigrants seeking a new life. A hard overseas journey was the first obstacle they had to overcome. Most immigrants lived first with relatives, and then ventured out on their own. Families were critical for most immigrants as they worked together to build their futures. Most of these immigrants were a "tough breed" and knew how to survive under stressful conditions and how to deal with adjusting to their new culture in their new homeland. The Ellis Island Museum is one of New York's most moving sites. Roughly 40% of America's immigrants can trace their heritage to an ancestor who came through Ellis Island. For 62 years (from 1892 until 1954), Ellis Island was America's main entry point for immigrants and processed some 12 million people. Immigration through Ellis Island was brusque in the early years of the 20th century until 1924. The Ellis Island Immigration Museum skillfully relates the story of Ellis Island by placing emphasis on presenting each visitor with a personal experience. I wonder what immigrants thought as they disembarked from their ship at the dock and entered the Main Immigration Building Baggage Room? They then climbed the stairs to the Registry Room (with its dramatic vaulted tiled ceiling) and waited anxiously for medical, and legal processing. The Ellis Island Treasures Exhibit features 1,000 objects and photos donated by descendants of immigrants, including family heirlooms, religious articles, period clothing, and jewelry. The American Immigrant Wall of Honor at the Statue of Liberty on Liberty Island commemorates more than 500,000 immigrants and their families, from Myles Standish and George Washington's great-grandfather to the forebears of John F. Kennedy. Visitors can research their family's history at the interactive American Family Immigration History Center.

Immigration through Ellis Island, New York

In 1892, ten years after the Statue of Liberty's completion, America's largest and most famous immigration port, Ellis Island, was completed and dedicated for the single purpose of processing thousands of new immigrants. Ellis Island is in New York Harbor, next to Liberty Island. In the years that followed, the number of immigrations that passed through this facility increased drastically. This immigration explosion was due to several events that happen in Europe, including the Irish Potato Famine (1845-1847); Britons' massive exodus to America (one third of the United Kingdom population emigrated to other countries to live), religious persecution of the Jews in Russia and Eastern Europe, religious persecution of the Mormons in Great Britain and Scandinavia, and a massive exodus from Europe during and following World Wars. Between 1892 and 1954, Ellis Island processed 17 million immigrants, but only 12 million were admitted into America. Around five million were deported by ship back to their countries of origin, or died in custody and were cremated at the Ellis Island disease detention facility on Hoffman Island. For those who were deported back to their port of emigration, Ellis Island became referred to as "Heartbreak Island" or "the Isle of Tears." One can only imagine what it must have been like to spend all your money to get to America, have no resources left after having endured a potentially deadly and devastating voyage by ship, only to be humiliated, quarantined, and then sent back home on another ship, or worse yet, dying while in custody.

Healthy Ellis Island immigrants were processed, approved, and quickly released to become participants in the "American Dream." Money made a great difference in how one was processed on arrival at Ellis Island. For instance, the poor steerage passengers (called the "great unwashed") were required to depart their ship and continue through Ellis Island's Main Immigration Facility. Many first class and second class passengers received their medical examinations by the Immigration Authority while onboard their ships and were often released to travel anywhere they pleased without ever entering Ellis Island. There are some immigrant accounts that describe how immigration agents changed immigrants' given and surnames while processing them. However, imagine, if you can, what it was like having the responsibility of handling and processing millions of immigrants from so many different cultures, religions, and languages. It must have been a monumental task, to say the least. Also, don't forget the high quality of the architecture and the facilities on Ellis Island, and the other islands (including the hospitals, living quarters, dining halls, and transportation). It is well known that Ellis Island immigrants were herded into chain-link cages, often referred to as "pens," and everyone was forced to remain in custody until they passed the last processing station. Unfortunately, this processing environment was a necessary part of the immigration experience of the time.

In November of 1954, all facilities on Ellis Island were closed. In the year 2000, funds were raised for the restoration of the island (now known as the National Immigration Museum). The Ellis Island National Immigration Museum and the Statue of Liberty are now under the care and management of the U.S. National Park Service. These facilities have been closed several times for repairs (most recently during Hurricane Sandy; that struck New York in October 2012 and caused considerable damage). As of 2014, Ellis Island and the Statue of Liberty had reopened to visitors.

Ocean Voyages to America, 1800-1950
Many immigrant family stories describe what it was like for them to say goodbye to their loved ones, step aboard an oceangoing ship, and watch the shoreline disappear, never to be reunited with their family again. It was an enormous risk taken my millions of immigrants who believed (rightly or not) that America held the "promise of fortune and fame." Some immigrants had nothing to lose if they succeeded and stayed alive. Many immigrant families sold all their worldly possessions, took enormous risks during their voyage across the ocean, and landed in the country of unfamiliar languages and customs.

The majority of immigrations to America came by way of sailing ships called "schooners." These vessels were often considered undesirable and frequently proved to be dangerous (if not deadly) for passenger sea travel. They were slow, had small quarters, were unkempt, riddled with diseases, and human waste. In the early 1900s, the mighty coal-fired steamships came into service. Steamships had large steel shells, offered large quarters, moved much faster than schooners, and had two or three classes of passenger accommodations. Wealthy passengers traveled in first class cabins located on the upper levels of the ship, and had almost all the comforts of home, including champagne and fine dining. Second class passengers traveled in the mid-ship cabins, usually on the second deck, and had excellent accommodations as well. Then, there were the steerage passengers, who were often referred to as the "unclean, or dirty immigrants." Steerage berths crowded into the hull of the ship (known as the "steerage deck"), where the steering cables ran through the ship's bowels. The hull area, never designed for human passengers, but instead for cattle and cargo. The steerage passengers were often taken on board in arrival ports, after the paid cargo was unloaded, and the ship's captain was expected to fill these spaces with more paying cargo or passengers upon return to their ports of origination. These steerage compartment hulls were usually composed of one large, open large floor, with no cabin rooms or any wall partitions for privacy. There was no running water, few if any sanitary toilets, and no fresh air. Steerage passengers were often fed spoiled food from communal kettles.

Immigration Stories

The voyage by ship to America was not an easy one for many of our ancestors. They had to deal with seasickness, crowded conditions, and the fear that when they arrived they could be turned away and deported to their country of origin. Millions of these immigrants passed through Ellis Island and other U.S. ports. Immigrants often shared oral stories about their immigration with their close family members, but too often these have been lost to time. Since 1973, the Ellis Island Oral History Program, run by the Ellis Island Immigration Museum, has been collecting oral histories from immigrants who came to America during the years when Ellis Island was in operation (1892-1954). Audio files of over 1,700 interviews can be listened to on this Ellis Island website. These oral histories are full of juicy details about their life in their mother country, their immigration journey and early experiences in America. Four such unedited immigration stories read as follows:

1. Rose Milazzo emigrated from Naples to America by steamship in 1901 when she was only seven years old, and she had this story to tell: "We started at Naples and boarded the ship and my last meal was in Naples and I got seasick and didn't eat another meal until we got to Ellis Island. My mother had funny ideas that if they caught me seasick, they'd throw me overboard, so she hid me from the authorities or even from a doctor (which maybe could have helped me a little bit). We used to be pushed on deck because they'd have to clean the steerage where we come from, so it was easy for my mother to hide me under a blanket. We spent Christmas on board the steamship. I hid under the blanket during Christmas, but I could see that they gave out figs and they gave out delicacies (that they wouldn't give out ordinarily). So we landed at Ellis Island and got a delicious soup with white bread."

2. Estelle Schwartz Belford (a Romanian Jewish immigrant) described her trip in 1905 when she was just five-years old: "I remember riding in this wagon to a certain cousin in this large town and that was the first time that we saw these large houses and you could see across from one house to another, and everything was just wonderful. We stayed in a town by the name of Beltz for two days. We also stayed for about two days with somebody else that we knew (I had an uncle there who was a politician and through him we were able to ride across the border because in those days you couldn't get out of that town). People had to really steal their way across, but we were able to ride across the border. Then we got to the seaport of Antwerp. And we stayed there only for about a day or so and that was the first time my mother saw a lot of people in one room (like in the waiting room) and she was telling us this story that when she went into the ladies room there were a lot of sinks there, and mirrors, and the toilets on the side and we children were standing by the mirrors. She came in and she saw us. She didn't see herself, she saw us in the mirror, she never saw a mirror before. And, she thought we were there and she started scolding us, Come over here, and then she realized, and she was very much embarrassed. My mother was a very sensitive person, and all the way through she would make one little mistake and people laughed and then she wouldn't say another word. About life on board the ship in steerage. It was terrible, the whole trip. You didn't change your clothing every day on board the ship. Once, a few people came down from upstairs and spoke to us children and gave us some candy, the first time that we ever saw any candy or sweets and we were so happy to get it. The meals were brought to you very sparingly. The food was so bad that sometimes my mom would say, Don't eat it. Or, Eat very little. She herself was very sick. She was confined to bed the whole trip through, and we three kids would stand around her. We were sometimes allowed to go out on the deck. And, people from first class would look down at us and they felt sorry for us. And, many times they would throw down an orange, or apples or some food, and the children would all stand by, and I remember, this one would catch this, and this one would catch that, and if you were lucky enough you'd get something, and being as my mother was sick, if it was an orange or so, we'd bring it to her. My mother had never seen a banana, none of us ever saw a banana. And, then all of a sudden we heard a big commotion. And, everybody started yelling that they see the lady Statue of Liberty. And, we all ran upstairs and my mother got out of bed. We went upstairs and everybody started screaming and crying. You were kissing each other —people that you didn't even

know before that were alongside of you and you previously never paid any attention. Everybody was so excited that you see America and you see the Lady with her hand up, you know."

3. The following is an anonymous observers description of what it was like to travel as a steerage passenger on an ocean going steamship in 1905: "I say, and witnessed, 900 steerage passengers crowded into the hold of so elegant and roomy a steamer as the Kaiser Wilhelm II (of the North German Lloyd line) and they were positively packed like cattle, making a walk on deck when the weather was good, absolutely impossible, while to breathe of clean air below is not existent in rough weather, and when the hatches are down is an equal impossibility. The stench became unbearable, and many of the emigrants have to be driven down; for they preferred the bitterness and dangers of the stormy weather on deck, to the pestilential air below. The division between the sexes is not carefully looked after, and the young women who are quartered among the married passengers have neither the privacy to which they are entitled, nor are they much more protected than if they were living promiscuously. The food, which is miserable, is dealt out of huge kettles into the dinner pails provided by the steamship company. When it is distributed, the stronger push and crowd, so that meals are anything but orderly procedures. On the whole, the steerage of the modern steamship ought to be condemned as unfit for the transportation of human beings. Take for example, the second cabin which costs about twice as much as the 'Steerage' and sometimes not twice so much; yet the second cabin passenger on the Kaiser Wilhelm II has six times as much deck room, much better located and well protected against inclement weather. Two to four sleep in one cabin, which is well and comfortably furnished; while in the steerage from 200 to 400 sleep in one compartment on bunks, one above the other, with little light and no comforts. In the second cabin the food is excellent, is partaken of in a luxuriantly appointed dining-room, is well cooked and well served; while in the steerage the unsavory rations are not served, but doled out, with less courtesy than one would find in a charity soup kitchen. The steerage ought to be and could be abolished by law. On many ships, even drinking water is grudgingly given, and on the steamer Statendam, four years ago, we had literally to steal water for the steerage from the second cabin, and that of course at night. On many journeys, particularly on the SS Prince Bismarck of the Hamburg American Line, five years ago, the bread was absolutely uneatable, and was thrown into the water by the irate emigrants."

4. There are hundreds of other compelling and heartbreaking immigration stories. Here is one story written by Beverly Vaillancourt whose grandparents immigrated to America through Ellis Island, New York: "My grandparents were among those who immigrated to America as steerage passengers when grandma was just 14 years old. Both of my grandparents emigrated from Lithuania. My grandfathers name was Bielevicous, which was shortened to Biele when he went through Ellis Island. I have visited Ellis Island several times. Looking down from the top level of the Main Immigration Building's Great Hall is like looking down where my grandparents stood as young hopeful immigrants making their way through the cattle runs set up down there. My grandfather escaped through the underground. He was a revolutionary. My grandmother was the oldest child and was sent to America for safekeeping as the firstborn. The second story of Ellis Island has the Exam Rooms and a few swinging cots. Walking through those halls is an experience. The main room museum area has incredible photos of immigrants all dressed in their finest clothes, before their review hearing in front of the Immigration Board. Some images are full size. The looks of sadness and heartache are captivating. So much said in the eyes of those immigrants. There is a photo there of some young men in an English classroom in Chicago. One of them looks like my grandfather. I stopped cold when I saw it. There is also a quote on one of the walls from a mother in Lithuania that states: "When I put my daughter on the train that would take her to the ship bound for America, it was like placing her in her coffin." That has always resonated with me because that must have been how my great-grandmother felt when she put my grandmother on a ship bound for America. Ellis Island is a very poignant place."

- End of Section -

Gallery

Immigration to America

Illustration of steerage passengers on a steamship's deck viewing the Statue of Liberty as they enter New York Harbor and the Ellis Island Immigration Station, July 2, 1887
Source: Frank Leslie's Illustrated Newspaper-Nation Park Service, National Monument-Liberty Island-Photo Collection

Steerage passengers on a steamship's deck entering the New York Harbor, c. 1892
Source: Statue of Liberty-Ellis Island Foundation, Inc.-Photo Collection

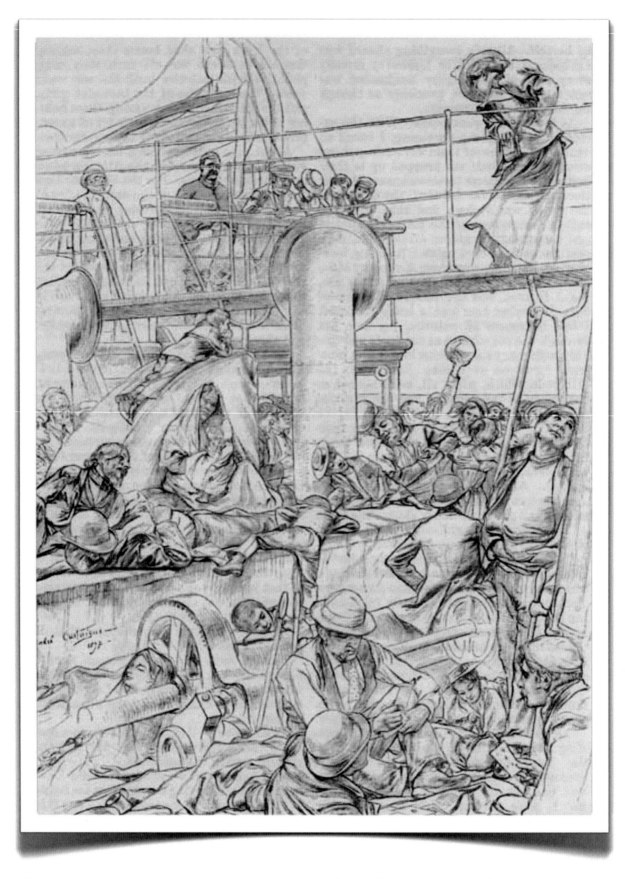

Illustration of steerage passengers on a steamship's deck during good weather, c. 1890
Source: Gjenvick & Gjonvik Photo Collection-Pinterest

Illustration of steerage passengers inside a ship's hull facing seasickness and cramped
quarters, c. 1890
Source: Gjenvick & Gjonvik Photo Collection-Pinterest

Steerage passengers on a steamship's deck entering New York Harbor, c. 1892
Source: The Statue of Liberty-Ellis Island Foundation, Inc.-Photo Collection

Immigrants arriving at Ellis Island, in New York Harbor, c. 1902
Source: The Statue of Liberty-Ellis Island Foundation, Inc.-Photo Collection

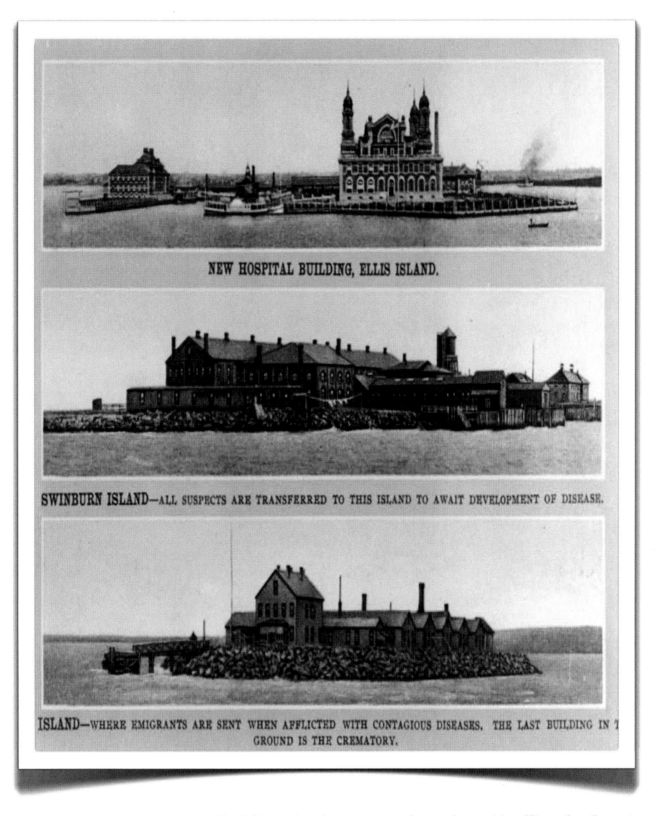

NEW HOSPITAL BUILDING, ELLIS ISLAND.

SWINBURN ISLAND—ALL SUSPECTS ARE TRANSFERRED TO THIS ISLAND TO AWAIT DEVELOPMENT OF DISEASE.

ISLAND—WHERE EMIGRANTS ARE SENT WHEN AFFLICTED WITH CONTAGIOUS DISEASES. THE LAST BUILDING IN 7 GROUND IS THE CREMATORY.

American immigration port buildings in the New York Harbor: (1) Ellis Island Main Building's immigration processing center and Hospital Building, (2) Swinburn Island was a holding center for all immigrants suspected of carrying disease, and (3) Hoffman Island was a contagious disease detention center with crematory. Photos c. 1902

Source: Library Of Congress-Quarantine Sketches-The Maltine Company Collection

Ellis Island, New York Harbor. Immigrants crossing the ferry landing and walking to the Main Immigration Building, c. 1902
Source: Library of Congress-Quarantine Sketches-The Maltine Company Collection

Uncle Sam providing a free meal to the immigrants at Ellis Island, c. 1902
Source: New York Public Library-Photo by Edwin Levick-Williams & Williams, Stephen A. Schwarzman Collection

Ellis Island, New York, Main Immigration Building, mental testing station, c. 1902
Source: National Park Service-The Statue of Liberty-Ellis Island Foundation, Inc. Photo Collection

Ellis Island, New York, Main Immigration Building railroad ticket office, the station where
immigrants who had been processed and approved are waited to be picked up by a ferry and
taken to New York to board a train to their destinations, c. 1905
Source: National Park Service-The Statue of Liberty-Ellis Island Foundation, Inc. Photo Collection

Immigrants on Ellis Island, processed, approved, waiting for a ferry to New York, c. 1902
Source: The Statue of Liberty-Ellis Island Foundation, Inc.-Photo Collection

German steamship *Prince Friedrich Wilhelm*, boarded by Karl Friedrich Wilhelm
Brinkmann during his immigration to America, 1909
Source: Ancestry.com-Steamship Photo Collection

Ellis Island, New York Harbor, as seen from immigration ship's top deck on arrival. The Statue of Liberty is in the background, c. 1910
Source: The Statue of Liberty-Ellis Island Foundation, Inc.-Photo Collection

Ellis Island, New York Harbor, Main Immigration Building dock where processed immigrants are waiting for a ferry to take them to New York, October 30, 1912.
Source: Library of Congress Photo Collection-Underwood & Underwood Collection

Three immigrants on Ellis Island looking at the Statue of Liberty and wondering what their futures will be like in their new home in American, c. 1915
Source: Nation Park Service, Nation Monument-Liberty Island-Photo Collection

Ellis Island, New York Harbor, Main Immigration Building entrance where newly arrived immigrants are awaiting processing, c. 1907
Source: Library Of Congress Photo Collection

Steerage passengers packed on a ship's deck for fresh air and sunlight, c. 1920
Source: Gjenvick & Gjonvik Photo Collection-Pinterest

Ellis Island Immigration Station - Main Building, New York, c. 1902-1913
Source: New York Public Library-Stephen A. Schwarzman Photo Collection

Ellis Island, New York Harbor, Main Immigration Building with ferry arriving with new immigrants, c. 1918-1922
Source: Library of Congress-Herbert A. French Photo collection

Ellis Island, New York, Main Dining Hall. Empty hall with immigrant's place settings of worn porcelain-enameled plates, with a fork, and knife, c. 1902-1913
Source: New York Public Library-Photo by Edwin Levick-Williams & Williams, Stephen A. Schwarzman Collection

Ellis Island, New York, N.Y. Main Building Dining Hall where each arriving new immigrant
received a free meal during processing. c.1920.
Source: U.S. Immigration & Naturalization Service-The Statue of Liberty-Ellis Island Foundation, Inc. Collection.

Ellis Island "holding pens" (processing stations) Main Immigration Building. These
immigrants passed mental inspections and are awaiting further processing, c.1902-1912
Source: New York Public Library-Photo by Edwin Levick-Williams & Williams, Stephen A. Schwarzman Collection

Ellis Island, New York, Main Hall Building with long benches installed after the "pen stations" were removed. Note the U.S. flag with 46 stars, c. 1907-1912.
Source: New York Public Library-Photo by Edwin Levick-Williams & Williams, Stephen A. Schwarzman Collection

U.S. passenger steamship *America*, docked in the New York Harbor, c. 1920
Source: The Statue of Liberty-Ellis Island Foundation, Inc.-Photo Collection

U.S. steamship *George Washington*, boarded by Ernestine Hermine (Hildebrandt)
Brinkmann and her daughter Elsie Louise Brinkman during their return trip home to
America after visiting Hermine's family in Nienburg, Germany, c. 1923
Source: Ancestry.com Ship Collection

U.S. steamship *George Washington,* crossing the Atlantic Ocean, c. 1923
Source: Ancestry.com Ship Collection

Immigrants in an English class given by the Training Service Department of Labor at the
Ford Motor Company Factory, Detroit, Michigan, c. 1930
Source: Library Of Congress-National Photo Collection

Immigrants in an English class given by the Training Service Department of Labor at the
Ford Motor Company Factory, Detroit, Michigan, c. 1930
Source: Library Of Congress-National Photo Collection

Ellis Island, New York, Main Immigration Building front entrance after its restoration into
a National Monument Immigration Museum, photo c. 2012
Source: The Statue of Liberty-Ellis Island Foundation, Inc. Photo Collection

Ellis Island Great Hall after its total restoration, photo c. 2012
Source: The Statue of Liberty-Ellis Island Foundation, Inc. Photo Collection

Ellis Island Immigration Museum, photo c. 2012
Source: The Statue of Liberty-Ellis Island Foundation, Inc. Photo Collection

Ellis Island, New York Harbor; Arial photograph after the completion of the buildings restoration and new bridge to connect Ellis Island with New Jersey, c. 2006
Source: Library Of Congress-National Photo Collection-Carol M. Highsmith Photo Collection

Chapter Three

Glassmaking History

Glassmaking History

Glassmaking & Glass Blowing, Brinkmann Family Trade History
Before this book introduces the Brinkmann family ancestors, I think it is critical to present what they did for a living in Germany. Many Brinkmann's were skilled *Glasmachers* (glassmakers) who worked in various German *Glashütten* (glass foundries). At its origin, glass blowing began as a novel idea invented by the Phoenicians around 50 B.C. (that coincided with the establishment of the Roman Empire). Later, the art of glass blowing was refined and advanced in the first century A.D. (with an injection of air into a ball of molten glass heated to 2,400 Fahrenheit Degrees). Roman Centurion outposts were established all over Europe to spread the dominance of the Roman Empire, and during this period the Romans set out to train apprentices in the growing glass blowing industry. One of the largest glass manufacturing centers in Europe was established in Cologne (near the Rhine River) in Germany. Glassmaking (and glasswares) were a very important part of all European economies. The *Glasflasche* (glass bottle) became the container of choice for all liquid goods, and commerce. Glass was also used as a media for making very ornate gifts and ornamentation. It was also used to make coins for a variety of monetary exchange systems. Several Brinkmann generations (from the early 1700s through the 1900s) were highly skilled glass blowers, and glass makers, in a variety of glass manufacturing trades. Glassmaking skills were trade secrets passed on from father to son, and became a very important part of the Brinkmann heritage. It is, therefore, important to understand the history of the glassmaking in Europe and Germany in particular.

A Brief History of Glassmaking
Glass artifacts have been found in Germany that date back hundreds of years. Early German *Goblets* (drinking glasses with a stem and base) were made in small villages using mud and stone kilns to heat sand into a molten form of glass that was cooled inside a stone form to create the desired shape. Later, glass blowing evolved to become one of the most important industries in Europe. Large *Glashütten* (glass foundries) or *Glasfabriken* (glass factories) were built to accommodate the demand for glass products. As production increased so did the need for skilled *Glasmachers* (glassmakers) who were recruited from all over Europe. Before the Industrial Revolution, each step in the glassmaking process required many skilled artisans who had been trained to master specific tasks. Some of these glass trades included: *Glas Verkäufer und Händler* (glass seller & merchant), *Glasverarbeitung Koller und Sand Ofen Füllstoff* (glass processing edge runner and sand furnace filler), *Glasbläser* (glass blower), *Balloonmacher* (large glass jug maker), *Packmeister* (shipping packer), *Schürer* (Keeper of the fire in the glass furnace), and the *Schmelzmeister* (glass melting master). There were also many other trades that supported these glassmaking artisans, such as weavers, who made the straw baskets that were woven around the large flasks (jugs) for protection during shipping; enamel masters, who applied gold gilding, etchings, and engravings; and glass artisans, who made glass objects that were considered works of art. Many of the German *Glashütte* (glass works) of the 1700s and 1800s built cottage living quarters for their workers as an incentive for them to remain close to the factory. The Brinkmanns are known to have lived, and died, in these cottages. Many of the earliest most remote glass factories eventually evolved into villages, towns, and cities that were often named for the original glass factories.

Work in the glass trade was not easy. It required multiple manual skills and muscle. The furnaces and the blowing of glass generated heat and fumes created by silica dust that made the work environment hazardous, and unhealthy. In 1901, German glass blowers organized into unions and led a national strike to improve their working conditions. As a result, glass production halted in Germany. Union-busting fights erupted, and many striking glass blowers (including Karl Friedrich Wilhelm Brinkmann) were "blacklisted" for several years. Many strikers were forced to find other ways of making a living. The 1901 glass bottle workers' strike eventually ended because their union ran out of funds, and glassmaking regained its previous production demand quotas.

Next came the Second Industrial Revolution, which permanently changed everything. Machines were invented that made skilled glass tradesmen a thing of the past. The glass industry evolved into a science with little need for thousands of workers. It was around this juncture in time, the early 1900s, when many of the younger Brinkmanns began immigrating to America. Karl Friedrich Wilhelm Brinkmann was one of the first to go. He immigrated to Platteville, Wisconsin in 1909 and took up farming. Soon, the Brinkmanns met other German families (such as the Grafs and Weisses) and intermarried. Many of the children of these Brinkmann ancestors were born as American citizens and have little or no knowledge of their original family histories.

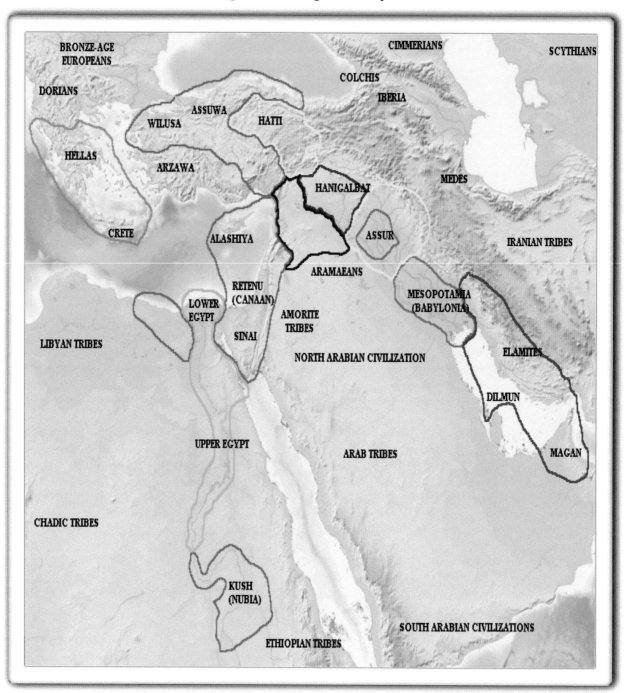

Bronze Age world map of ancient eastern civilizations where glass was discovered and introduced to Rome, the rest of Europe, and the world

Source: Wikimedia Commons

A History of Glassmaking Unions in Germany

The first union of *Glaskünstler* (glass artists) was founded in Dresden, Germany in 1875. Factory owners' responses were harsh, and none of the union's members received work. All labor unions were banned by the German *Sozialistengesetz* (Socialists' Act) which came into effect in 1878.

In 1890, the antiunion law had been repealed, and a new union for glass workers was founded in Hamburg, Germany. The organization had its headquarters in Berlin-Stralau and was the first union to include members from glass factories in Nienburg. The unions fight for better working conditions was aided by the opening of a new glass factory in Wilhelmshütte, which was much more worker-friendly than other established glass factories.

By 1900, many German glass factories had already begun switching to a more industrial approach to the production of glass, leading to poorer working conditions and a reduced need for laborers. In August 1900, the first strike broke out among the glass workers in an old established glass factory in Schaumburg. A Mr. Heye owned both the Schaumburg and Nienburg glass factories, which caused the Schaumburg laborers to demand working conditions and pay comparable to their colleagues in Nienburg. In February of 1901, the Nienburg Glass Workers' Union also went on strike to support the Schaumburg workers. This was the first sympathy strike in the history of German glassmaking.

The Nienburg Union members paid a heavy price for their solidarity. Many workers were evicted from their homes, and their children were no longer allowed to attend the Nienburg Glass Factory's schools. The strike dragged on for many months. To solve his labor shortage, Mr. Heye imported many Russian and Finnish glass blowers to keep up factory production. These replacement glassblowers were not informed that the local workers had gone on strike, and were not prepared for confrontations with the German glassworkers. In addition, Heye installed new automated bottle-making machines to increase production, which eliminated many jobs.

By July 1901, the strike had escalated into a strike of all glassmakers in Germany. By then, more than 4,000 glass blowers had left the country, unable to find work due to their affiliation with the union, or due to poor working conditions. On September 18, 1901, the unions cancelled the strike due to their lack of funding. Those who had led the strikes were unable to find employment in the glass industry, and many left the country. The remaining workers were only slowly employed back into the industry.

Despite Heye's vehement objection to unions, it should be noted that his factories in Germany contributed greatly to the local economy and employed many people. In addition, he had many worker welfare facilities (including schools, day care facilities, and homes) built for his factories' glass workers. In the end, the strike cost the tradesmen dearly and eroded the unions' strength for many years to come. The "old way" of making glass in Germany had ended.

As previously mentioned, some Brinkmanns, such as Karl Friedrich Wilhelm Brinkmann, are known to have been blacklisted in Germany and to have suffered great hardship, as a result, of their union affiliations. Karl was one of the glass workers who left Germany and immigrated to America in 1909. His immediate family (spouse and children) immigrated in 1910. Karl quickly discovered that there was no glassmaking industry in the Platteville, Wisconsin area, so he was forced to take on any work he could find, including mining work and heavy labor. Farming turned out to be Karl's most enduring source of income. However, after his boys returned from military service in the U.S. Army in World War I, Karl packed up his family and moved to Milwaukee, Wisconsin and never returned to the rural lifestyle.

Records Search, Glassmaking Industry Locations in Germany

Glassmaking factories were located in many different parts of Germany, including Lower Saxony, as early as the 1700s, and some still operate today. To properly conduct research regarding where glass factories are located, a request was sent February 2013 to the Nienburg-Weser Museum in Nienburg, Germany. This request asked for assistance in finding research authorities who specialized in the location of German glass factories, in the hope that such factories and villages might have church parish records for the ancestors of this Brinkmann family.

Note: A response to this request was received in 2013. The Nienburg Museum referred our search to a German history book entitled *A 100 Year History of Glass Factories in Nienburg, Germany, 1891-1991.*[6] This book was bought by this author and contains a great history of the glassmaking industry in Nienburg/Weser. This is recommended reading, even though it is available only in German.

Records Search, Letter Sent to *Hans Otto Schneegluth*, Nienburg, Germany

In 2013, this author sent a letter to Hans-Otto Schneegluth[7] (author of the book *Glassmaking in Nienburg, Germany*) to see if he could assist with the location of other German glass factories in Lower Saxony where Brinkmann family members may have worked.

Note: No response was received. Letters and packages exchanged between the U.S., and Germany can take 2 to 3 weeks for delivery and there is no way to know if they arrived at their proper German destination. Undeliverable mail is a common problem. Sending an email is much preferred, and can be used to confirm mailings, but not all Germans are willing to provide their email addresses to American strangers.

- End of Section -

Gallery

Glassmaking in Germany

Photographs in this gallery were provided courtesy of the following:

The Museum of Nienburg, Nienburg/Weser, 1991 publication-*100 Years of Glassmaking in Nienburg (1891-1991),* by Dr. Dietmar Obsto and Dr. Eilbert Ommen (ISBN 3-9802037-8-6), published by Druckerei J. Hoffmann Gmb H & Co., Nienburg/Weser, Germany, and from Wikipedia & Wikimedia Commons, Open Source Media. All original photographs were from period-specific locations within Germany and secured in protected personal archives or public history museums.

Roman blown-glass pitcher, c. 4th century A.D.

Ancient symbol of glassmaking, c. 1200

A glassmakers' crest, c. 1300

Glass factory in a German village, c. 15th century

Glass merchant, c. 16th Century

White glass goblet, c. 1600

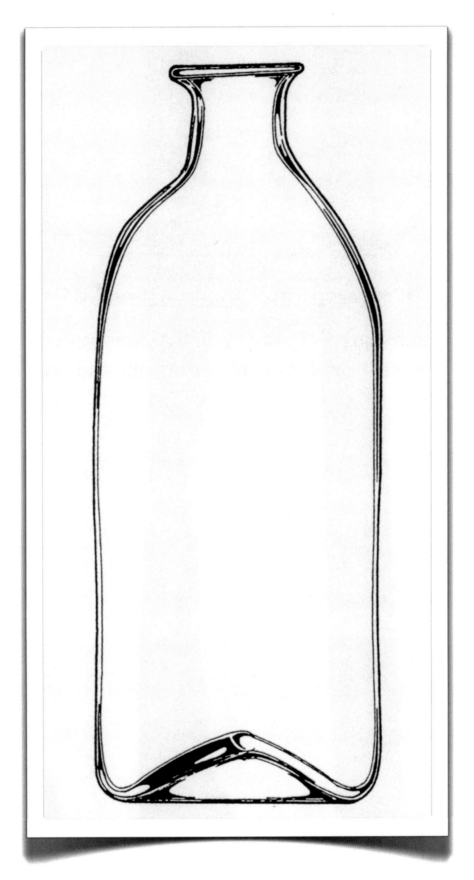

Simple four-sided flattened bottle, c. 1600

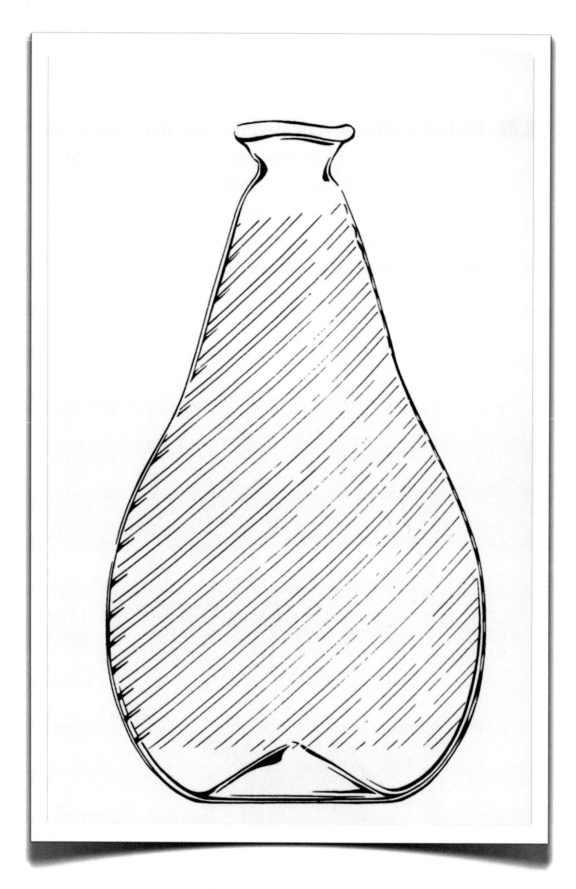

Bulbous ribbed bottle, c. 1600

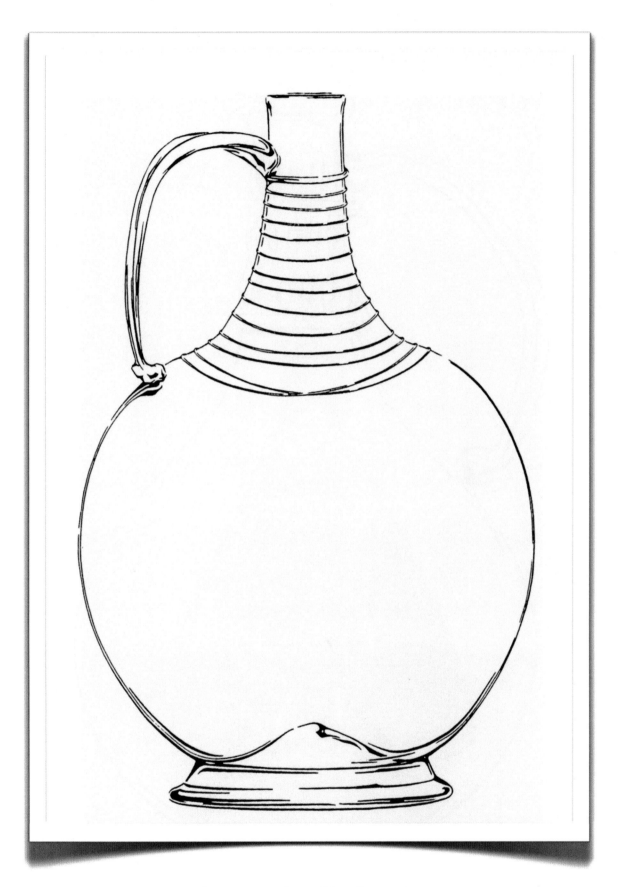

Blown pear-shaped bottle, c. 1600

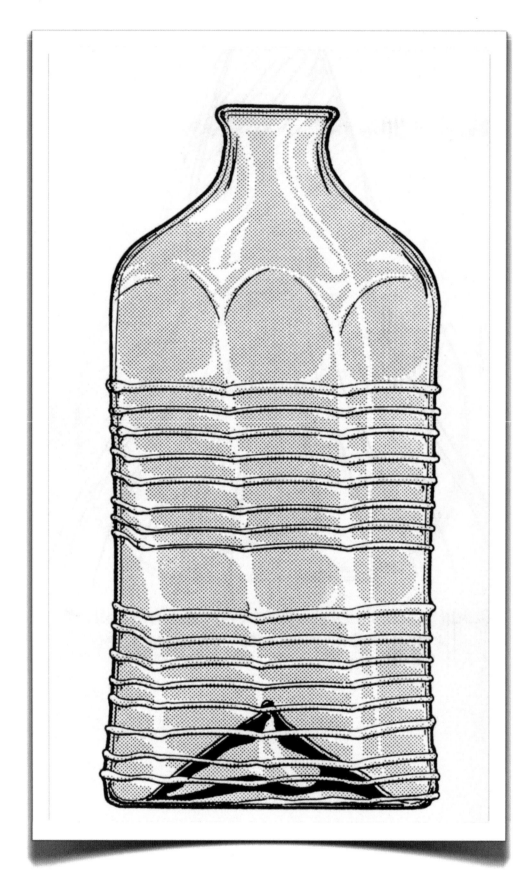

Octagonal bottle, c. 1700

Decorative goblet, c. 1600

Ruby ribbed glass set in a solid gold cradle with a walking man figure at its crown, c. 1700

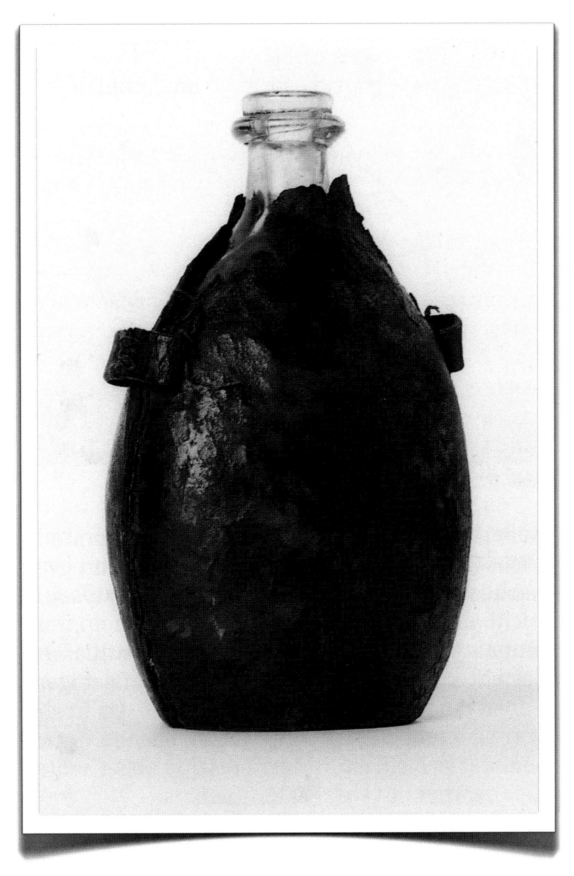

Army field flask, glass wrapped in leather, c.1800

Tinted four-sided bottles, c. 1800

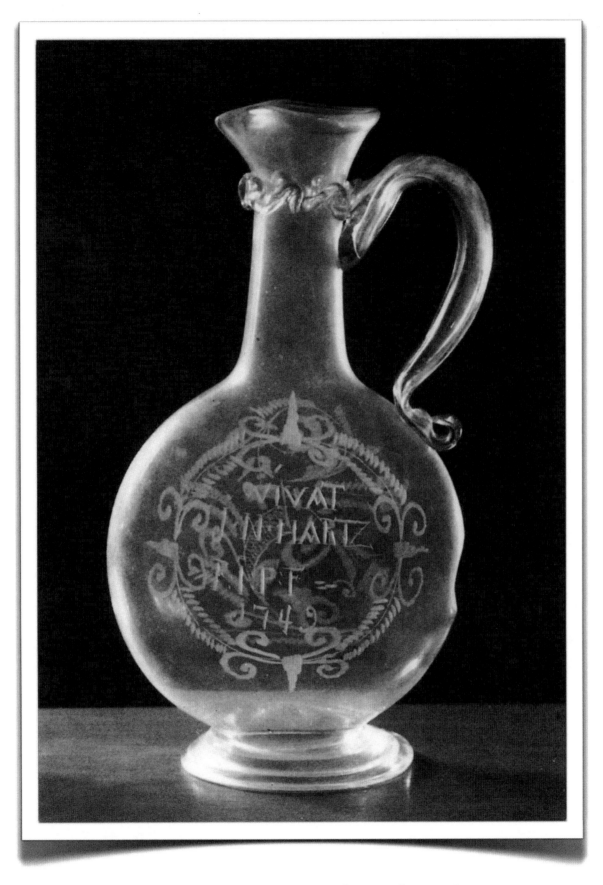

Frosted fancy flask-style bottle with etching and engraving, c. 1800

Glass balloon maker working at the furnace kiln, c. 1900

Glass blowing workstation "on the block," c. 1903

H. Heye Glass Factory, Nienburg, Germany, c. 1906

H. Heye Glass Factory, Nienburg, Germany (south view), c. 1910

Feeding sand (silica) into the glassmaking furnaces, c. 1950

Batch Plant at the Wilhelmshütte Glass Factory, Germany, c. 1950

White sand (silica) pit excavation quarry, Germany, c. 1950

Blowing glass balloons in an open form, c. 1950

Blowing glass balloons into a closed form, c. 1950

Balloon railroad shipping yard, c. 1955

Large balloon basket weaver, c. 1950

Modern gas injection glass bottle production line, Germany, c. 1983

Modern gas injection bottle line, Germany, c. 1988

Modern 3-liter jugs with woven basket, c. 2000.

Modern balloon jugs, c. 2000

Modern production line water bottles, c. 2000

Modern production line juice bottles, c. 2000

Wilhelmshütte, Nienburg/Weser Glass Factory, Germany, c. 2010
Source: Museum of Nienburg, Germany 1991 publication. *100 Years of Glassmaking in Nienburg*. (1891-1991).

Chapter Four

Brinkmann Descendants Family List

Brinkmann Descendants Family List

1-1.Johann Friedrich Wilhelm Brinkmann-b.abt.Dec-27-1769-(est.-based on death record)-(not in Einbeck or Wetteborn Parish), m.(1/2)-Nov-1796*-[*Maria Dorothea Sophia (Gundelach) Brinkmann*]-Winzenburg Catholic Parish Church-Winzenburg-Niedersachsen-Germany, m.(2/2)-Unknown-(not in Schönhagen or Wetteborn Parish)-[*Maria (Hutlach) Brinkmann*], d.3-Jan-1851*-Westerberger Glashütte-(Westerberger Glass Factory)-Landkreis-Hildesheim-Niedersachsen-Germany, bur.7-Jan-1851*-Evangelical Lutheran Church-Wetteborn Parish Cemetery-Landwehr-Hildesheim-Niedersachsen-Germany.

1-1.Spouse-2/2: Maria (Hutlach) Brinkmann (placed out of order) & Johann Friedrich Wilhelm Brinkmann-b.Unknown, m.(2/2)-abt.1825*-Unknown location)-Not found in Schönhagen, the Winzenburg Catholic Church-Winzenburg-Germany, or in the Wetteborn Parish), d.Unknown. No birth, marriage, or death records. Parents: Unknown. No birth, baptism, or marriage death records have been located for *Maria (Hutlach) Brinkmann*. However, there is a birth and death record for her daughter, born to *Wilhelm Brinkmann* (Thought to be *Johann Friedrich Wilhelm Brinkmann*) and *Maria Hutlach-"born stillborn"* on 1-Jul-1825.* The written Brinkmann family history has no citation of this marriage or the stillborn child. It is thought (but not certain) that this *Wilhelm Brinkmann* is the correct Brinkmann for this Brinkmann family. This stillborn child's birth record cites her father as *Wilhelm Brinkmann* "the glass trader." Both parents are cited as living in "the glass factory" (thought to be the Westerberger Glass Factory) in the Wetteborn Parish.

Children: Maria (Hutlach) Brinkmann & Johann Friedrich Wilhelm Brinkmann.

    2-1.Ms. Brinkmann-b.1-Jul-1825*-(Stillborn daughter)-Evangelical Lutheran Church-Wetteborn Parish-Landwehr-Hildesheim-Niedersachsen-Germany. This child is cited as the "Legitimate-daughter," bur.1-Jul-1825*-Evangelical Lutheran Church-Wetteborn Parish-Landwehr-Hildesheim-Niedersachsen-Germany.

1-1.Spouse-1/2: Maria Dorothea Sophia (Gundelach) Brinkmann & Johann Friedrich Wilhelm Brinkmann-b.abt.1766*-Germany-(not in Wetteborn Parish), m.Nov-1796*-[*Johann Friedrich Wilhelm Brinkmann*]-Winzenburg Catholic Parish Church-Winzenburg-Niedersachsen-Germany, d.9-Apr-1824*-Westerberger Glashütte-(Westerberger Glass Factory Cottage)-Landkreis-Hildesheim-Niedersachsen-Germany, bur.10-Apr-1824*-Wetteborn Parish Church Cemetery-Landwehr-Hildesheim-Niedersachsen-Germany.

Children of Spouse-1/2: Maria Dorothea Sophia (Gundelach) Brinkmann & Johann Friedrich Wilhelm Brinkmann.

    2-1.Johann Philipp Brinkmann-b.abt.-1797*-green glass factory near Winzenburg-Germany-(not in Einbeck, Schönhagen, or Wetteborn Parish), bap.12-Feb-1797*-Winzenburg Catholic Church-Winzenburg-Germany, m.(1/2)-24-Nov-1818,*-[*Johanne Justine Charlotte (Düen) Brinkmann*]-Evangelical Lutheran Church-Wetteborn Parish Church-Landkreis-Hildesheim-Niedersachsen-Germany, m.(2/2)-1-Jun-1841,*-[*Louise Antoinette (Stender) Brinkmann*], d.Unknown. No birth-baptism-death records were found at the Evangelical Lutheran Church-Wetteborn Parish-Landwehr-Hildesheim-Niedersachsen-Germany. *Johann Philipp's* marriage record lists his place of birth as "born at the green glass factory near Winzenburg" (thought to be the Westerberger Glass Factory) within the Wetteborn Parish.

    2-1.Spouse-1/2: Johanne Justine Charlotte (Düen) Brinkmann & Johann Philipp Brinkmann-b.16-May-1796*-Rothenkirchen-Dassensen-Einbeck Parish Church-Einbeck-Northeim-Niedersachsen-Germany. Source-1: *Mr. Rolf Nowak*, researcher using the *Local Family Book of Dassensen* (family name resource for genealogy research). Source-2: Hannover Archive-Evangelical Lutheran Church-St. Jacobi Parish Church Book-Einbeck-Northeim-Niedersachsen-(Lower Saxony)-Germany, bp.Unknown-(not in St. Jacobi Church Parish-Einbeck-Germany), m.24-Nov-1818,*-[*Johann Philipp Brinkmann*]-Evangelical Lutheran Church-Wetteborn Parish Church-Landkreis-Hildesheim-Niedersachsen-Germany, d.11-Mar-1840*-Westerberger Glass Factory-Westerberg-Germany, bur.14-May-1840*-Wetteborn Parish-Landwehr-Hildesheim-Niedersachsen-Germany.

Children of Spouse-1/2: Johanne Justine Charlotte (Düen) Brinkmann & Johann Philipp Brinkmann.

    3-1.Johanne Sophie Henriette Brinkmann-b.27-Nov-1818*-Einbeck-Northeim Niedersachsen-Germany, bap.3-Dec-1818*-Evangelical Lutheran Church-St. Jacobi Church Parish-Einbeck-Northeim-Niedersachsen-Germany, Godparents: *Widow-Johanne Düen-Mrs. Sophia Brinkmann,* con.1833*-Evangelical Lutheran Church-Wetteborn Parish Church-Landwehr-Hildesheim Niedersachsen-Germany, d.Unknown.

    3-2.Dorothee Charlotte Brinkmann-b.9-Oct-1820*-Einbeck-Northeim-Niedersachsen-Germany, bap.15-Oct-1820*-Evangelical Lutheran Church-St. Jacobi Parish Church-Einbeck-Northeim-Niedersachsen-Germany, Godparent: *Mrs. Ebbighausen,* con.-1835*-Evangelical Lutheran Church-Wetteborn Parish Church-Landwehr-Hildesheim-Niedersachsen-Germany, d.Unknown.

    3-3.Johann Heinrich Brinkmann-b.10-Jul-1823*-Westerberger Glass Factory-Westerberg-Hildesheim-Niedersachsen-Germany, bap.13-Jul-1823*-Evangelical Lutheran Church-Wetteborn Parish-Landwehr-Hildesheim-Niedersachsen-Germany, Godparents: *J. Hr. Lange-J.P. Brinkmann-Charlotte Hutlach,* con.-1837*-Evangelical Lutheran Church-Wetteborn Parish Church-Landwehr-Hildesheim-Niedersachsen-Germany, d.Unknown.

    3-4.Gottfried Brinkmann-b.11-Nov-1825*-Westerberger Glass Factory-Westerberg-Hildesheim-Niedersachsen-Germany, bap.20-Nov-1825*-Evangelical Lutheran Church-Wetteborn Parish-Landwehr-Hildesheim-Niedersachsen-Germany, Godparents: *Franz Seadler-Gottfiried Kaufle-Karlina Peters,* d.Unknown.

    3-5.Ferdinand Heinrich Julius Brinkmann-b.26-Feb-1828*-Westerberger Glass Factory-Westerberg-Hildesheim-Niedersachsen-Germany, bap.1-May-1826* Evangelical Lutheran Church-Wetteborn Parish-Landwehr-Hildesheim-Niedersachsen-Germany, Godparents: *Julius Staender; Louise Schorr; and Ferdinand Peters,* d.Unknown.

    3-6.Wilhelm August Ludwig Brinkmann-b.26-Apr-1831*-Westerberger Glass Factory Westerberg-Hildesheim-Niedersachsen-Germany, bap.1-May-1831*-Evangelical Lutheran Church-Wetteborn Parish-Landwehr-Hildesheim-Niedersachsen-Germany, Godparents: *Herr Heinrich Ludwig Stender* of the Lamspringe Glass Factory; *Herr Thon's spouse (Bock)* of Westerberg, d.Unknown.

    3-7.August Heinrich Carl Brinkmann-b.17-Nov-1833*-Westerberger Glass Factory-Westerberg-Hildesheim-Niedersachsen-Germany, bap.30-Nov-1833*-Evangelical Lutheran Church-Wetteborn Parish-Landwehr-Hildesheim-Niedersachsen-Germany, Godparents: *H. Brinkmann,* m.25-Feb-1859* to *Johanne Sophie Louise Friedrike (Hirsch) Brinkmann,* d.15-Mar-1906*-Mitterteich-Tirschenreuth-Bavaria-Germany.

    3-7.Spouse: Johanne Sophie Louise Friederike (Hirsch) Brinkmann & August Heinrich Carl Brinkmann-b.10-Apr-1839*-Braunlage-Goslar-Niedersachsen-Germany, m.25-Feb-1859*-(*Johann Friedrich Wilhelm Brinkmann*)-Braunlage-Goslar-Niedersachsen-Germany, d.29-Dec-1928*Mitterteich-Tirschenreuth-Bavaria-Germany.

    Children: Johanne Sophie Louise Friederike (Hirsch) Brinkmann & August Heinrich Carl Brinkmann.

        4-1.Friedrich Ludwig Carl Brinkmann-b.13-Apr-1856*-Braunlage-Goslar-Niedersachsen-Germany, bp.27-Apr-1856-Braunlage Parish-Braunlage-Goslar-Niedersachsen-Germany, Godparents: *Louis Hirsch-Fritz Becker-Caroline Kamm,* con.24-Apr-1870*-Braunlage-Goslar-Niedersachsen-Germany, m.Unknown, d.Unknown.

        4-2.Louis Heinrich Hermann Brinkmann-b.4-Mar-1859*-Braunlage-Goslar-Niedersachsen-Germany, bp.20-Mar-1859*-Braunlage Parish-Braunlage-Goslar-Niedersachsen-Germany, Godparents: *Ludwig Hirsch* (glass factory overseer); *Henriette (Achtermann* [Spouse of the glass maker *Heinrich Hirsch*]; *Magdalene (Kamm)*-(wife of the glass maker *Joseph Herzog);* (all from Braunlage), con.20-Apr-1873*-Braunlage Parish-Braunlage-Goslar-Niedersachsen-Germany, res. 1898*-Mitterteich-Germany, d.abt.-1904.*

        4-2.Spouse: Frieda (Unknown) Brinkmann & Louise Heinrich Herman Brinkmann-b.Unknown, m.Unknown, res.-1942*-Mitterteich, Germany.

        Children: Frieda Brinkmann & Louise Heinrich Herman Brinkmann.

            5-1.Friedrich Louis Brinkmann-b.15-May-1909*-Mitterteich-Germany, res.2003*- Zimdorf-Germany, d.6-Mar-2003*-Zimdorf-Germany.

            5-1.Spouse: Unknown & Friedrich Louis Brinkmann-b.Unknown, m.Unknown, d.Unknown.

Children: Friedrich Louis Brinkmann & Unknown.
> **6-1.Peter Brinkmann**-b.*Unknown, m.Unknown, liv.2014*-Germany, res.2003-2007*-Nümberg-Nuremberg-Bavaria Germany, occ.textile engineer, res.Nuremberg, Bavaria, Germany.

5-2.Walter Brinkmann-b.bef-1922*, res.1942-1960*-Mitterteich-Germany, occ.glassmaker's assistant-Mitterteich-Germany.*

5-3.Philippine Brinkmann-b.bef.-1940*, res.1960*-Mitterteich-Germany, d.aft.1960.*

5-3.Spouse: Mrs. (Fink) & Philippine Brinkmann-b.Unknown, m. 1960*, d.Unknown.

5-4.Ms. Brinkmann-b.Unknown, d.Unknown.

5-4.Spouse: Ernst Neff & Ms. Brinkmann-b.bef.1920,* m.bef.1960,* res.1942*-Mitterteich-Germany, occ.glass factory director, d.Unknown.

Children: Ernst Neff & Ms. Brinkmann.
> **6-1.George Neff**-b.bef.1940,* res.1960*-Mitterteich-Germany, occ. 1960*-police officer-Mitterteich-Germany.

4-3.Wilhelmine Marie Helene Brinkmann-b.26-Jan-1864*-Braunlage-Goslar,Niedersachsen-Germany, bp.18-Feb-1864*-Braunlage Parish-Goslar, Niedersachsen-Germany, Godparents: *Wilhelm Otte* (glass maker); *Marie Hirsch* (virgin); *Mrs. Magdalene (Kamm) Herzog* (all from Braunlage, Germany), m.Unknown, d.Unknown.

4-4.Albertine Pauline Martha Brinkmann-b.13-Oct-1872*-Braunlage-Goslar-Niedersachsen-Germany, bp.8-Nov-1872*-Braunlage Parish-Goslar, Niedersachsen-Germany, Godparents: *Albert Hirsch*; *Paulus Winkler* (looking-glass manufacturer in Fürth); and *Minna (Paul) Brinkmann* (spouse of the glass maker *Wilhelm Brinkmann* in Gifhorn, Germany), m.Unknown, d.Unknown.

4-4.Spouse: Christoph Caspar Carl Christian Büchner & Albertine Pauline Martha Brinkmann-b.16-Mar-1866*-Weinheim-Germany, c.28-May-1866*-Weinheim-Germany, res.-Sep-1866-Bamberg-Germany, m.23-Oct-1893*-Mitterteich-Germany, d.29-Oct-1950*-Miesbach-Germany.

Children: Christoph Caspar Carl Christian Büchner & Albertine Pauline Martha Brinkmann.

5-1.Karl Theodor Alfred Büchner-b.23-Nov-1897*-(by citation only, no records)-Mitterteich-Tirschenreuth-Bavaria-Germany, bp.12-Dec-1897*-Mitterteich Parish-Tirschenreuth-Bavaria-Germany, d.14-Nov-1916*-Mitterteich-Germany-(German Army causality of World War I).

5-2.Ema Babette Louise Büchner-b.10-Apr-1899*-(by citation only, no records)-Widen-Germany, m.(1/2)-1930,* m.(2/2)-10-Jun-1939,* d.7-Mar-1979*-Bad-Bergzabem-Germany.

5-2.Spouse: Mr. Reiland & Ema Babette Luise Büchner- b.Unknown (by citation only, no records), m.abt.1930*, d.abt.1970*-Germany.

5-2.Spouse: Karl Friedrich Sturn & Ema Babette Luise Büchner- b. 23-Sep-1894*-(by citation only, no records), m.10-Jun-1939*-Heidelberg-Germany, res.1957*-Landau-Germany, occ.1957*-Lawyer, d.Unknown.

5-3.Elfriede Paula Amanda Büchner-b.15-Oct-1905,* m.1950,* d.abt. 1984*-Nümberg-Germany.

5-3.Spouse: Erich Oskar Albert Baer & Elfriede Paula Amanda Büchner- b.1-Jul-1904*-(By citation only, no records)-Saaralben-France, m.abt.1950*, res.1979*-Nuremberg-Germany, occ.1979*-Director of Court, d.Unknown.

5-4.Doris Sophie Maria Büchner-b.21-Nov-1906*-(by citation only, no records)-Steinmühle-Germany, m.5-Oct-1933*-Bad Bruckenau-Germany, d.1-Nov-1956*-München-Germany.

5-4.Spouse: Anton Ferdinand Pelikan & Doris Sophie Maria Büchner-b.13-Oct-1886*-(By citation only, no records)-München-Germany, m.5-Oct-1933*-Bad Bruckenau-Germany, d.21-May-1957*-München-Germany.

Children: Mr. Pelikan & Doris Sophie Maria Büchner

146

6-1.Sylvia Frieda Maria Pelikan-b.3-Dec-1933-Bad Bruckenau-Germany,* m.Unknown, d.Unknown.

6-2.Theodor Karl Tonci Pelikan-b.1-Sep-1938*-(by citation only, no records), d.2004*-Wangen-Germany.

4-5.Karl Brinkmann-b.aft.1873*-(by citation only), occ.*Huttenmeister*-(overseer), d.Unknown.

4-5.Spouse: Unknown & Karl Brinkmann.

Children: Unknown & Karl Brinkmann.

5-1.Carla Paula Büchner-b.1940,*m.Unknown, d.Unknown.

5-1.Spouse: Mr. Wiegand-b.Unknown, m.Unknown, d.1960*-Mitterteich-Germany.

3-8.Heinrich Carl Wilhelm Brinkmann-b.5-Jun-1836*-Westerberger Glass Factory-Westerberg-Hildesheim-Niedersachsen-(Lower Saxony)-Germany, bap.19-Jun-1836*-Evangelical Lutheran Church-Wetteborn Parish-Landwehr-Hildesheim-Niedersachsen-Germany, Godparents: *Wilhelm Schmietut-Carl Topp-Henriette Brinkmann*, d.Unknown.

3-9.Dorothee Marie Brinkmann-b.15-Oct-1838*-Westerberger Glass Factory-Westerberg-Hildesheim-Niedersachsen-Germany, bap.26-Oct-1838*-Evangelical Lutheran Church-Wetteborn Parish-Landwehr-Hildesheim-Niedersachsen-Germany, Godparents: *August Thon-Friederike Ruhlender-Amalie Brinkmann* (all from the glass factory), d.Unknown.

2-1.Spouse-2/2: Louise Antoinette (Stender) Brinkmann & Johann Philipp Brinkmann-b.20-Nov-1798*-Bursfelden-Hemeln-Hannoversch-Müden-Göttengen-Niedersachsen-Germany, m.28-Feb-1841,*-Evangelical Lutheran Church-Lamspringe-Hildesheim-Niedersachsen-Germany. d.Unknown. Louise's birth and surname are cited within the *Glass Maker Name Book by Klaus Kunze-1820-(copyright-2000)* along with her sibling, her parents, and Godparents: *Johann Heinrich Stender-Johann Carl Kauffeld*. There is a proclamation of marriage on file and a marriage record for *Louise and Johann Philipp Brinkmann*. The Kunze source listed above cites Louise's parents as *Johann Christoph Ferdinand Ständer (Stender)*, Occ.glass worker at Braunwald Glass Factory-Hannoversch-Münden-Göttingen-Niedersachsen-Germany, and *Anna Catharina Sophie (Liphard-Lippert)*-whose parents were *Johann Cord Liphard* and *Marie Catharine (Backhaus) Liphard*.

Children of Spouse-2/2: Louise Antoinette (Stender) Brinkmann & Johann Philipp Brinkmann.

3-1.Karl Daniel August Brinkmann-b.25-Apr-1841*-Westerberger Glass Factory-Westerberg-Landkreis-Hildesheim-Niedersachsen-Germany, bap.4-May-1841*-Evangelical Lutheran Church-Wetteborn Parish-Landwehr-Hildesheim-Niedersachsen-Germany, m.Unknown, d.Unknown.

2-2.Anna Maria Carolina Brinkmann-b.10-Aug-1799*-(cited in baptism record)-Winzenburg-Hildesheim-Niedersachsen-Germany, bap.11-Aug-1799*-Winzenburg Catholic Parish Church-Winzenburg, Hildesheim-Niedersachsen-Germany, d.Unknown-Germany. This child's birth and death records are not available. However, an August 11, 1799* baptism record is on file in the Winzenburg Catholic Parish church, Winzenburg, Germany. It is known that the death record for *Maria Dorothea Sophia (Gundelach) Brinkmann* of April 10, 1824* cites that she died and left behind her spouse *Johann Friedrich Wilhelm Brinkmann*, and 3 *"major"* (of age) children, and 2 *"minor"* (not of age) children. *Anna* is thought to be one of the major children cited in this death record. The search is still in progress. No other records are in this file.

2-3.Liborius Friedrich Brinkmann-b.abt-1802*-Germany-(based on baptism citation record)-(not born/did not die in the Einbeck, Schönhagen, or Wetteborn parishes), bap.16-May-1802*-Winzenburg Catholic Church Parish-Winzenburg-Germany, m.19-Feb-1826,*-[*Henriette (Lange) Brinkmann*], Wetteborn Parish Church-Wetteborn-Landwehr-Hildesheim-Niedersachsen-Germany, d.aft.1864-Germany, occ.1826*-"Schmelzmeister" (glass melting master) at the Westerberger Glass Factory-Westerberg-Hildesheim-Niedersachsen-Germany, occ. 1828-1829*-"Schürer" (keeper of the fire)-Osterwald-Hemmendorf-Hameln-Pyrmont-Niedersachsen-Germany, occ.1830-1832*-"Schmelzmeister" (glass melting master) at the Westerberger Glass Factory-Westerberg-Hildesheim-Niedersachsen-Germany, occ.1832*-glass blower at the Ziegenhagen Glass Factory-Witzenhausen-Werra-Meissner-Hesse-Germany. occ. 1865*-glass blower a the Ziegenhagen Glass Factory-Ziegenhagen-Witzenhausen-Werra-Meissner-Hesse-Germany. It is thought that *Friedrich* moved his family to another location after his son *Christian Karl Brinkmann* was born in 1832 in the Westerberger Glass Factory in the Wetteborn Parish. *Friedrich Brinkmann* is known to have been living at the Westerberger Glass

Factory, Westerberg, Germany in 1826* when, at the age of 23 (estimated birth 1802*), he married *Henriette (Lange) Brinkmann* in the Wetteborn Parish Church. It is thought that around 1832 *Friedrich* may have moved back to Winzenburg, Ziegenhagen, Freden, or Einbeck, Germany. *Friedrich Brinkmann* was living in Westerberg, Germany in 1864,* when *Friedrich's* son *Christian Karl Brinkmann's* married *Marie Elizabeth (Merker) Brinkmann*. *Friedrich Brinkmann's* son *Christian Karl Brinkmann's* first child *Friedrich Ernst August Brinkmann's* baptism record lists *Christian's* father as *Friedrich Brinkmann* a "glass blower" at the Ziegenhagen Glass Factory in Ziegenhagen, Germany in 1865. *

2-3.Spouse: Henriette (Lange) Brinkmann (Unmarried partner) & Friedrich Achilles- b.abt.1792-1793*-Germany-(not in Wetteborn Parish), m.19-Jan-1826*-[*Liborius Friedrich Brinkmann*] at the Evangelical Lutheran Church-Wetteborn Parish-Landwehr-Hildesheim-Niedersachsen-Germany, d.Unknown-Germany-(Not in Wetteborn Parish). *Henriette's 1826** marriage record list her parents as *Johann Heinrich Brinkmann* & *Rosina (Lange) Brinkmann*, d.26-May-1826*-Westerberger Glass Factory-Hildesheim-Niedersachsen-Germany, bur.30-May-1826*-Wetteborn Parish Cemetery-Wetteborn-Landwehr-Hildesheim-Germany.

Illegitimate Children: Henriette (Lange) & Friedrich Achilles.

> **3-1.Heinrich Ferdinand Lange**-b.5-Jun-1822*-Illegitimate son-Wetteborn Parish Birth Record-Wetteborn-Landwehr-Hildesheim-Germany. Child's cited Father: *Friedrich Achilles* of the Lamspringe Glass Factory-Germany, bp.9-Jun-1822*-Wetteborn Parish Church, m.Unknown-(not in Wetteborn), d.Unknown.

Legitimate Children: Henriette (Lange) Brinkmann (Married) & Laborious Friedrich Brinkmann.

> **3-1.Maria Sophia Henriette Brinkmann**-b.7-Nov-1826*-Westerberger Glass Factory-Winzenburg-Hildesheim-Niedersachsen-Germany, bp.12-Nov-1826*-Wetteborn Church Parish-Wetteborn-Landwehr-Hildesheim-Germany, Godparents: *Maria Sophia Langen-Henriette Brinkmann*, con.Unknown (not found in Wetteborn Parish records 1844-1848), d.19-Apr-1828*-Osterwald Glass Factory-Osterwald-Salzhemmendorf-Hameln-Pyrmont-Niedersachsen-Germany, bur.21-Apr-1828*-Hemmendorf-Parish Cemetery-Hemmendorf-Salzhemmendorf-Hameln-Pyrmont-Niedersachsen-Germany.

> **3-2.Hanna Luise Charlotte Brinkmann**-b.7-Dec-1829*-Osterwald Glass Factory-Osterwald-Salzhemmendorf-Hameln-Pyrmont-Niedersachsen-Germany, bp.13-Dec-1829* -Hemmendorf Parish-Niedersachsen-Germany, m.Unknown, d.Unknown.

> **3-3.Christian Karl Brinkmann**-b.13-Feb-1832*-Westerberger Glass Factory-Westerberg-Landkreis-Hildesheim-Niedersachsen-Germany, bp.19-Feb-1932*Wetteborn Parish-Wetteborn-Landwehr-Hildesheim-Germany, Con.Unknown-(not found at the Wetteborn Parish Church in 1846-age 14), m.19-Nov-1864*-Sülbeck Parish-Nienstädt-Schaumburg-Niedersachsen-Germany, d.abt.-1906*-Unknown location-(Possibly: Hamburg-Ottensen-or-Bergedorf-Germany)-(not found in Nienburg/Weser Municipal records for 1906).

> **3-3. Spouse: Marie Elisabeth (Merker) Brinkmann & Christian Karl Brinkmann-** b.22-Sep-1831*-Ziegenhagen-Werra-Meissner-Kreis-Hessen-Germany, bp.16-Oct-1831*-Evangelical Lutheran Church-Ziegenhagen-Werra-Meissner-Kreis-Hessen-Germany, m. 19-Nov-1864*-[*Liborius Friedrich* Brinkmann-Evangelical Lutheran Church-Sülbeck Parish-Nienstädt-Schaumburg-Niedersachsen-Germany], d.7-Apr-1895*-Nienburg/ Weser-Niedersachsen-Germany. *Marie's* parents are clearly identified in her 1832* birth record, and in her marriage record to *Christian Karl Brinkmann* in 1864* as [*Jacob Merker-b.abt.-1790*-Germany, Par.-Unknown, res.-1864*-known to have lived in Ziegenhagen-Germany, occ.-1864*-Packmeister (one who packs the glass wares for shipping)* at the Ziegenhagen Glass Factory-Ziegenhagen-Germany, *d.Unknown-Germany* & his wife *Friederike Ernestine Antoinette (Fiege-Fige) Merker-b.abt.-1790*-Germany, Par.Unknown, m.bef.-1831*-Germany, d.bef.-1864*-Germany].

> **Children: Marie Elisabeth (Merker) Brinkmann & Christian Karl Brinkmann.**

>> **4-1.Friedrich Ernst August Brinkmann**-b.28-Oct-1865*-Schierbach Glass Factory-Nienstädt-Schaumburg-Niedersachsen-Germany, bap.12-Nov-1865*-Evangelical Lutheran Church-Sülbeck Parish-Nienstädt-Schaumburg-Niedersachsen-Germany, wit.*Carl Warnik*; *Carl Merker*; and *Friedrich Brinkmann*-(glass blower in Ziegenhagen-absent at the baptism), m.abt.1894*-Unknown location-Germany, d.abt.1946*-Germany. *Friedrich Ernst August Brinkmann* is cited in the Sülbeck Parish birth record as the (First child, first son, first marriage) of *Christian Karl Brinkmann and Marie Elisabeth (Merker) Brinkmann.*

4-1.Spouse: Edith (Erman) Brinkmann & Friedrich Ernst August Brinkmann-b.Unknown, par.Unknown, m.abt.-1890-1894*-Germany, d.Unknown.

Children: Edith (Erman) Brinkmann & Friedrich Ernst August Brinkmann.

  5-1.Walter Brinkmann-b.1894*, d.1935*-Germany.

  5-2.Marie Brinkmann-b. 1895*-Germany, d.Unknown.

  5-3. Paul Brinkmann-b.1906*-Germany, d.Unknown.

4-2.Louise Auguste Sophie Brinkmann-b.2-May-1868*-Schierbach Glass Factory-Nienstädt-Schaumburg-Niedersachsen-Germany, bap.17-May-1868*-Evangelical Lutheran Church-Sülbeck Parish-Nienstädt-Schaumburg-Niedersachsen-Germany, m.abt.-1886*-Germany, d.Unknown-Germany. *Louise Auguste Sophie Brinkmann's* birth and baptism record cites parents as living in house Number 12, Nienstädt-Germany, and cites *Christian Karl Brinkman* as being from the Westerberger Glass Factory in Westerberg-Germany. *Louise's* mother *Marie Elisabeth (Merker) Brinkmann* is cited as coming from Ziegenhagen near Witzenhausen, Germany. *Louise's* spouse, *Karl Micka,* and all the children listed below are known by citation only (no records) within the written Brinkmann family history.

4-2.Spouse: Karl Micka & Louise Auguste Sophie Brinkmann-b.Unknown, par.Unknown, m.abt.-1886*-Germany, d.Unknown.

Children: Karl Micka & Louise Auguste Sophie Brinkmann

  5-1.Hermine Micka-b.1895*-Germany, d.Unknown.

  5-2.Marie Micka-b.Unknown-Germany,*, d.Unknown.

  5-3.Evina Micka-b.Unknown-Germany,* d.Unknown.

  5-4.Frieda Micka-b.Unknown-Germany,* d.Unknown.

  5-5.Paul Micka-b.Unknown-Germany,* d.Unknown.

  5-6.Elizabeth Micka -b.Unknown-Germany,* d.Unknown.

  5-7. Henry Micka-b.Unknown-Germany,* d.Unknown.

  5-8.Rose Micka-b.Unknown-Germany,* d.Unknown.

  5-9.Paula Micka-b.Unknown-Germany,* d.Unknown.

4-3.Mr. Brinkmann-b.14-Feb-1871*-Schierbach Glass Factory-Nienstädt-Schaumburg-Niedersachsen-Germany, d.14-Feb-1871*-(Stillborn-second son)-Evangelical Lutheran Church-Sülbeck Parish-Nienstädt-Schaumburg-Niedersachsen-Germany.

4-4.Karl Friedrich Wilhelm Brinkmann-b.5-Jun-1872*-Schierbach Glass Factory-Nienstädt-Schaumburg-Niedersachsen-Germany, bap.23-Jun-1872*-Evangelical Lutheran Church-Sülbeck Parish-Nienstädt Schaumburg-Niedersachsen-Germany, m.1895*-Nienburg/Weser-Nienburg-Niedersachsen-Germany, im.1909*-Platteville-Wisconsin-USA, d.27-Aug-1948*-Milwaukee-Wisconsin, bur.31-Aug-1948*-Lincoln Memorial Cemetery-Milwaukee-Wisconsin.

4-4.Spouse: Ernestine Hermine (Hildebrandt) Brinkmann & Karl Friedrich Wilhelm Brinkmann-b.12-Dec-1876*-Nienburg/Weser-Nienburg-Niedersachsen-Germany, m.25-May-1895*-Nienburg/Weser-Nienburg-Niedersachsen-(Lower Saxony)-Germany, im.1910*-Platteville-Wisconsin-USA, d.17-Dec-1947*-Milwaukee-Wisconsin-USA, bur.Dec-20-1947*-Lincoln Memorial Cemetery-Milwaukee-Wisconsin. Parents: *Carl Christian Hildebrandt*-b.1846*-Germany, d.1926*-Germany. *Hanne Louise Friederike Caroline (Pfennig) Hildebrandt*-b.1844*-Germany, m.1873*-Germany, d.1930*-Germany.

Children: Ernestine Hermine (Hildebrandt) Brinkmann & Karl Friedrich Wilhelm Brinkmann.

  5-1.Adolf Carl Christian Brinkmann (See Volume 2).

  5-2.Alwin August Adolf Brinkmann (See Volume 2).

  5-3.Hugo Frank Brinkmann (See Volume 2).

  5-4.Frieda Brinkmann (See Volume 2).

  5-5.Karl Wilhelm Hermann Heinrich Brinkmann (See Volume 2).

  5-6.Elsie Louise Brinkmann (See Volume 2).

2-4.Henriette Wilhelmine Brinkmann-b.1809*-(based on baptism record)-Winzenburg-Hildesheim-Niedersachsen-Germany-(Not in Schönhagen or Wetteborn Parish), m.6-May-1838*-Wetteborn Parish-Wetteborn-Landwehr-Hildesheim-Niedersachsen-Germany. Parents: *Johann*

Christoph Huck-b.25-Dec-1803,* d.14-Mar-1857*), d.Unknown. No birth, baptism, or death records have been located for *Henriette* who is known to have had two illegitimate children with *Heinrich Fasterling* from Winzenburg-Germany before her legitimate 1838* marriage to *Johann Christoph Huck*. *Henriette* is known to have been godmother to a niece (born in 1826),* and to two nephews (born in 1833,* and 1836).*

2-4.Spouse-1/2: Heinrich Fasterling & Henriette Wilhelmine Brinkmann-b.Unknown, not married, d. Unknown.

Illegitimate Children: Heinrich Fasterling & Henriette Wilhelmine Brinkmann.

> **3-1.Mr. Brinkmann**-b.16-Feb-1835*-(stillborn son)-Westerberger Glass Factory-Westerberg-Landkreis-Hildesheim-Niedersachsen-Germany, par.Unmarried-*Henriette Wilhelmine Brinkmann and Heinrich Fasterling* (of Winzenburg, Germany), d.16-Feb-1835*-Evangelical Lutheran Church-Wetteborn Parish Church Book-Niedersachsen-Germany.

> **3-2.George Heinrich Carl Fasterling**-b.8-Jun-1837*-Westerberger Glass Factory-Westerberg-Landkreis-Hildesheim-Niedersachsen-(Lower Saxony)-Germany, par.Unmarried-*Henriette Wilhelmine Brinkmann* and *Heinrich Fasterling* of Winzenburg, Germany, bp.18-Jun-1837*-Westerberg Parish-Hildesheim-Niedersachsen-Germany, Godparents: *Heinrich Krumsick; Amalie Brinkmann; Augusta Munten* (all from the glass factory), im.1857*-New Orleans-America-(Not verified), m.Unknown, d.Unknown.

2-4.Spouse-2/2: Johann Christoph Huck & Henriette Wilhelmine Brinkmann.-b.25-Dec-1803*-Everode-Niedersachsen-(Lower Saxony)-Germany, m.6-May-1838*-Wetteborn Parish-Wetteborn-Landwehr-Hildesheim-Niedersachsen-Germany, d.14-Mar-1857*-Westerberg-Niedersachsen-Germany. Birth and death by citation only in the Ancestry Tree (*Hartmann-9-24-2013*).* *Johann Christoph Huck* is cited as being a renter and journeyman mason in Everode-Freden-Hildesheim-Niedersachsen-Germany, and is also cited in the Ancestry Tree (*Hartmann-9-24-2013*) as the son of [*Christoph Huck*-b.1758*-Niedersachsen-Germany, m. 27-Jul-1778*-Winzenburg-Niedersachsen-Germany, d.21-Dec-1838*-Unknown location-Germany, res.Renter in Everode, Germany whose wife was *Marie Gertrude (Bock) Huck*-b.12-Aug-1768,* m.27-Jul-1778*-Winzenburg-Niedersachsen-Germany, d.25-Jan-1838*-Unknown location-Germany]. No birth, marriage, death records are on file for *Johann Christoph Huck, Christoph Huck, or Marie Gertrude (Bock) Huck.*

Children: Johann Christoph Huck & Henriette Wilhelmine Brinkmann.

> **3-1.Wilhelmine Dorothea Huck**-b.6-Feb-1854*-Westerberg-Landkreis-Hildesheim-Niedersachsen-Germany, m.Unknown, d.30-Nov-1918*-Hannover-Linden-Niedersachsen-Germany. By citation only in the Ancestry Tree-(Hartmann-9-24-2013).* No birth, marriage, or death records have been located.

> **3-1.Spouse: Johann Goslar & Henriette Wilhelmine Brinkmann**-b.24-Dec-1849*Duderstadt-Göttingen-Niedersachsen-Germany, m.Unknown, d.Unknown. By citation only in the Ancestry Tree-(Hartmann-9-24-2013).

> **Children: Johann Goslar & Henriette Wilhelmine Brinkmann.**

> > **4-1.Elsie Therese Henriette Julie Goslar**-b.7-Aug-1878*-Hannover-Linden-Niedersachsen-(Lower Saxony)-Germany, m.Unknown, d.19-Jan-1970*-Hannover-Niedersachsen-(Lower Saxony)-Germany. By citation only in the Ancestry Tree (Hartmann-9-24-2013).

2-5.Maria Amalie Brinkmann-b.abt.-1812*-(based on citation in the Hannover Baptismal Records from the Wetteborn Parish-Hildesheim-Niedersachsen-Germany-(Not on microfiche at the Lutheran Church Hannover Archive-Hannover-Germany-2013 search)-birth record was not located at the Hannover State Archive, and is thought lost due to World War II destruction, m.Unknown, d.Unknown. No other records are on file. The birth record for *Maria Amalie Brinkmann* is by citation only and needs verification. It is not certain if *Maria Amalie* was born to *Johann Friedrich Wilhelm Brinkmann & Maria Dorothea Sophie (Gundelach) Brinkmann, or to Johann Friedrich Wilhelm Brinkmann & Maria (Hutlach) Brinkmann*. There are also the following record citations for *Maria Amalie*: (1) Godmother to *George Heinrich Carl Fasterling* in 1837*, and (2) Godmother to *Dorothee Marie Brinkmann* in 1839.* No marriage records are on file. No parents names on are on file. No birth record is on file. It is thought (until proven otherwise) that no other unrelated *Brinkmann* family lived at the Westerberger Glass Factory from 1812 to 1824 and that *Maria Amalie Brinkmann* was the youngest daughter of *Johann Friedrich Wilhelm Brinkmann and Maria Dorothea Sophie (Gundelach) Brinkmann.*

2-5.Spouse: Wilhelm Conrad Lüttge & Maria Amalie Brinkmann-b.Unknown, m.Unknown, d.Unknown.

Illegitimate Children: Wilhelm Conrad Lüttge & Maria Amalie Brinkmann.

    3-1.Mr.Lüttge-b.29-May-1839,*(stillborn son)-Westerberger Glass Factory-Westerberg-Landkreis-Hildesheim-Niedersachsen-Germany, par.[*Amalie Brinkmann* and *"Schürer"* (keeper of the fire) and *Wilhelm Conrad Lüttge*],* bur.29-May-1839*-Evangelical Lutheran Church-Wetteborn Parish Cemetery-Landwehr-Hildesheim-Niedersachsen-Germany. There are no birth or marriage records on file for this child's parents.

    3-2.Wilhelmine Henriette Brinkmann-*Wilhelmine Henriette Brinkmann*-b.abt.-Feb-1841*-Maternity Hospital-Hildesheim-Niedersachsen, par.Amalie Brinkmann and Unknown father, d.9-Jun-1842*-(age 1 year, 3 months, 20 days)-Westerberger Glass Factory-Westerberg-Landkreis-Hildesheim-Niedersachsen-Germany, bur.11-Jun-1842*-"poor in silence of hooping couch"-Evangelical Lutheran Church-Wetteborn Parish Cemetery-Landwehr-Hildesheim-Niedersachsen-Germany. The father is not listed in this death record of this child, and the birth record of this child is not on file.

- Continue Family List in Volume 2 -

The red asterisk (*) represents an event that is verified by documents on record.
The blue asterisk (*) represents an event that is cited from a source with no record on file.

Abbreviations: abt. (about), bef. (before), b. (born), bap. (baptized), bur. (buried), c. (circa), ch. (christened), con. (confirmation), d. (died), div. (divorces), god. (godparents), im. (immigrated), liv. (living), m. (married), occ. (occupation), par. (parents),   res. (residence), sib. (siblings), wit. (witnesses), and (-) (parenthesis indicates maiden surname).

- End of Section -

Chapter Five

The Johann Friedrich Wilhelm Brinkman Family
The Johann Philipp Brinkmann Family
The Liborius Friedrich Brinkmann Family
The Christian Karl Brinkmann Family

Descendants of Johann Friedrich Wilhelm Brinkmann

Johann Friedrich Wilhelm Brinkmann.
& *Spouse 1/1 - Maria Dorothea Sophia (Gundelach) Brinkmann.*

- Johann Philipp Brinkmann.
  Spouse 1/2 - Johanne Justine Charlotte (Düen) Brinkmann.
  - Johanne Sophie Henriette Brinkmann.
  - Dorothee Charlotte Brinkmann.
  - Johann Heinrich Brinkmann.
  - Gottfried Brinkmann.
  - Ferdinand Heinrich Julius Brinkmann.
  - Wilhelm August Ludwig Brinkmann.
  - August Heinrich Carl Brinkmann.
    Spouse - Johanne Sophie Louise Friederike (Hirsch) Brinkmann.
  - Heinrich Carl Wilhelm Brinkmann.
  - Dorothee Marie Brinkmann.
  Spouse 2/2 - Louise Antoinette (Stender) Brinkmann.
  - Karl Daniel August Brinkmann.
- Anna Maria Carolina Brinkmann.
- Liborius Friedrich Brinkmann.
  Spouse - Henriette (Lange) Brinkmann.
  Illegitimate Children.
  Partner - Friedrich Achilles.
  - Heinrich Ferdinand Lange.
  Spouse - Liborius Friedrich Brinkmann.
  - Maria Sophia Henriette Brinkmann.
  - Hanna Luise Charlotte Brinkmann.
  - Christian Karl Brinkman.

- Henriette Wilhelmine Brinkmann.
  Illegitimate Children.
  Partner - Heinrich Fasterling.
  - Mr. Fasterling.
  - George Heinrich Carl Fasterling.
  Spouse - Johann Christoph Huck.
  - Wilhelmine Dorothea Huck.
- Maria Amalie Brinkmann.
  Illegitimate Children.
  Partner 1/2 - William Conrad Lüttge.
  - Mr. Lüttge.
  Partner 2/2 - Unknown.
  - Wilehelmine Henriette Brinkmann.

& *Spouse 2/2 - Maria (Hutlach) Brinkmann.*
- Ms. Brinkmann.

Source: Brinkman Family Tree

The Johann Friedrich Wilhelm Brinkmann Family

Johann Friedrich Wilhelm Brinkmann, b. c. 1769, d. 1851

Introduction

As of 2014, Johann Friedrich Wilhelm Brinkmann, also known as Wilhelm Brinkmann, is the earliest known member of this Brinkmann family line. Johann is this author's *fourth-great grandfather*. Johann's birth is estimated based on his death record, and he is thought to have been born in Prussia/Germany sometime between December 1769 and 1970. His birth records have not been located, but he is known to have died on January 3, 1851, at age 81, in the town of Westerberg, Germany. Johann was buried in the nearby Evangelical Lutheran Church's, Wetteborn Parish Cemetery. Johann was a *Glasverkäufer* or *Glashändler* (glass seller and merchant) for the *Westerberger Glashütte* (Westerberger Glass Factory) located in what was once the hamlet of Westerberg, Germany, which is located within the Hildesheim District of the German State of Niedersachsen (Lower Saxony), Germany. This rural area was historically part of the Evangelical Lutheran Church and its Wetteborn Parish.

Note: Wetteborn Parish Church records show that Johann's first spouse Maria Dorothea Sophie (Gundelach) Brinkmann died on April 9, 1824, and that she was buried in the Wetteborn Parish Church Cemetery. Johann lived in the Westerberger Glass Factory housing cottages for many years. Wetteborn Parish records show that Johann died on January 3, 1851, as "poor widower." Parish records show that Johann and Maria had five known children: (1) Johann Philipp Brinkmann, (2) Anna Maria Carolina Brinkmann, and (3) Liborius Friedrich Brinkmann, and (4) Henriette Wilhelmina Brinkmann, and (5) Maria Amalie Brinkmann. The German map below shows the locations where this Brinkmann family lived and worked, circa 1744.

History of Westerberg, Germany

The village of Westerberg, Germany was founded around 1744 as a small rural hamlet outside the *Westerberger Glashütte* (Westerberger Glass Factory). Originally, it was intended only to be a temporary location for the factory, and the land was rented rather than owned. The factory was founded by the Franz brothers and Jürden Nicholas Stender. After the eighth year extension of the Factory's lease, the Westerberg village settlement became permanent. In 1840, the Thon family bought the factory. The Probst family later owned the factory from 1864 to 1875. It was then managed by the Limburg family. The Westerberger Glass Factory was very productive and employed many skilled workers who came to Westerberg from all over Germany. Westerberg is the area where many Brinkmanns (belonging to this author's Brinkmann family line) moved to work in the glass industry, and where Brinkmann family records are found at the Evangelical Lutheran Church in Wetteborn Parish (the jurisdictional Lutheran Parish Church in Westerberg, Germany). Brinkmann records are also found in the Catholic Parish Church of Winzenburg, Germany. Around 1876, after many years of glass production, the factory closed its doors. The village of Westerberg went on to manufacture bricks in the existing kilns. Sand (used for making glass and bricks) was once quarried by digging large pits, which are now filled with water and host fishing and wildlife sporting events. Westerberg is one of four communities in the municipality of Winzenburg, which is in the district of Hildesheim, of Niedersachsen (Lower Saxony), Germany. The early (c. 1744) maps of the area show where the Westerberger Glass Factory, and the *Glasfabrik Schildhorst Glashütte* (Schildhorst Glass Factory) were located, south of the larger town of Winzenburg. Today there are four communities in the municipality of Winzenburg: Winzenburg, Westerberg, Klump, and Schildhorst. Each belongs to a joint Municipal Association administered by the town of Freden. Around 1800, the village of Westerberg was under the jurisdiction of the Evangelical Lutheran Church, Wetteborn Parish, which kept all Lutheran records of births, baptisms, marriages, and deaths for the local communities.

The Schildhorst Glass Factory is thought to have been equally important (or even more productive) than the Westerberger Glass Factory. Schildhorst, which is near the railroad station in Freden, is a village surrounded by forests, plenty of white sand (required for clear glass), and a bountiful source of water, making it another ideal location for a white glass production factory. The town of Schildhorst was of great significance in the eighteenth and nineteenth centuries, primarily due to the presence of the Schildhorst Glass Factory. However, in the twentieth century, the glass industries in the region (which employed hundreds of workers) left the area, and the prosperity of the villages of Westerberg and Schildhorst greatly declined. In 2011, the total population of Winzenburg was 735, and the village of Schildhorst had only one remaining small sawmill, a cheese maker, and a total population was about 70. Today, very little physical structural evidence of these once massive glass factories can be found. The sand quarries that were previously excavated to provide the silicone for glassmaking are now a major fishing and sporting location for tourists. Some of the glass artifacts recovered from the Schildhorst Glass Factory site show a wide variety of items produced from its glass factory. The *Wetteborn* (The Bright Mountain) Parish Church is still standing, and sits on a ridge that is part of a famous set of mountains.

Note: Johann Friedrich Wilhelm Brinkmann and his wife Maria Dorothea Sophie (Gundelach) Brinkmann both died in the village of Westerberg and lived in the Westerberger Glass Factory cottages. They were buried in the Wetteborn Parish Church Cemetery in Germany. The glass blowing (or glassmaking) trade was passed on to many descending Brinkmann descendants, and may still be practiced by some yet-to-be-discovered Brinkmanns still be living in Germany today.

Map of Freden, Germany and the location of several historic glass factories, c. 1585
Source: Heimatbund, Hildesheim, Germany website photo

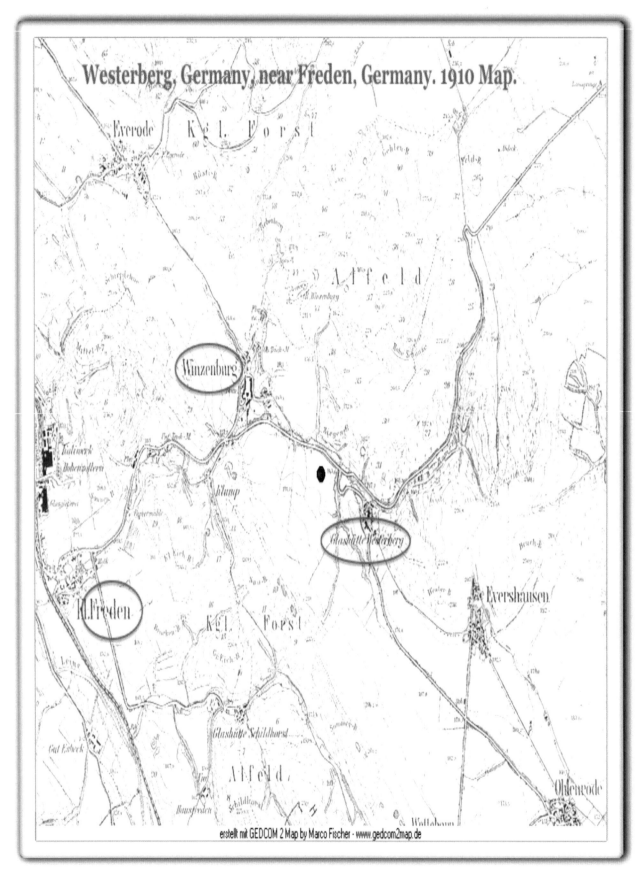

Old German map showing the Westerberg Glass Factory, nearby towns, & villages, c. 1744
Source: GEDCOM-Marco Fischer map

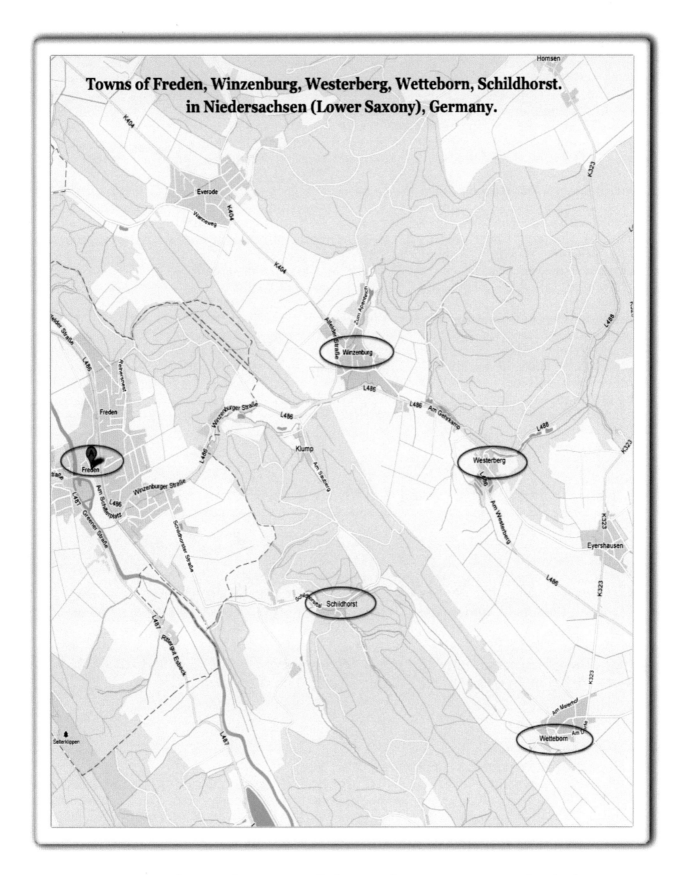

2013 map of towns that surrounded Westerberg, Germany. Freden is the
administrative area parish center, with railroad and river access.
Source: Google Maps

Written Brinkman Family History

The only known surviving written Brinkman family history was originally compiled and written by Elsie Louise (Brinkman) Mertig in the early 1900s. Elsie's family history identified Karl Von Brinkenhausen and his spouse Louise (Mueller) Von Brinkenhausen as the oldest known members of this Brinkmann family line. This information has been proven incorrect. There is a remote chance that further research into the 1600s may reveal a Brinkmann surname of nobility, or another spelling of the Brinkmann surname (such as Brincmann). In spite of this, the majority of information Elsie gave in her written Brinkman family history has turned out to be accurate.

Records Search, Wetteborn Parish

In 2012, German genealogist Gabriele Fricke did a search in the Wetteborn Parish. These records from this parish are now available on microfiche at the Landeskirchliches Archiv in Hannover (Evangelical Lutheran Church Archive). Her search did not reveal a birth or marriage record for Johann Wilhelm Friedrich Brinkmann, or his spouse Maria Dorothea Sophie (Gundelach) Brinkmann. However, death records for Johann and Maria were found in the Wetteborn Parish Church records (see death records listed below).

Residence Search, Germany, 1818-1851

In 1818, Johann Friedrich Wilhelm Brinkmann was living and working in 1818 at the *Grün Glashütte* (Green Glass Factory, otherwise known as the Westerberger Glass Factory) in Westerberg. He lived there until his death at the factory in 1851. He and his first spouse Maria Dorothea Sophie (Gundelach) Brinkmann, are known to have lived in the factory-owned cottages and to have had five children: (1) Johann Philipp Brinkmann, (2) Anna Maria Carolina Brinkmann;, (3) Liborius Friedrich Brinkmann, (4) Henriette Wilhelmina Brinkmann, and (5) Maria Amalie Brinkmann.

Marriage, First Spouse, Winzenburg, 1796

In 2014, German genealogist Jens Kaufmann did a search in the Catholic Dioceses Archive of Hildesheim,[8] in the Winzenburg Parish. A 1796 marriage record was found for Johann Wilhelm Brinkmann and his first spouse Maria Sophia (Gundelach) Brinkmann. This marriage record includes the following:

- Marriage Record -

Groom - Johann Friedrich Brinkmann [Johann Friedrich Wilhelm Brinkmann].
Bride - Maria Sophia (Gundelach) Brinkmann [Maria Dorothea Sophia (Gundelach) Brinkmann].
Date, Place of Marriage - November of 1796, Winzenburg Catholic Church Parish, Winzenburg, Germany.
Witnesses - Joachim Joseph Flugge and Johannes Diesing.
Source - Catholic Dioceses Church Archive of Hildesheim, Winzenburg Parish Church Book, Volume: (1784), Page: (472).

Marriage, Second Spouse, Winzenburg, 1824-1825

Around 1824 or 1825, Johann Friedrich Wilhelm Brinkmann married his second spouse Maria (Hutlach) Brinkmann, while living at the Westerberger Glass Factory, Westerberg. This marriage record has not yet been located and is based on the birth of an unnamed "stillborn child" born on July 1, 1825, in Westerberg, Germany (the child's birth record is in the Evangelical Lutheran Church, Wetteborn Parish records).

Residence, Winzenburg, 1826

Johann Friedrich Wilhelm Brinkmann was present at the Wetteborn Parish Church during his son Friedrich Brinkmann's wedding to Henriette (Lange) Brinkmann on January 19, 1826. His other places of residence included Einbeck, Hannoversch-Münden, Everode, Freden, and Braunlage, Germany.

Death & Burial, Wetteborn Parish, 1851

In 2013, German genealogist Jens Kaufmann did a search in the Evangelical Lutheran Church, Wetteborn Parish. This search provided a January 3, 1851, death record for Johann Wilhelm Brinkmann, who died in a factory-owned cottage in Westerberg at the age of 88. Johann's death record states he died as a "poor man" and a widower who was "buried in silence." Apparently, no Brinkmann family members were present at his burial. Johann was not known to have participated in labor-intensive work during his career in the glass industry. To the contrary, he was consistently described as a *Glashändler* (glass merchant). His spouse is not listed on his death record, but he is known to have remarried sometime between 1824 and 1825. Johann's death record includes the following:

-Death & Burial Record-

Record Type - Death Record.
Date - January 3, 1851, at 10 o'clock in the morning.
Name - Johann Brinkmann [Johanne Friedrich Wilhelm Brinkmann].
Location of Death - Village of Westerberg, Germany - Westerberg Glass Factory Housing Cottage.
Cause of Death - Old age. Cited to be 81 years and 7 days old at time of death.
Buried - January 7, 1851, in the Wetteborn Church Parish Cemetery, Germany.
Notation - Widower. Died as a poor man and was buried in silence on 7th of January 1851.
Occupation - Formerly a glass trader in Westerberg.
Source - Evangelical Lutheran Church, Wetteborn Church Parish, Church Book, Death Register: 1851, Page: (52), No: (1).

Occupation, Glass Merchant

As previously mentioned, Johann was a glass merchant. He never worked inside a glass factory making glassware. He was considered an upper level manager who was not required to do manual labor. However, all of his sons in the Westerberg village worked in the factory at various glass trades (for which they were trained as apprentices).

Note: The making and selling of glass products was an important part of the Brinkmann family's story for than six generations. Johann previously worked in the town of Winzenburg (and several other glass manufacturing towns in Germany). Individuals who worked in the glass manufacturing trades moved around the country, relocating to different factories (as factory sites shifted based on supply and demand). Because of this constant relocation, genealogy records for glass workers are often hard to find. In this author's case, I had never before communicated with, or written to German speaking persons. I recognized that I needed the services and assistance of a professional German genealogist in Germany who was familiar with glassmaking history. Knowing where historic glass factories are located helps narrow down relevant geographic parish church locations, and civil record searches. There are many German books that contain histories of German families who worked in various German glass factories (and towns). These resources should be evaluated before launching an expensive search of church and civil records. In most cases, researchers need to be able to read German because most historic German publications are not available in English.

Search for Documents, Freden Parish

In 2013, Germany genealogist Tiger Young[9] sent a letter to the Freden Parish, Evangelical Lutheran Church[10] in Freden, Germany. The Freden Parish is the central headquarters for the surrounding parishes (including the Wetteborn & Winzenburg Parishes). This letter requested a search of the Wetteborn Parish Church Book for the death record of Johann Friedrich Wilhelm Brinkmann, who died, and was buried in the Wetteborn Parish Cemetery. In February 2013, an answer was received that did not provide any answers to the questions presented. Rather, it simply said that the Freden Parish has church microfiche films from some unstated date, up to 1897 and that these film records are available at the Church Archives in Göttingen, Germany. No further information was provided.

Life Story by Alvin Brinkman, Jr.

I define citations as notes from a researcher regarding their interpretation of a given document name, date, location, or other details, which they came across during their research. If possible, it is best to obtain a copy of every document found during the entire process, and then commission a qualified English translation of the text before adding a copy of it (and its translation) into one's genealogy history. It is expensive to have a professional German genealogist make a paid trip to an archive, complete the research, pay for copies of original or film versions of documents, then forward them to the researcher (such as this author). This research is a very labor-intensive process. As of 2014, most German genealogy records were not available online, except for some Latter Day Saints' microfilm records. German genealogy research is complicated and difficult to navigate, but don't let that discourage you! Any novice American genealogy researcher needs to know that most German archives are currently available only at specific physical archive sites where the records are made available to the public. Not all German archive records are available for public review. Some German records can only be searched through church parish-approved German researchers at their parish. Always demand a copy of each record your researcher finds in his or her work, including an English translation of each record's heading and all text entries. Never accept citations unless it is your only option. Know that, at some point, you will have to get the original document to make certain you have the correct family line. If you fail to make this your record-gathering process standard, you risk the worst genealogy tragedy imaginable, that of following the wrong tree members, rendering all your future work worthless! Check, and then double check, any new family members and their supporting documents.

-End of Life Story-

Marie Dorothea Sophia (Gundelach) Brinkmann, b. c. 1766, d. 1824

Introduction

Maria Dorothea Sophia (Gundelach) Brinkmann, also known as Marie and Aunt Sophie, is believed to have been born around 1766 to 1767 in Germany. Maria is this author's *fourth-great-grandmother*. She was the first spouse of Johann Friedrich Wilhelm Brinkmann. Maria died on April 9, 1824, in the Westerberger Glass Factory, in Westerberg, and was buried on April 10, 1824, in the Evangelical Lutheran Church, Wetteborn Parish Church Cemetery, in Landwehr.

Birth Citation, Schönhagen, Germany, 1766

In 2013, German genealogist Jens Kaufmann found several new Brinkmann family citation links. Considering the Kunze Klaus Directory, it is believed that Maria Dorothea Sophie Brinkmann was born on February 26, 1766, in Schönhagen, Uslar, Northeim, Niedersachsen, Germany, but according to the Hartmann Family Tree, she was born on June 14, 1767, in Winzenburg. This 1766 birth citation matches other similarly dated documents and will be used in this record until proven otherwise. The birth citation lists Maria's parents and includes the following:

-Birth Citation Record-
Record Type - Birth Citation.
Date of Birth - February 26, 1766.
Name - Maria Dorothea Sophie Gundelach.
Location - Schönhagen, Uslar, Northeim, Niedersachsen, Germany. Parish church not listed.
Parents - Father: Johann Justus Gundelach, Mother: Christina Louise (Sturm) Gundelach.
Family Members Listed - Father of child: Johann Friedrich Gundelach, Mother of child: Anna Dorothea (Sturm) Gundelach, Brother of child: Johann Hermann Gundelach, and Johann Friedrich Gundelach.

Godfather - Johann Hermann Gundelach.
Note - Gundelach extended family marriages are listed in Silberborn, Schönhagen, Mecklenburg, and Winzenburg, Germany.
Source - Kunze Klaus Book: Glasmacher-Sippenbuch Werra-Weser-Bergland und Ortssippenbuch Bursfelde-Glashütte bis 1820, Page: (156), Uslar 2000.

Marriage, Winzenburg, Germany, 1796

In 2013, German genealogist Jens Kaufmann did a search in the Evangelical Lutheran Church in Wetteborn Parish, in Landwehr, Germany. No marriage record for Johann or Maria was found suggesting that Johann and Maria married in another location several years before moving their family to the Westerberger Glass Factory. However, in 2014, Kaufmann contacted the Catholic Diocese Archive of Hildesheim, Germany.[11] This archive contains the church records for the Mariä Geburt Parish in Winzenburg. Kaufmann discovered that Johann and Maria were married in November 1796 at the Catholic Church in Winzenburg, now known as the Mariä Geburt Parish of Winzenburg. Their children were also born and baptized in this Catholic Church, even though Johann and Maria were Lutheran, not Catholic. However, it was common practice at the time for families to use the church nearest to their village, rather than travel long distances to a church of their faith. This appears to be the case for Johann and Maria, who lived in the town of Winzenburg, a distance from the nearest Lutheran Church in Wetteborn. These Catholic records were written in Latin, and have Latin and feature spellings of both their given and surnames. This marriage record contains the following:

- Marriage Record -

Groom - Johann Friedrich Wilhelm Brinkmann.
Bride - Maria Sophia (Gundelach) Brinkmann.
Date, Place of Marriage - November of 1796, Winzenburg Catholic Church Parish, Winzenburg, Germany.
Witnesses - Joachim Joseph Flugge and Johannes Diesing.
Source - Catholic Dioceses Church Archive of Hildesheim, Winzenburg Parish Church Book, Volume: (1784), Page: (472).

Note: This was a great learning experience. It is essential that one check all parishes (of all religions) in any known area where one's ancestors lived. One never knows what one might find.

Death & Burial Record - Westerberg, Germany-1824

In 2013, German genealogist Jens Kaufmann did a search in the Wetteborn Parish, Landwehr, Germany. A death record dated April 9, 1824, was found for Maria Sophia (Gundelach) Brinkmann, who died (at the early age of 57 years) from "breast disease." Maria died while living in her factory-cottage in the Westerberger Glass Factory, Westerberg, Landkreis. She left behind her widowed spouse Johann Friedrich Wilhelm Brinkmann, and five children. When Maria died, it must have been a difficult time for all members of this Brinkmann family. There were still two known minor children living in the Brinkmann household. Maria's death record includes the following:

-Death & Burial Record-

Record Type - Death Record - Wetteborn Evangelical Lutheran Church Parish.
Date - April 9,1824.
Name - Sophia Brinkmann [Maria Dorothea Sophia Brinkmann]. Wife of the glass trader Wilhelm Brinkmann [Johann Friedrich Wilhelm Brinkmann].
Age of Deceased - 57 years, 4 Months (Estimated born 1767).

Survivors of Deceased - Left behind a widower, three major children, two minor children.
Day & Time of Death - April 9,1824 at six o'clock in the morning.
Cause of Death - Breast disease.
Priest Attending - Local pastor, J.H. Brunker, received the news of the death and is sure that the deceased is the same as the one reported to him, as she was described.
Day of Burial - April 10, 1824.
Burial Place - Took place in the church yard in Wetteborn, Germany.
Source - Wetteborn Parish Church Book, Death Register-1824, Page: (148), No: (10).

Children of Johann Friedrich Wilhelm Brinkmann & Maria Dorothea Sophia (Gundelach) Brinkmann

1. Johann Philipp Brinkmann, b. c. 1797, d. Unknown
(See corresponding history section for details).

2. Anna Maria Carolina Brinkmann, b. c. 1799, d.Unknown

Introduction.
Anna Maria Carolina Brinkmann was baptized on August 11, 1799, as the daughter of Johann Wilhelm Brinkmann and Maria Sophia (Gundelach) Brinkmann in the Winzenburg Catholic Church Parish, Winzenburg, Germany. She is not cited within the written Brinkmann family history. No further records have been located.

3. Liborius Friedrich Brinkmann, b. c. 1802, d. c. 1864
(See corresponding history section for details).

4. Henriette Wilhelmina Brinkmann, b.1809, d.Unknown

Introduction
In 2013, German genealogist Jens Kaufmann did a search in the Evangelical Lutheran Church, Wetteborn Parish, Landwehr, Germany. No birth record was found for Henriette Wilhelmina Brinkmann. However, a marriage record was found for her and establishes her as part of this Brinkmann family line. Henriette is thought to have been born in May 1809 in the town of Winzenburg, Germany. She baptized on May 11, 1809, as the daughter of Johann Wilhelm Brinkmann and Maria Sophia (Gundelach) Brinkmann in the Winzenburg Catholic Church Parish. Henriette does not appear in the written Brinkman family history, and was not known to be part of this Brinkman family line, until her 1838 marriage to Johann Christoph Huck was discovered in the Evangelical Lutheran Church, Wetteborn Parish Church Book. This search also found birth records for two illegitimate children born to her before her marriage to Huck.

Birth Citation, Winzenburg, Germany 1809
In 2013, this author was working on the Brinkmann Family Tree and discovered the Hartmann Family Tree, which had exact matches to several Brinkmann family members (including Henriette Wilhelmina Brinkmann and her parents Johann Friedrich Wilhelm Brinkmann and Maria Dorothea

Sophie (Gundelach) Brinkmann. The Hartmann Family Tree citation listed Henriette's birth date, place of birth, and parents, and contains the following:

-Birth Citation Record-

Record Type - Birth Citation.
Birth Date - November 5, 1809.
Child's Name & Parents - Henriette Wilhelmina Brinkmann. Daughter of Johann Friedrich Wilhelm Brinkmann and Maria Dorothea Sophie (Gundelach) Brinkmann.
Birth Location - Winzenburg, Hildesheim, Niedersachsen (Lower Saxony), Germany.
Source - Hartmann Family Tree. Citation only.

Baptism, Winzenburg Catholic Parish, Winzenburg, Germany, 1809

In 2014, German genealogist Jens Kaufmann did a search in the Catholic Dioceses Archive of Hildesheim, where all the Catholic Parish Church records are archived for the Winzenburg Catholic Parish Church in Winzenburg, Germany. A baptism record was found for Henrietta Wilhelmina Brinkmann dated May 11, 1809, which contains the following:

-Baptism Record-

Record Type - Baptism.
Birth Date - May 11, 1809.
Child's Name & Parents - Henrietta Wilhelmina Brinkmann. Legitimate daughter of Wilhelm Brinkmann [Johann Friedrich Wilhelm Brinkmann] and Maria Sophie Gundelach [Maria Dorothea Sophie (Gundelach) Brinkmann].
Baptism Location - Winzenburg, Hildesheim, Niedersachsen (Lower Saxony), Germany.
Godparents - Wilh Kessemeyer and Ludow Broseke.
Source - Catholic Dioceses Church Archive of Hildesheim, Catholic Parish Church Book, Volume: (1784), Page: (112).

Illegitimate Children

In 2013, German genealogist Jens Kaufmann did a search in the Evangelical Lutheran Church, Wetteborn Parish Church Book, Landwehr, Germany. This search yielded birth records for two illegitimate children born to Henriette Wilhelmine Brinkmann and Heinrich Fasterling. At the time of the births, Henriette and Heinrich were living at the Westerberger Glass Factory. Heinrich Fasterling is cited as being from the nearby town of Winzenburg. There is no marriage record for Henriette and Heinrich, and no other birth or death records have been located for Heinrich Fasterling. It is not known what happened to Heinrich Fasterling after 1837, when his second illegitimate son was born. Henriette married her first legal spouse, Johann Christoph Huck, in 1838. The two illegitimate children's birth records contains the following:

-Birth & Death Record-

Record Type - Birth & Stillborn Death Record.
Birth Date - February 16, 1835.
Death Date - February 16, 1835.
Child's Name & Parents - Unnamed "Stillborn Child-Illegitimate son" of Henriette Brinkmann [Henriette Wilhelmine Brinkmann] and Heinrich Fasterling in Winzenburg (Germany).
Parents Residence - Westerberg Glass Factory, Niedersachsen (Lower Saxony), Germany.
Burial - Not listed.
Source - Wetteborn Parish Church Book, 1835, Page: (17), No.: (11).

-Birth & Baptism Record-

Record Type - Birth & Baptism Record.

Birth Date - June 8, 1837.

Child's Name & Parents - George Heinrich Carl Fasterling-"Illegitimate son" of Henriette Brinkmann [Henriette Wilhelmine Brinkmann] and Heinrich Fasterling in Winzenburg (Germany).

Parents Residence - Westerberg Glass Factory (Niedersachsen-Lower Saxony, Germany).

Baptized - June 18, 1837, Wetteborn Parish Church, (Wetteborn, Germany).

Godparents - Heinrich Krumsick, Amalie Brinkmann, and Augusta Munten, all from the Glass Factory (Westerberger Glass Factory, Germany).

Source - Wetteborn Parish Church Book, 1837, Page: (25), No.: (21).

Marriage Record - 1838 - Wetteborn Parish, Germany

In 2013, German genealogist Jens Kaufmann searched in the Evangelical Lutheran Church's Wetteborn Parish Church Book, Landwehr, Germany. The May 6, 1838, marriage record was found for Henriette Wilhelmine Brinkmann, citing her parents and confirming her place in the Brinkmann family. She was not previously cited in the written Brinkman family history or known to be part of this Brinkman family line. Henriette was the daughter of Wilhelm Brinkmann (Johann Friedrich Wilhelm Brinkmann) and Marie Sophie Gundelach (Maria Dorothea Sophia (Gundelach) Brinkmann]. The marriage record contains the following:

-Marriage Record-

Record Type - Marriage.

Proclamation - Sundays "Quasimodogeniti and Misericordias Domini."

Marriage Date & Location - May 6, 1838, (at the Evangelical Lutheran Church), Wetteborn Parish, (Niedersachsen, Germany).

Groom - Johann Christoph Huck - Renter and journeyman mason in Everode, (Germany), and the legitimate son of the renter Christoph Huck and of Marie Gertrud (Bock).

Bride - Henriette Wilhelmina Brinkmann - legitimate daughter of Wilhelm Brinkmann [Johann Friedrich Wilhelm Brinkmann] and of the deceased Marie Sophia Gundelach [Maria Dorothea Sophie (Gundelach) Brinkmann].

Source - Wetteborn Parish Church Book, Marriage Record, 1838, Page: (18), No.: (2).

Children of Johann Christoph Huck & Henriette Wilhelmina (Brinkmann) Huck

In 2013, this author conducted an internet search for any Brinkmann family trees. Two were located: (1) Crone Deutscher Stammbaum (Ingolf Crone) and (2) Hartmann Familienstammbaum (mh544). Both sources cited Johann Christoph Huck and Henriette Wilhelmina (Brinkmann) Huck as having married (unknown date) and producing one daughter, Wilhelmine Dorothea Huck, born February 6, 1854, in Westerberg. She died on November 30, 1918, in Hannover-Linden, Niedersachsen (Lower Saxony), Germany. Wilhelmine is also cited as having married Johann Goslar, born on December 24, 1849, in Duderstadt, Gottengen, Niedersachsen (Lower Saxony), Germany. Wilhelmine and Johann had one daughter Elsie Therese Henriette Julie Goslar, born August 7, 1878, in Hannover-Linden, Germany. She died January 19, 1970, in Hannover, Niedersachsen (Lower Saxony), Germany.

Note: Due to the extreme complexity of this Brinkman family line, research this author set some limits on the research time spent on each family tree, and their individual descending generations. At some future date, research into this branch of the Brinkmann family line should be continued in depth.

Introduction

Maria Amalia Brinkmann is believed born around 1812 (based on her baptism record), as the daughter of Johann Friedrich Wilhelm Brinkmann and Maria Dorothea Sophia (Gundelach) Brinkmann in the Westerberger Glass Factory, Westerberger, Germany. Her August 11, 1799, baptism record is in the Winzenburg Catholic Parish Church Book, Winzenburg, Germany. Her birth and death records were not found in searches of the Wetteborn Parish Church Book, or the Winzenburg Catholic Parish Church Book.

Birth & Baptism Record Search

In 2014, German genealogist Jens Kaufmann did a search in the Evangelical Lutheran Church, Wetteborn Parish, Germany and in the Catholic Dioceses Church Archive of Hildesheim, Germany. No Brinkmann birth or baptism records were found for Maria Amalia Brinkmann.

Illegitimate Children, 1839 & 1841

Two Wetteborn Lutheran Parish Church birth records for Maria cite two illegitimate children which include: (1) a stillborn son, born May 29, 1839, in the Westerberger Glass Factory to Amalie Brinkmann and Wilhelm Conrad Lüttge (not married), and (2) Wilhelmine Henriette Brinkmann, born about February 1841 in Hildesheim, Niedersachsen at the Entbindungshaus Maternity Hospital, (with no father cited). The second child died June 9, 1842, at 1 years old, and was buried on June 11, 1842, in the Wetteborn Church Parish Cemetery, Wetteborn, Germany. These two birth and death records contains the following:

-Birth & Death Record-

Record Type - Stillborn Birth & Death Record.
Date of Birth & Death - May 29, 1839.
Name - Unnamed stillborn illegitimate son.
Parents' Names - Amalie Brinkmann and the Schürer (keeper of the fire) Wilhelm Conrad Lüttge.
Buried - May 29, 1839, (In the Wetteborn Church Parish Cemetery).
Parent's Residence - Westerberger Glass Factory.
Source - Evangelical Lutheran Church, Wetteborn Parish Church-1839, Page: (30), No.: (18).

-Death Record-

Record Type - Death Record.
Date of Death - June 9, 1842, at 3 o'clock in the morning.
Cause of Death - Hooping-Cough Disease; Age: 1 year, 3 months, 20 days.
Deceased's Name - Henriette Wilhelmine Brinkmann. Illegitimate daughter.
Parents' Names - Amalie Brinkmann, from the Westerberger Glass Factory (father not listed).
Buried - June 11, 1842, buried "as a poor man, in silence." (In the Wetteborn Church Parish Cemetery.
Remarks - The deceased was born at the maternity hospital in Hildesheim (Germany).
Source - Evangelical Lutheran Church, Wetteborn Parish Church-1842, Page: (98), No.: (8).

Note: One of the supporting facts that make Maria a part of this Brinkmann family line is that she was the godmother to George Heinrich Carl Fasterling, born in 1837 and Dorothee Marie Brinkmann, born 1839.

Introduction

In 2013, German genealogist Jens Kaufmann [5] searched in the Evangelical Lutheran Church, Wetteborn Parish, Landwehr, Germany. Kaufmann discovered a new record for Maria (Hutlach) Brinkmann, who was not otherwise cited in the written Brinkmann family history. Maria is the second spouse of this author's *fourth-great-grandfather*. As of 2013, no birth, baptism, marriage, or death records for Maria. However, a July 1, 1825, birth record was found in the Wetteborn Parish Church Registry for a "stillborn child," cited as the "legitimate daughter" of Wilhelm Brinkmann (thought to be Johann Friedrich Wilhelm Brinkmann) and his cited spouse, Maria Hutlach. Johann's first spouse Maria Dorothea Sophie (Gundelach) Brinkmann had died in 1824, one year before this stillborn child was born. Johann and Maria (Hutlach) Brinkmann may have married about 1824 (just after Johann's first spouse's death). Johann would have been about 55 years old when the stillborn child was born. No other living children are known from Johann's second marriage.

Note: Because little information is available for Maria (Hutlach) Brinkmann, it is believed that she may have died before Johann Friedrich Wilhelm Brinkmann's death in 1851 (wherein he is listed as a widower). More work needs to be completed to fill in the missing pieces regarding this marriage.

Children of Johann Friedrich Wilhelm Brinkmann & Maria (Hutlach) Brinkmann

1. Stillborn Daughter, b. 1825, d. 1825

Introduction

In 2013, German genealogist Jens Kaufmann did a search in the Evangelical Lutheran Church, Wetteborn Parish Registry, Landwehr, Germany. Kaufmann found a new birth and death record for an unnamed "stillborn daughter" of Johann Friedrich Wilhelm Brinkmann and Maria (Hutlach) Brinkmann. This July 1, 1825, birth and death record confirms that there was a "legitimate" child born to this marriage. The birth and death record do not state the child's age from birth to death, the cause of death, or burial arrangements. No marriage record for Johann Friedrich Wilhelm Brinkmann or Maria (Hutlach) have been located. This child's birth and death record contains the following:

-Birth & Death Record-

Record Type - Stillborn Birth & Death Record.
Date - July 1, 1825, at 1 o'clock p.m.
Name - No name stillborn daughter (Miss Brinkmann).
Day & Hour of Birth - The 1st of July, at 1 o'clock p.m.
Whether Legitimate or Illegitimate - Born legitimate.
Father's Name & Occupation - Wilhelm Brinkmann [Johann Friedrich Wilhelm Brinkmann], glass trader.
Mother's Name - Maria Hutlach [Maria (Hutlach) Brinkmann].
Parent's Residence - The (Glass) Factory (Westerberger Glass Factory) is the parents' place of residence.
Source - Wetteborn Parish Church Book, Birth Register-1825, Page: (67), Number: (23).

- End of Section -

Gallery

Johann Friedrich Wilhelm Brinkmann

Exhibit of archeological glass products from the Schildhorst Glass Factory, Germany, c. 1845-1875.
Source: Heimatbund-Hildesheim District Federal History Association, Germany

Main road to Wetteborn Parish Church, Germany, c. 2010
Location where the Brinkmann family worshiped, and were buried
Source: Google-Panoramio-Vincentvangogh

Winzenburg, Germany, photo c. 2010
Location where the Johann Wilhelm Brinkmann Family lived and married in 1796
Source: Google-Panoramio-Vincentvangogh

Mariä Geburt Catholic Church Parish in Winzenburg, Germany, photo c. 2000
Location where Johann Wilhelm Brinkmann and Maria Dorothea Sophia (Gundelach) Brinkmann
were married in 1796, and where they baptized their children
Source: Diocese Archive of Hildesheim, Germany-postcard

156 · Glasmacher-Sippenbuch

ℋℋ

Gundelach 1762, NN, vmtl. Hütte Winzenburg
  ∞Maria Elisabeth **Ständer** *um 1742 †Winzenburg (kath.) 27.11.1804, 62J. 4Mo. 14Tage

Gundelach 1763, Johann Justus, ~Bu.25.1.1736 S.v. Johann Friedrich und Anna Dorothea **Sturm**
  1766 (Kb.) am M...berge bei Schönhagen. Die Familie steht am 4.11.1766 im Einwohnerverzeichnis
  von Silberborn, darunter seine Brüder Johann Hermann und Johann Friedrich Gundelach[476]
  Okt.1769 Silberborn: „auf der Nieme gebürtig, nährt sich von Holzhauen und von seinen Pferden und
  Wagen"[477]
    1.∞Schönhagen 23.6.1763 Christina Louise **Sturm**
    ✔ 1. Maria Dorothea Sophie, gen. 1766, *Schönhagen 26.2.1766 P: Johann Hermann Gundelach
       2. Johann Christoph Ludwig *Schönhagen ..12.1769 Paten u.a. Just Wilhelm Sturm
    2.∞Schönhagen 24.5.1772 Catharina Sophie **Ruländer**
       1. Marie Christine *Schönhagen 30.5.1773, †Silberborn 30.6.1778 Pocken ☐Schönhagen 5.7.1778 5J. 1
          Mo. 1Tag
       2. Sophie Catharina Henriette *Silberborn (~Schönhagen) 20.4.1775
       3. Sophie Dorothea Wilhelmine *Schönhagen 26.3.1777
       4. Justine Sophie *Silberborn (~Schönhagen) 29.5.1779
       5. Christine Louise *Silberborn (~Schönhagen) 12.3.1781

Gundelach 1764, Georg Rudolf ~Hellenthal 29.1.1732 S.v.Christoph und Ilse Catharina **Lokamp**
  1764 auf der Glashütte Winzenburg
  ∞Winzenburg 25.11.1764 Maria Elisabeth **Ständer**

Gundelach 1766, Heinrich Christoph ~Hellenthal 9.8.1724 S.v Christian.
  ∞Schönhagen 18.2.1766 Sophia Dorothea **Göbels**
    1. Rebecca *Schönhagen 10.10.1766
    2. Justina Hanne *Schönhagen 1774, XE †Wiensen 1840

Gundelach 1769, Johann Hermann, *1744 S.v.Johann Friedrich und Anna Dorothea **Storm**
  1755 in Einwohnerliste von Silberborn, 11J., Am 4.11.1766 im Einwohnerverzeichnis von Silberborn.[478]
  Okt.1769 Silberborn: ...geboren auf der ehemaligen Glasehütte am Dasselschen Mittelberge[479], ein
  Holzhauer.
  ∞Silberborn 3.10.1769 Sophie Catharina **Pape** (~Uslar 11.11.1742)

Gundelach 1774, Johann Conrad, *um 1745, †Winzenburg 31.3.1817, 72J.
  ∞vmtl. Witwe Elisabeth **Gundlach** *um 1754 †Winzenburg 16.11.1823, 69J.

Gundelach 1780, Georg Rudolph ~Schönhagen 6.8.1758 S.v.Johann Andreas und Catharina **Sturm**
  ∞Dorothee Juliane **Dörries** *err.6.11.1758 †Silberborn 3.3.1824
    1. Christoph Ludwig *1800 †Silberborn 14.3.1800 alt 15Tage

Gundelach 1781, Johann Georg, *Mecklenburg
  ∞Isselt (Niederlande) Gerichtsakten 25.5.1781 Jannetje **Schneider** („Snijder") T.v.Arnoldus
    1. Sara ∞Isselt (Niederlande) 10.6.1806 Matthias **Beurs**

---

[476] BRODHAGE-MÜLLER, Silberborn, S.39 nach StA Hannover 106 Han 88 D Uslar 721.
[477] BLOß, Die Glashütte am Silberborn, S.69.
[478] BRODHAGE-MÜLLER, Silberborn, S.35 und 39 nach StA Hannover 106 Han 88 D Uslar 721.
[479] Das soll nach BLOß, Die Glashütte am Silberborn, S.68 mit der Glashütte Silberborn identisch sein; im übrigen nach einem
  Einwohnerverzeichnis des Amts Uslar.

Birth citation, February 26, 1766, Maria Dorothea Sophia (Gundelach) Brinkmann
Location of birth, Schönhagen, Uslar, Northeim, Niedersachsen, Germany
Source: Klaus Kunze Book: Glasmacher-Sippenbuch, Werra-Weser-Bergland to 1820, Uslar 2000

M:	Copulati 1796 à Liborio Pieper pastore.	Nomina.
Julii	Copulati sunt ex commissione mea à R.P. Seraphin Wachter primissario adolescens Laurentius Hagemann, ex Everode, et Maria Christina Klooth virgo ex majore Freden, præsentibus testibus Conrado Hagemann, et Christiano Klooth ex majore Freden.	Hagemann, et Klooth.
Octobris	Copulati sunt honestus adolescens Wilhelmus Scholle, et pudica virgo Maria Magdalena Brandis, præsentibus testibus Andrea Munter, et Clemente Dickehucth.	Scholle, et Brandis.
Octobris	Obtenta dispensatione à R^{mo} Vicariatu hildesino in tertio consanguinitatis gradu æquali copulati sunt Joannes Maximilianus Hagemann, et Maria Christina Heuth ex Everode, præsentibus testibus Joanne Bernardo Hagemann, et Leopoldo Heuth ex Everode.	Hagemann, et Heuth.
Octobris	Copulati sunt Franciscus Kindervater, honestus adolescens lammspringensis et Friderica Klooth ex minore Freden virgo, præsentibus testibus Andrea Hagemann ex Everode, et Joachimo Josepho Flügge.	Kindervater, et Klooth.
Novembris	Copulati sunt ex officina vitriaria Joannes Wilhelmus Brinkmann, et Maria Sophia Gundelach; testes fuere Joachimus Josephus Flügge, et Joannes Diesing.	Brinkmann et Gundelach.
Novemb^r	Copulati sunt adolescens Joannes Deppen ex Breidenborn, et virgo Maria Angela Heine ex minore Freden; testes fuere Adolphus Preusse, et Henricus Rühmer.	Deppen, et Heine.
die	Copulati sunt honestus adolescens Joannes Conradus Schünemann, et pudica virgo, Joanna Justina Dieser, à c; testes fue—	Schünemann et Dieser.

Marriage record - November 1796
Johann Friedrich Wilhelm Brinkmann & Maria Dorothea Sophia (Gundelach) Brinkmann
Winzenburg Catholic Parish Church, Winzenburg, Niedersachsen, Germany
Source: Catholic Diocese, Church Archive of Hildesheim, Germany

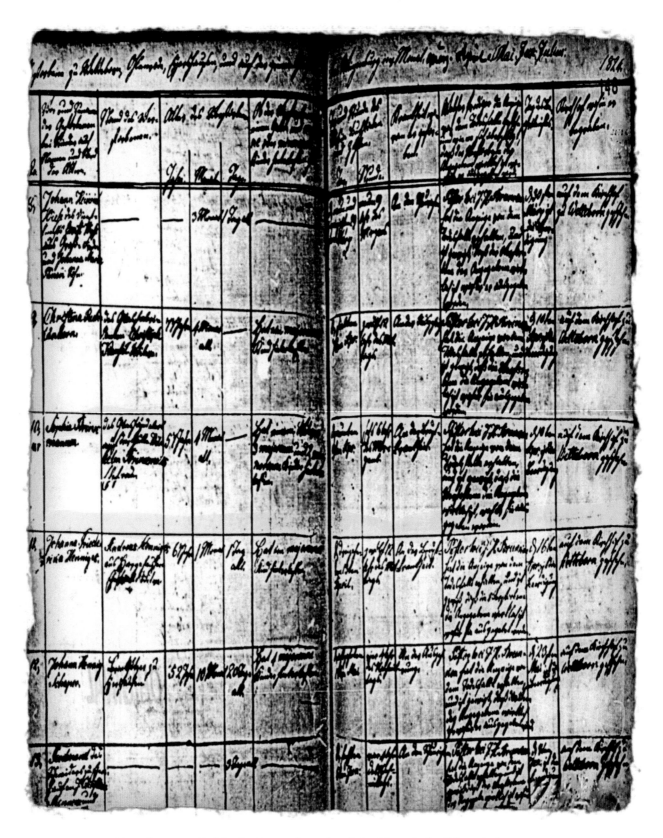

Death record, Maria Dorothea Sophia (Gundelach) Brinkmann
Died: April 9, 1824, Westerberger Glass Factory, Germany
Buried: April 10, 1824, Wetteborn Church Parish Cemetery, Germany
Source: Wetteborn Parish Church Records

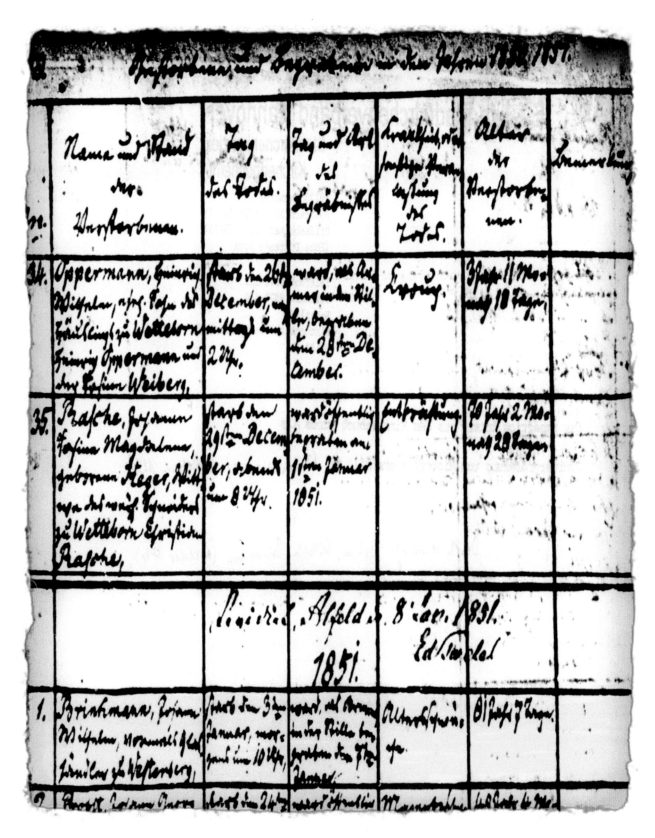

Death record, Johann Friedrich Wilhelm Brinkmann
Died: January 3, 1851, Westerberger Glass Factory, Germany
Buried: January 7, 1851, Wetteborn Church Parish Cemetery, Germany
Source: Wetteborn Parish Church Records

Descendants of Johann Philipp Brinkmann

Johann Philipp Brinkmann.
& *Spouse* 1/2 - Johanne Justine Charlotte (Düen) Brinkmann.

- Johanne Sophie Henriette Brinkmann.
- Dorothee Charlotte Brinkmann.
- Johann Heinrich Brinkmann.
- Gottfried Brinkmann.
- Ferdinand Heinrich Julius Brinkmann.
- Wilhelm August Ludwig Brinkmann.
- August Heinrich Carl Brinkmann.
    - *Spouse* - Johanne Sophie Louise Friederike (Hirsch) Brinkmann.
        - Friedrich Ludewig Carl Brinkmann.
        - Louis Heinrich Hermann Brinkmann.
        - Wilhelmine Marie Helene Brinkmann.
        - Albertine Pauline Martha Brinkmann.
        - Karl Brinkmann.
- Heinrich Carl Wilhelm Brinkmann.
- Dorothee Marie Brinkmann.

& *Spouse* 2/2 - Louise Antoinett (Ständer) Brinkmann.
- Karl Daniel August Brinkmann.

The Johann Philipp Brinkmann Family

Johann Philipp Brinkmann, b. c. 1797, d. Unknown

Introduction
Johann Philipp Brinkmann is this author's *third-great-grand-uncle*. His birth and death records were not been located. However, his February 12, 1781, baptism records were found in the Winzenburg Catholic Parish Church, Winzenburg, Germany. Johann Philipp is known to have been married twice. He had nine children with his first spouse, Johanne Justine Charlotte (Düen) Brinkmann, and one child with his second, Louise Antoinette (Stender) Brinkmann.

Baptism, Winzenburg, Germany, 1797
In 2014, German genealogist Jens Kaufmann did a search at the Catholic Dioceses Church Archive of Hildesheim where all the Catholic Parish Church records are microfilmed and stored for the old Winzenburg Catholic Parish Church. A February 12, 1797, baptism record was found for Johann Philipp Brinkmann in the Catholic Parish Church Book, Winzenburg, Germany. This baptism record contains the following:

-Baptism Record-
Name - Johann Philipp Brinkmann.
Birth Date and Location - February 12, 1797.
Parents - Legitimate son of Johann Wilhelm Brinkmann [Johann Friedrich Wilhelm Brinkmann] and his wife Maria Sophia Kundelach [Maria Dorothea Sophia (Gundelach) Brinkmann].
Statement - Baptized by Pastor Liborius Pieper; Godparents: Johannes Stender and Philipp Seiths.
Source: Catholic Dioceses Church Archive of Hildesheim, Volume: (1781), Page: (288).

Residences
Various related records indicate that Johann Philipp Brinkmann originally lived and worked in Einbeck, Germany. Around 1823, he moved to Westerberg, and remained there through 1841. It is not known where he and his family moved to after leaving Westerberg.

Military Service, Germany, 1818
In 2013, German researcher Jens Kaufmann did a search at the Wetteborn Parish for any records of Johann Philipp Brinkmann. An 1818 marriage record was found containing information that Johann Phillip was a *Tambour* (infantry drummer) in the Einbeck Landwehr Battalion of the German Army. It is believed that this was his profession for several years. No other military records have been located.

Occupation 1818-1841
In 2012, German researcher Gabriele Fricke did a search at the Wetteborn Parish for any documents related to Johann Philipp Brinkmann. Several records were located during this search verifying that Johann Philipp was a skilled *Schürer* (one who kept the furnaces hot and ready for glassmaking). He was separated by his training status from the day laborers and apprentices. Johann worked for six years (1818-1823) in the Einbeck Glass Factory. He then moved his family to the Westerberger Glass Factory in Westerberg, Germany, where he worked for 18 years (1823-1841).

Search for Birth & Death Records, Wetteborn Parish, Germany
In 2012, German researcher Gabriel Fricke did a search at the Wetteborn Parish for Johan Philipp Brinkmann's birth and death records. None were found.

Marriage Records, Wetteborn Parish, Germany, 1818 & 1841
In 2013, German researcher Jens Kaufmann did a search at the Wetteborn Parish for a marriage record for Johann Philipp Brinkmann. An 1818 marriage proclamation and a marriage record were located for Johann and his first spouse, Johanne Justine Charlotte (Düen) Brinkmann. Also, an 1841 marriage proclamation and marriage record was located for Johann and his second spouse, Louise Antoinette (Stender) Brinkmann. Johann's first marriage produced a total of nine children (listed below). His second marriage produced one child, Karl Daniel August Brinkmann (listed below).

Johanne Justine Charlotte (Düen) Brinkmann, b. 1796, d. 1840

Introduction
Johanne Justine Charlotte (Düen) Brinkmann was the first spouse of this author's *third-great-grand-uncle*. No birth record was found. However, there is a citation of her birth, including her parents and siblings, and an 1840 death record. Johanne was the first of two spouses married to Johann Philipp Brinkmann.

Birth Citation, Germany, 1796
In 2013, German genealogist Jens Kaufmann did a search at the Wetteborn Parish for a birth record for Johanne. No birth record was found, but the *Local Family Book of Dassensen* (Source: Nowak Rolf, 1999 edition, page 96, No. 762) does list Johanne Justine Charlotte (Düen) as having been born May 16, 1796. Her parents and siblings are also listed in that book.

Marriage, Westerberg, Germany, 1818
In 2013, German genealogist Jens Kaufmann did a search at the Wetteborn Parish for a marriage record for Johanne and Johann Philipp Brinkmann. A November 4, 1818, marriage record was located and shows that they were married at the Evangelical Lutheran Church, Wetteborn Parish, Niedersachsen, Germany while Johann was living and working at the Westerberger Glass Factory. They were married for 22 years and had nine children. The marriage ended with Johanne's unexpected death in 1840 from "nervous fever." This proclamation and marriage record contain the following:

-Marriage Record-
Record Type - Proclamation and Marriage.
Proclamation - 26th & 27th Sunday after Trinity in 1818, at the Evangelical Lutheran Church, Jacobi Parish, Einbeck, Germany.
Marriage Date - November 4, 1818, at the Evangelical Lutheran Church, Wetteborn Parish, Niedersachsen, Germany.
Groom - Johann Philipp Brinkmann, the German Army drummer from the Landwehr Battalion, Einbeck, Germany; Born the legitimate son of the glass trader Johann Friedrich Wilhelm Brinkmann from the green glass factory near Winzenburg, (Germany).
Bride - Johanne Justine Charlotte (Düen) Brinkmann, the legitimate daughter of the deceased linen weaver Johann Düen. Born: 1796 (Dassausen Directory).
Source - St. Jacobi Parish Church Proclamation Record, 1818, Page: (17); and the Wetteborn Parish Church Book, Marriage Record, 1818-1819, Dated: November 24, 1818.

Note: Proclamations were public announcements made either in front of the parish church or in the town's central square on a scheduled day when important news was to be announced. Usually, the announcers were professionals who were approved by their monarch through the kingdom's governmental agencies. They were; one might say, licensed to travel and announce the King's news of importance. Weddings were held after proclamations, and marriages were often recorded separately in parish church records and contained many more details not found in the proclamations.

Death, Westerberg, Germany, 1840
In 2013, German genealogist Jens Kaufmann did a search at the Wetteborn Parish for a death record for Johanne. A death record dated March 11, 1840, was located for her. She died unexpectedly at the age of 43 and left behind nine children, ranging from 2 to 22 years old. Johanne's death led to a great hardship for her spouse Johann Philipp Brinkmann. Johann married again (within ten months of the death of Johanne's death). The death record contains the following:

-Death & Burial Record-
Record Type - Death & Burial - Wetteborn Evangelical Lutheran Church Parish.
Date - March 11, 1840.
Name - Johanne Justine Charlotte Brinkmann, wife of the *Schürer* (keeper of the fire), Philipp Brinkmann in Westerberg [Germany].
Cause of Death - Nervous Fever. Age: 43 years and 24 days old.
Place of Death - Westerberg, Glass Factory Cottage, Germany.
Date of Burial - March 14, 1840.
Place of Burial - Evangelical Lutheran Church-Wetteborn Parish Cemetery.
Notation - Was buried (as a poor woman in silence) on 14th of March.
Source - Wetteborn Parish Church Book, Death Record, 1840, Page: (32), No: (11).

Records Search, Freden Parish, Germany
In 2013, German genealogist Tiger Young sent a letter to the Evangelical Lutheran Church, Freden Parish, in Germany requesting a search of the Wetteborn Parish for the death record of Johanne. The Freden Parish is the central administrative office for the surrounding parishes (including the Wetteborn & Winzenburg Parishes). In February 2013, the response was received that did not provide any answers to the questions presented. Rather, it simply said that the Freden Parish has church microfiche from an unstated date (up to 1897) and that these records are available at the Church Archives in Göttingen, Germany. No further information was provided. This was a very disappointing search.

Children of Johann Philipp Brinkmann & Johanne Justine Charlotte (Düen) Brinkmann

1. Johanne Sophie Henriette Brinkmann, b. 1818, d. Unknown

Introduction
Johanne Sophie Henriette Brinkmann was the first child of Johann Philipp Brinkmann and Johanne Justine Charlotte (Düen) Brinkmann. She was born in 1818 in Einbeck, Germany and then moved with her family to Westerberg, Germany. No marriage or death records have been located for her, and no records were found at the Wetteborn Parish.

Birth & Baptism, 1818
In 2013, German genealogist Jens Kaufmann did a search at the Evangelical Lutheran Church Archives, of the Wetteborn Parish for Brinkmann records. A birth and baptism record were found for Johanne Sophie Henriette Brinkmann, born November 27, 1818, in Einbeck, Northeim,

Niedersachsen, Germany. She was baptized on December 3, 1818, at the Evangelical Lutheran Church, St. Jacobi Parish, in Einbeck. Her godparents are listed as Widow-Johanne Duen and Mrs. Sophia Brinkmann. The birth and baptism record contains the following:

-Birth & Baptism Record-

Record Type - Birth & Baptism.
Child's Name - Johanne Sophie Henriette Brinkmann.
Date of Birth - November 27, 1818, born legitimate.
Father's Name & Occupation - Johann Philipp Brinkmann; *Tambour* (drummer) in the Landwehr Battalion of the Germany Army in Einbeck, Germany.
Mother's Name - Johanne Justine Charlotte (Düen) Brinkmann.
Date of Baptism - December 3, 1818, (at the Evangelical Lutheran Church, St. Jacobi Parish, Einbeck, Germany).
Godparents - Widow Johanne Duen, and Mrs. Sophia Brinkmann.
Source - Evangelical Lutheran Church, St. Jacobi Parish Church Book, 1818, Page: (979), No: (33).

Confirmation, 1833
A citation dated 1833 states that Johanne's confirmation was held in the Evangelical Lutheran Church, Wetteborn Parish.

---

2. Dorothee Charlotte Brinkmann, b. 1820, d. Unknown

Introduction
Dorothee Charlotte Brinkmann was the second child of Johann Philipp Brinkmann and Johanne Justine Charlotte (Düen) Brinkmann. She was born in 1820 in Einbeck, Germany, and then moved with her family to Westerberg, Germany where her father worked in the Westerberger Glass Factory. No marriage or death records have been found for her, and no records were found at the Wetteborn Parish.

Birth & Baptism, 1820
In 2013, German genealogist Jens Kaufmann did a search at the Evangelical Lutheran Church Archives of the Wetteborn Parish for Brinkmann records. A birth and baptism record were found for Dorothee Charlotte Brinkmann. She was born October 9, 1820, in Einbeck, and was baptized on October 15, 1820, at the Evangelical Lutheran Church, St. Jacobi Parish, Einbeck. The birth and baptism record contains the following:

-Birth & Baptism Record-

Record Type - Birth & Baptism.
Child's Name - Johanne Sophie Henriette Brinkmann.
Date of Birth - October 9, 1820, Born legitimate.
Father's Name & Occupation - Johann Philipp Brinkmann; *Tambour* (drummer) in the Landwehr Battalion of the German Army in Einbeck, Germany.
Mother's Name - Johanne Justine Charlotte (Düen) Brinkmann.
Date of Baptism - October 15, 1820, (at the Evangelical Lutheran Church, St. Jacobi Parish, Einbeck, Germany).
Godparent - Mrs. Ebbighausen.
Source - Evangelical Lutheran Church, Wetteborn Parish Book, 1818, Page: (104), No: (33).

Confirmation, 1835
A citation dated 1835 states that Dorothee's confirmation was held in the Evangelical Lutheran Church, Wetteborn Parish.

---

3. Johann Heinrich Brinkmann, b. 1823, d. Unknown

Introduction
Johann Heinrich Brinkmann was the third child of Johann Philipp Brinkmann and Johanne Justine Charlotte (Düen) Brinkmann. He was born in 1823 in a Westerberger *Glashütte* (glassworks cottage). No marriage or death records have been located for him, and no records were found at the Wetteborn Parish.

Birth & Baptism, 1823
In 2013, German genealogist Jens Kaufmann did a search at the Evangelical Lutheran Church Archives of the Wetteborn Parish for Brinkmann records. A birth and baptism record were found for Johann Heinrich Brinkmann, born July 10, 1823, in a Westerberger *Glashütte* (glassworks cottage) in Landkreis, Hildesheim, Niedersachsen Germany. He was baptized on July 13, 1823, at the Evangelical Lutheran Church, Wetteborn Parish Church. Godparents are listed as J.H. Lange, J.P. Brinkmann, and Charlotte Hutlach. The birth and baptism record contains the following:

-Birth & Baptism Record-
Record Type - Birth & Baptism.
Child's Name - Johann Heinrich Brinkmann.
Date of Birth - July 10, 1823, at 2 o'clock in the morning, born legitimate.
Father's Name & Occupation - Philipp Brinkmann, [Johann Philipp Brinkmann] working as the *Schürer* (Keeper of the fire) at the Westerberger Glass Factory, Westerberg, Germany.
Mother's Name - Sophie Charlotte Düen [Johanne Justine Charlotte (Düen) Brinkmann].
Residence of Parents - The Glass Factory (Westerberger Glass Factory) is the parents' place of residence.
Date of Baptism - July 13, 1823, (at the Evangelical Lutheran Church, Wetteborn Parish).
Pastor's Name - Baptism was performed by the local pastor J.H. Brunken.
Godparents - J.H. Lange, J.P. Brinkmann, and Charlotte Hutlach.
Source - Evangelical Lutheran Church, Wetteborn Parish Church Book, 1825, Page: (59), No: (22).

Confirmation, 1837
An 1837 citation states that Johann Heinrich's confirmation was held in the Evangelical Lutheran Church, Wetteborn Parish.

---

4. Gottfried Brinkmann, b. 1825, d. Unknown

Introduction
Gottfried Brinkmann was the fourth child of Johann Philipp Brinkmann and Johanne Justine Charlotte (Düen) Brinkmann. He was born in 1825 in a Westerberger *Glashütte* (glassworks cottage). No confirmation, marriage or death records have been located for him, and no records were found at the Wetteborn Parish.

Birth & Baptism, 1825

In 2013, German genealogist Jens Kaufmann did a search at the Evangelical Lutheran Church Archives of the Wetteborn Parish for Brinkmann records. A birth and baptism record were found for Gottfried Brinkmann, born November 11, 1825, in a Westerberger *Glashütte* (glassworks cottage) in Landkreis, Hildesheim, Niedersachsen, Germany. He was baptized on November 20, 1825, at the Evangelical Lutheran Church, Wetteborn Parish. Godparents are listed as Franz Standler, Gottfried Kaufel, and Karolina Peters. The birth and baptism record contains the following:

-Birth & Baptism Record-

Record Type - Birth & Baptism.
Child's Name - Gottfried Brinkmann.
Date of Birth - November 11, 1825, at 12 o'clock at night, born legitimate.
Father's Name & Occupation - Philipp Brinkmann [Johann Philipp Brinkmann] working as the *Schürer* (keeper of the fire) at the Westerberger Glass Factory, Westerberg, Germany.
Mother's Name - Scharlotte Düen [Johanne Justine Charlotte (Düen) Brinkmann].
Residence of Parents - The Glass Factory (Westerberger Glass Factory) is the parents' place of residence.
Date of Baptism - November 20, 1825, (at the Evangelical Lutheran Church, Wetteborn Parish).
Pastor's Name - Baptism was performed by the local pastor J.H. Brunken.
Godparents - Franz Standler, Gottfried Kaufel, and Karolina Peters.
Source - Evangelical Lutheran Church, Wetteborn Parish Church Book, 1825, Page: (69), No: (37).

Confirmation, Marriage, and Death Record Search

No confirmation, marriage or death records were located for Gottfried Brinkmann in the Wetteborn Parish Church records. This indicates that the Brinkmann family most likely moved after 1825.

---

5. Ferdinand Heinrich Julius Brinkmann, b. 1828, d. Unknown

Introduction

Ferdinand Heinrich Julius Brinkmann was the fifth child, of Johann Philipp Brinkmann and Johanne Justine Charlotte (Düen) Brinkmann. He was born in 1828 in a Westerberger *Glashütte* (glassworks cottage). No confirmation, marriage or death records have been located for him, and no records were found at the Wetteborn Parish.

Birth & Baptism, 1828

In 2013, German genealogist Jens Kaufmann did a search at the Evangelical Lutheran Church Archives of the Wetteborn Parish for Brinkmann records. A birth and baptism record were found for Ferdinand Heinrich Julius Brinkmann, born February 26, 1828, in a Westerberger *Glashütte* (glassworks cottage) in Landkreis, Hildesheim, Niedersachsen, Germany. He was baptized on May 1, 1828, at the Evangelical Lutheran Church, Wetteborn Parish. Godparents are listed as Julius Stander, Louise Schorr, and Ferdinand Peters. The birth and baptism record contains the following:

-Birth & Baptism Record-

Record Type - Birth & Baptism.
Child's Name - Ferdinand Heinrich Julius Brinkmann.
Date of Birth - February 26, 1828, at 8 o'clock in the morning, born legitimate.
Father's Name & Occupation - Johann Philipp Brinkmann, *Schürer* (keeper of the fire) at the Westerberger Glass Factory, Westerberg, Germany.
Mother's Name - Sophie Scharlotte Düen [Johanne Justine Charlotte (Düen) Brinkmann].

Residence of Parents - The Glass Factory (Westerberger Glass Factory) is the parents' place of residence.
Date of Baptism - March 2, 1828, (at the Evangelical Lutheran Church, Wetteborn Parish).
Pastor's Name - Baptism was performed by the local pastor J.H. Brunken.
Godparents - Julius Staender, Louise Schorr, and Ferdinand Peters.
Source - Evangelical Lutheran Church, Wetteborn Parish Church Book, 1825, Page: (79), No: (5).

---

6. Wilhelm August Ludewig Brinkmann, b. 1831, d. Unknown

Introduction
Wilhelm August Ludewig Brinkmann was the sixth child of Johann Philipp Brinkmann and Johanne Justine Charlotte (Düen) Brinkmann. He was born in 1831 in a Westerberger *Glashütte* (glassworks cottage). No confirmation, marriage or death records have been located for him, and no records were found in the Wetteborn Parish records.

Birth & Baptism, 1831
In 2013, German genealogist Jens Kaufmann did a search at the Evangelical Lutheran Church Archives of the Wetteborn Parish for Brinkmann records. A birth and baptism record were found for Wilhelm August Ludewig Brinkmann, born April 26, 1831, in the Westerberger *Glashütte* (glassworks cottage), Landkreis, Hildesheim, Niedersachsen, Germany. He was baptized on May 1, 1831, at the Evangelical Lutheran Church, Wetteborn Parish. His godparents were Herr Stender of the Lamspringer Glass Factory, and Herr (Bock) Thon's wife of Westerberg. The birth and baptism record contains the following:

-Birth & Baptism Record-
Record Type - Birth & Baptism.
Child's Name - Wilhelm August Ludewig Brinkmann.
Date of Birth - April 26, 1831.
Father's Name & Occupation - Johann Philipp Brinkmann, *Schürer* (keeper of the fire) at the Westerberger Glass Factory, Westerberg, Germany.
Mother's Name - Sophie Charlotte Düen [Johanne Justine Charlotte (Düen) Brinkmann].
Residence of Parents - The Glass Factory (Westerberger Glass Factory) is the parents' place of residence.
Date of Baptism - May 1, 1831, (at the Evangelical Lutheran Church, Wetteborn Parish).
Godparents - Herr Stender of the Lamspringer Glass Factory, and Herr (Block) Thon's wife of Westerberg, Germany.
Source - Evangelical Lutheran Church, Wetteborn Parish Church Book, 1825, Page: (5), No: (20).

Confirmation, Marriage, and Death Records Search
No confirmation, marriage, or death records were located for Wilhelm August Ludewig Brinkmann in the Wetteborn Parish Church records.

---

7. August Heinrich Carl Brinkmann, b. 1833, d. 1908

Introduction
August Heinrich Carl Brinkmann was the seventh child of Johann Philipp Brinkmann and Johanne Justine Charlotte (Düen) Brinkmann. He was born in 1833 in a Westerberger *Glashütte* (glassworks cottage). No church confirmation record has been located for him, and no records were found at the Wetteborn Parish.

Birth & Baptism, 1833
In 2013, German genealogist Jens Kaufmann did a search at the Evangelical Lutheran Church Archives of the Wetteborn Parish for Brinkmann records. A birth and baptism record were found for August Heinrich Carl Brinkmann, born November 17, 1833, in a Westerberger *Glashütte* (glassworks cottage) in Landkreis, Hildesheim, Niedersachsen, Germany. He was baptized on November 30, 1833, at the Evangelical Lutheran Church, Wetteborn Parish. The birth and baptism record contains the following:

-Birth & Baptism Record-
Record Type - Birth & Baptism.
Child's Name - August Heinrich Carl Brinkmann.
Date of Birth - November 17, 1833.
Father's Name & Occupation - Philipp Brinkmann [Johann Philipp Brinkmann], *Schürer* (Keeper of the fire) at the Westerberger Glass Factory, Westerberg, Germany.
Mother's Name - Sophie Charlotte Düe [Johanne Justine Charlotte (Düen) Brinkmann].
Residence of Parents - The Glass Factory (Westerberger Glass Factory) is the parents' place of residence.
Date of Baptism - November 30, 1833, (at the Evangelical Lutheran Church, Wetteborn Parish).
Godparents - The Child's father, and H. Brinkmann of the Glass Factory.
Source - Evangelical Lutheran Church, Wetteborn Parish Church Book, 1833, Page: (9), No: (45).

Loan Record, Braunlage, Germany, 1850
August Heinrich Carl Brinkmann took out a loan 550 Thaler in 1850 while living in Braunlage, Germany. He used the money to invest in a glassmaking business as indicated by the record of this transaction found at the State Archives of Wolfenbüttel, 1850, Page 67, No. 250.

Note: Details of this loan are not clear and may require further investigation.

Marriage Citation with List of Children, 1859
In 2013, German genealogist Jens Kaufmann searched historic family name publications in Germany for any other members of this Brinkmann line. A February 25, 1859, marriage citation was found for August Heinrich Carl Brinkmann and his bride Johanne Sophie Louise Friederike (Hirsch) Brinkmann. This citation listed August Heinrich Carl Brinkmann, his parents, his marriage to Johanne Sophie, four children's names from their marriage, for a godparent Minni (Pahl) Brinkmann-wife of the *Glasmacher* (glassmaker) Wilhelm Brinkmann from Gifhorn, and the location of where Johanne Sophie was born in Russia. This citation is from the *Braunlager Family Book*, 1815-1875, © 2003. This citation contains the following:

-Marriage Citation Record-
Record Type - Braunlage Family Book, Name Directory 1815-1875.
Name - August Heinrich Carl Brinkmann, Born: Westerberger Glasshütte November 17, 1833, Occupation: *Glasarbeiter* (glassworker) Carlshütte Glass Factory-Rhade Parish (1859), and Braunlage (1864), Father: Phillip Brinkmann, *Schürer* (keeper of the fire), Westerberg Glashütte (glassworks); Mother: Sophie Charlotte Dui (Duen).
Marriage - August Heinrich Carl Brinkmann was married on February 25, 1859 to Johanne Sophie Louise Friedrike (Hirsch); Born: April 10, 1839 in Tewer, Nowoselskie, Russia; Father: Johann Gottlieb Ludwig Louis Hirsch, Occupation: *Tafelglasmacher* (Tafel Glass Factory glass maker) in

1839, and *Glashüttenmeister* (glass factory overseer) in 1855; Mother: Johanne Sophie (Gelpke), Born: April 8, 1818 in Blankenburg, Germany.

Children Born in Marriage - (1) Friedrich Ludewig Carl Brinkmann born April 13, 1856, (2) Louise Heinrich Hermann Brinkmann, born March 4, 1859, (3) Wilhelmine Marie Helene Brinkmann, born January 26, 1864, and (4) Albertine Pauline Martha Brinkmann, born October 13, 1872.

Godparents: 1872: Minna (Pahl) Brinkmann-Wife of the *Glasmacher* Wilhelm Brinkmann in Gifhorm, and godparent to Albertine Pauline Martha Brinkmann.

Notation - Johanne Sophie Louise Friedricke (Hirsch) is known to be a godmother in 1861, when she was known as Louise Brinkmann, born in Tewer, Nowoselskie,Russia.

Source - Braunlage Family Book, Name Directory 1815-1875, Page: (54), No: (2153); and Page: (132), No. (2429), © 2003.

Marriage, Braunlage, Germany, 1859

In 2013, German genealogist Jens Kaufmann did a search within the State Archives of Wolfenbüttel, Germany for Brinkmann records. These archives contain church records for the years 1815 thru 1875 for the Evangelical Lutheran Church, Braunlage Parish, Germany. This search looked for any marriage record for August Heinrich Carl Brinkmann. A marriage record for August and Johanne Sophie Friedricke Louise (Hirsch) Brinkmann was found dated February 25, 1859. The record contains the following:

-Marriage Record-

Record Type - Marriage.

Date of Marriage - February 25, 1859.

Groom's Name - August Heinrich Carl Brinkmann, glass worker on the Carlshütte, Rhade parish (born at Westerberger Glass Factory on November 17, 1833). Legitimate son of Philipp Brinkmann, keeper of the fire at Westerberger Glass Factory, and his wife Sophie Charlotte Dui (Düen) Brinkmann.

Bride's Name - Johanne Sophie Friedrike Louise (Hirsch) Brinkmann, (born on April 10, 1839), legitimate daughter of Ludewig Hirsch, overseer of the glass factory here, and his wife Sophie Dorothea (Gelpke) Hirsch.

Source - Evangelical Lutheran Church, Braunlage Parish Book, 1859, Page: (401), No: (2).

Child's Birth & Baptism, Braunlage, Germany, 1856

In 2013, German genealogist Jens Kaufmann did a search in the State Archives of Wolfenbüttel, Germany for Brinkmann records. A birth and baptism record was located for Friedrich Ludewig Carl Brinkmann, dated April 13, 1856. The record contains the following:

-Birth & Baptism Record-

Record Type - Birth & Baptism (Illegitimate child).

Child's Name - Friedrich Ludewig Carl Brinkmann

Date of Birth - April 13, 1856, at one o'clock in the morning.

Date of Baptism - April 27, 1856.

Father's Name & Occupation - August Heinrich Carl Brinkmann, glassmaker in Carlshütte near Rhade (well known to be born at Westerberger Glass Factory on November 17,1833). Declared to be the father of the child and proven by subsequent marriage in 1859.

Mother's Name - Johanne Sophie Friedrike Louise (Hirsch) Brinkmann, born on April 10, 1839, the legitimate daughter of the glass maker Gottlieb Ludewig Hirsch, living here.

Godparents - 1. Single man Louis Hirsch; 2. Single Man Fritz Becker; 3. Virgin Caroline Kamm; (all of Braunlage).
Source - Evangelical Lutheran Church, Braunlage Parish Book, 1856, Page: (4 to 5), No: (11).

Child's Birth & Baptism, Braunlage, Germany, 1859

In 2013, German genealogist Jens Kaufmann did a search at the State Archives of Wolfenbüttel, Germany for Brinkmann records. A birth and baptism record for Louise Heinrich Herman Brinkmann was found, dated March 4, 1859. The birth record contains the following:

-Birth & Baptism Record-

Record Type - Birth & Baptism (Legitimate child).
Child's Name - Louise Heinrich Hermann Brinkmann.
Date of Birth - March 4, 1859, born half past 6 0'clock in the morning.
Date of Baptism - March 20, 1859.
Father's Name & Occupation - August Heinrich Carl Brinkmann, glassmaker in Carlshütte near Rhade parish.
Mother's Name - Johanne Sophie Friedrike Louise (Hirsch) Brinkmann, born on April 10, 1839.
Godparents - 1. Glass Factory's overseer Ludewig Hirsch; 2. Henriette (Achitermann), wife of the glass maker Heinrich Hirsch; 3. Magdalene (Kamm), wife of the glass maker Joseph Herzog (all from Braunlage).
Source - Evangelical Lutheran Church, Braunlage Parish Book, 1856, Page: (50 to 51), No: (8).

Child's Birth Record, Braunlage, Germany, 1864

In 2013, German genealogist Jens Kaufmann did a search at the State Archives of Wolfenbüttel, Germany for Brinkmann records. A birth and baptism record for Wilhelmine Marie Helene Brinkmann was found dated January 26, 1864. The birth and baptism record contains the following:

-Birth & Baptism Record-

Record Type - Birth & Baptism (Legitimate child).
Child's Name - Wilhelmine Marie Helene Brinkmann.
Date of Birth - January 26, 1864, born at 11 0'clock in the morning.
Date of Baptism - February 8, 1859.
Father's Name & Occupation - August Heinrich Carl Brinkmann, glassmaker in Braunlage.
Mother's Name - Johanne Sophie Friedrike Louise (Hirsch) Brinkmann, born on April 10, 1839.
Godparents - 1. Glassmaker Wilhelm Otte; 2. Virgin Marie Hirsch; 3. Mrs. Magdalene Herzog (Kamm), all here in Braunlage.
Source - Evangelical Lutheran Church, Braunlage Parish Book, 1856, Page: (130 to 131), No: (7).

Death, Bavaria, Germany, 1908

German genealogist Sabine Schleichert determined that August Heinrich Carl Brinkman died in Mitterteich, Tirschenreuth, Bavaria, Germany on March 15, 1908. No death record has been located.

Record search from Ancestry.com Message Board, 2013

In 2013, a new contact was discovered with German genealogist Sabine Schleichert[12] while this author was viewing old postings on the Ancestry Family Tree website.[13] I emailed Schleichert, who provided many new Brinkmann ancestors who were previously unknown to me. Although the original research by Schleichert in 2003 did not primarily focus on Brinkmann surnames, it did lead to new Brinkmann family members. Schleichert went back into her records and sent this author a Brinkmann family tree of the previous reconstructions she had completed in 2003. Based on that tree we were able to reconstruct the citation records for the family of August Heinrich Carl Brinkmann, his spouse Johanne Sophie Louise Friederike (Hirsch) Brinkmann, and their nine known children. Schleichert's citations listed an additional child born to August Heinrich Carl Brinkmann and Johanne Justine Charlotte (Duen) Brinkmann whose name is Karl Brinkmann, born about 1873 (this has not yet been verified).

---

8. Heinrich Carl Wilhelm Brinkmann, b. 1836, d. Unknown

Introduction
Heinrich Carl Wilhelm Brinkmann was the eighth child of Johann Philipp Brinkmann and Johanne Justine Charlotte (Düen) Brinkmann. He was born in 1836 in a Westerberger *Glashütte* (glassworks cottage). No confirmation, marriage, or death records have been located for him, and no records were found at the Wetteborn Parish.

Birth & Baptism, Westerberg, Germany, 1836
In 2013, German genealogist Jens Kaufmann did a search in the Evangelical Lutheran Church Archives of the Wetteborn Parish for Brinkmann records. A birth and baptism record was discovered for Heinrich Carl Wilhelm Brinkmann, born June 5, 1836, in a Westerberger *Glashütte* (glassworks cottage) in Landkreis, Hildesheim, Niedersachsen, Germany. He was baptized on June 19, 1836, at the Evangelical Lutheran Church, Wetteborn Parish. His godparents were listed as Wilhelm Schmietut, Carl Topp, and Henriette Brinkmann. The birth and baptism record contains the following:

-Birth & Baptism Record-
Record Type - Birth & Baptism.
Child's Name - Heinrich Carl Wilhelm Brinkmann.
Date of Birth - June 5, 1836.
Father's Name & Occupation - Philipp Brinkmann [Johann Philipp Brinkmann], *Schürer* (keeper of the fire) at the Westerberger Glass Factory, Westerberg, Germany.
Mother's Name - Sophie Charlotte Düe [Johanne Justine Charlotte (Düen) Brinkmann].
Residence of Parents - The Glass Factory (Westerberger Glass Factory) is the parents' place of residence.
Date of Baptism - May 1, 1831, (at the Evangelical Lutheran Church, Wetteborn Parish).
Godparents - Herr Stender of the Lamspringer Glass Factory, and Herr (Bock) Thon's wife of Westerberg, Germany.
Source - Evangelical Lutheran Church, Wetteborn Parish Church Book, 1836, Page: (22), No: (23).

Confirmation, Marriage, and Death Records Search
No confirmation, marriage, or death records were located for Heinrich Carl Wilhelm Brinkmann in the Wetteborn Parish Church records.

---

9. Dorothee Marie Brinkmann, b. 1838, d. Unknown

Introduction
Dorothee Marie Brinkmann was the ninth child of Johann Philipp Brinkmann and Johanne Justine Charlotte (Düen) Brinkmann. She was born in 1838 at the Westerberger *Glashütte* (glassworks cottage). No confirmation, marriage or death records have been located for her, and no records were found at the Wetteborn Parish.

Birth & Baptism, Westerberg, Germany, 1838
In 2013, German genealogist Jens Kaufmann did a search at the Evangelical Lutheran Church Archives of the Wetteborn Parish for Brinkmann records. A birth and baptism record were discovered for Dorothee Marie Brinkmann, born October 15, 1838, in the Westerberger *Glashütte* (glassworks cottage) in Landkreis, Hildesheim, Niedersachsen, Germany. She was baptized on October 26, 1838, at the Evangelical Lutheran Church, Wetteborn Parish. Her godparents are listed as August Thon, Friederike Ruhlender, and Amalie Brinkmann. The birth and baptism record contains the following:

-Birth & Baptism Record-
Record Type - Birth & Baptism.
Child's Name - Dorothee Marie Brinkmann.
Date of Birth - October 15, 1838.
Father's Name & Occupation - Philipp Brinkmann [Johann Philipp Brinkmann], *Schürer* (keeper of the fire) at the Westerberger Glass Factory, Westerberg, Germany.
Mother's Name - Sophie Charlotte Düe [Johanne Justine Charlotte (Düen) Brinkmann].
Residence of Parents - Westerberger Glass Factory.
Date of Baptism - October 26, 1838, (at the Evangelical Lutheran Church, Wetteborn Parish).
Godparents - August Thon, Friederike Ruhlender, and Amalie Brinkmann of the factory (Westerberger Glass Factory).
Source - Evangelical Lutheran Church, Wetteborn Parish Church Book, 1838, Page: (28), No: (40).

Confirmation, Marriage, Death Record Search.
No confirmation, marriage, or death records were located for Dorothee Marie Brinkmann in the Wetteborn Parish Church records.

Louise Antoinette (Stender) Brinkmann, b. Unknown, d. Unknown

Introduction
Louise Antoinette (Stender) Brinkmann's surname in German is *Ständer,* which is pronounced in English as "stender." Louise was the second spouse of this author's *third-great-grand-uncle.* Louise's birth and death records have not been located. She married Johann Philipp Brinkmann ten months after Johann's first spouse died. Louise then assumed the responsibility of caring for the nine remaining children, who ranged from 22 to 2 years of age. It must have been a very difficult time for all to adjust to their new stepmother. Later, one additional child Karl Daniel August Brinkmann was born to this second marriage.

Birth & Death, Germany
No birth or death records have been located for Louise Antoinette (Stender) Brinkmann.

Marriage Proclamation, Second Spouse, Lamspringe, Germany, 1841
In 2012 a search was conducted by German genealogist Gabriele Fricke for records of Johann Philipp Brinkman. An 1841 marriage proclamation for Johann Philipp Brinkmann and his second spouse Louise Antoinette (Stander) Brinkmann was located. The marriage bond proclamation is dated February 14, 1841, when their intended marriage was publicly announced in the village of

Lamspringe, Hildesheim, Niedersachsen (Lower Saxony), Germany. This marriage proclamation contained the following:

-Marriage Proclamation Record-
Record Type - Marriage Proclamation.
Proclamation - February 14 and 21,1841, in Lamspringe, Hildesheim, Niedersachsen, Germany.
Groom - Johann Philipp Brinkmann, *Schürer* (keeper of the fire) at the Westerberger Glass Factory, thus far a widower.
Bride - Louise Antoinette (Stender). Legitimate daughter of the deceased glass worker Ferdinand Stender in Braunwald, and of his deceased wife Katharine Sophie (Lippert) Stender.
Source - Lamspringe Parish Church Book of 1841, Page: (24), No: (a).

Marriage, Second Spouse, Lamspringe, Germany, 1841
In 2013, German genealogist Jens Kaufmann did a search at the Lamspringe Church Parish for a marriage record for Johann Philipp Brinkmann and Louise Antoinette (Stender) Brinkmann. A marriage record was found dated February 28, 1841, at the Evangelical Lutheran Church, Lamspringe Parish, Hildesheim, Niedersachsen, Germany. Johann was then 44 years old, and Louise was 45 years old. This marriage record contains the following:

-Marriage Record-
Record Type - Marriage.
Marriage - February 28, 1841,Lamspringe Church Parish, Hildesheim, Niedersachsen, Germany.
Groom - Johann Philipp Brinkmann. Glass melter at the Westerberger Glass Factory. Age: 44.
Groom's Father - Johann Wilhelm Brinkmann, retired old father at the Westerberg Glass Factory.
Bride - Louise Antoinette (Stender). From the Glass Factory near Lamspringe.
Bride's Father - Ferdinand Stender, formerly glassworker at the Brammwalder Glass Factory. Bother of the Bride's parents are dead. Bride was previously unmarried.
Source - Lamspringe Parish Church Book of 1841, Page: (43), No: (4).

Children of Johann Philipp Brinkmann & Louise Antoinette (Stender) Brinkmann

---

1. Karl Daniel August Brinkmann, b. 1841, d. Unknown

Introduction
Karl Daniel August Brinkmann was the first born child of Johann Philipp Brinkmann and Louise Antoinette (Stender) Brinkmann. Confirmation, marriage, and death records for Karl Daniel August Brinkmann have not been located.

Birth & Baptism, Westerberger Glass Factory, Germany, 1841
In 2013, German genealogist Jens Kaufmann did a search at the Evangelical Lutheran Church Archives of the Wetteborn Parish for Brinkmann records. A birth and baptism record was discovered for Karl Daniel August Brinkmann, born April 25, 1841, in the Westerberger *Glashütte* (glassworks cottage) in Landkreis, Hildesheim, Niedersachsen, Germany. He was baptized on May

4, 1841, at the Evangelical Lutheran Church, Wetteborn Parish. His godparents are listed as Daniel Kaufel, Karl Kaufel, and Madame Stender of the Lamspringer Glass factory. The birth and baptism record contains the following:

-Birth & Baptism Record-

Record Type - Birth & Baptism.
Child's Name - Karl Daniel August Brinkmann.
Date of Birth - April 25, 1841.
Father's Name & Occupation - Johann Philipp Brinkmann, *Schürer* (keeper of the fire) at the Westerberger Glass Factory, Westerberg, Germany.
Mother's Name - Louise Antoinette (Stender) Brinkmann.
Date of Baptism - May 4, 1841, at the Evangelical Lutheran Church, Wetteborn Parish.
Godparents - Daniel Kaufel, Karl Kaufel, and Madame Stender, of the Lamspringer Glass Factory.
Source - Evangelical Lutheran Church, St. Jacobi Parish Church Book, 1841, Page: (35), No: (20).

Confirmation, Marriage, and Death Record Searches
No confirmation, marriage, or death records have been located for Karl Daniel August Brinkmann.

- End of Section -

Gallery

Johann Philipp Brinkmann

7o Januar.	Maria Theresia filia legitima Wilhelmi Meyer, et Maria Elisabetha Messer, conjugum habitantium in Eyershausen : baptizabat Liborius Pieper, parochus proprius ; levabat Maria Theresia Weddemeyer, nata Alberti.	Maria Theresia Meyer ex Eyershausen
9 Januar.	Baptizatus est Joannes Theodorus filius legitimus Petri Reyenhard, et Maria Theresia Peters, conjugum habitantium in Everode ; baptizabat Liborius Pieper, parochus proprius ; levabat Joannes Theodorus Stoer.	Joannes Theodorus Reyenhard ex Everode.
Februar.	Joannes Henricus filius legitimus Joannis Maximiliani Hagemann, et Maria Christina Heuth, conjugum : baptizabat Liborius Pieper, parochus proprius ; levabat Joannes Henricus Heuth, frater matris assistentiby testiby Joanne Brinkmann, Elisabetha Maria Giesecke, et Elisabetha Schlorr.	Hagemann ex mi Freden.
Februar.	Joannes Josephus filius legitimus Francisci Becker, et Elisabetha Hagemann, conjugum : baptizabat L. Pieper, parochus proprius ; levabat Joannes Arnoldus Zahren conjugatus, hujus	Becker ex Everode.
Februar.	Joannes Philippus filius legitimus Joannis Wilhelmi Brinkmann et Maria Sophia Kurdelach conjugum ; baptizabat Liborius Pieper, parochus proprius ; levabat Joannes Stender et Philippus Seitts.	Brinkmann ex officina vitriaria.
Februarii	Joachimus Franciscus Carolus filius legitimus praenobilium conjugum, D. Joannis Joachimi Toss, et Carolina Francisca Sievers die 15ta Februarii natus : baptizabat Liborius Pieper, parochus proprius ; levabat praenobilis Dominus Joachimus Franciscus Balla, postarum praefectus in Bönzingen.	Toss.

Baptism record, Johann Phillip Brinkmann, February 12, 1797
Winzenburg Catholic Parish Church, Winzenburg, Germany
Source: Catholic Dioceses Church Archive of Hildesheim

Marriage record page 1 of 2, November 24, 1818
Johann Phillip Brinkmann and Johanne Justine Charlotte (Düen) Brinkmann
Source: Wetteborn Parish Church Records

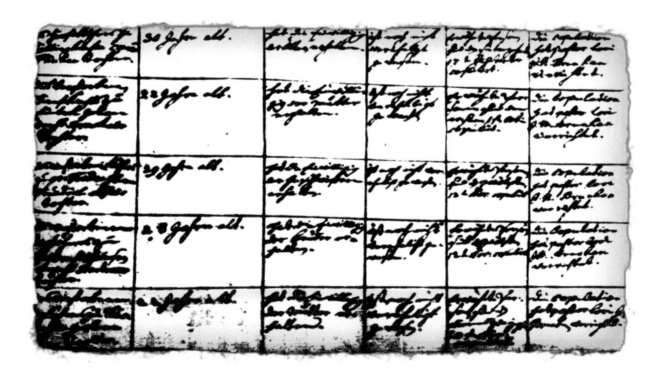

Marriage record page 2 of 2, November 24, 1818
Johann Phillip Brinkmann and Johanne Justine Charlotte (Düen) Brinkmann
Source: Wetteborn Parish Church Records

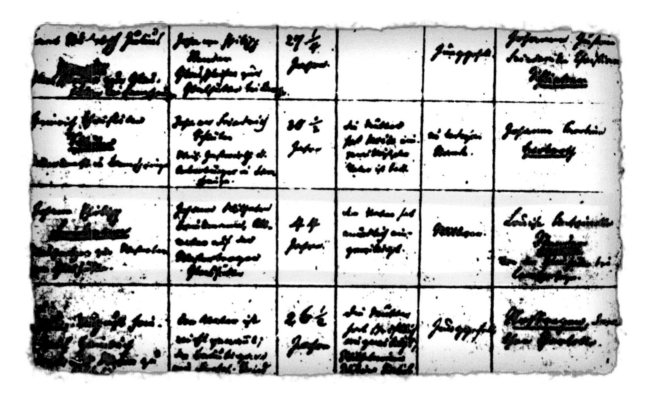

Marriage record page 1 of 2, February 28, 1841
Johann Phillip Brinkmann and Louise Antoinette (Stender) Brinkmann
Source: Lamspringe Parish Church Records

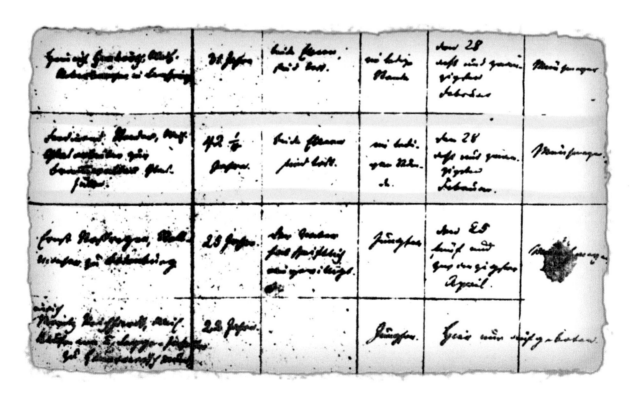

Marriage record page 2 of 2, February 28, 1841
Johann Phillip Brinkmann and Louise Antoinette (Stender) Brinkmann
Source: Lamspringe Parish Church Records

Descendants of Liborius Friedrich Brinkmann

Liborius Friedrich Brinkmann.
& *Spouse* - Henriette (Lange) Brinkmann.

- Marie Sophia Henriette Brinkmann.

- Hanna Luise Charolette Brinkmann.

- Christian Karl Brinkmann.
  Spouse - Marie Elisabeth (Merker) Brinkmann.
  - Friedrich Ernst August Brinkmann.
    Spouse - Edith (Erman) Brinkmann.
  - Louise August Sophie Brinkmann.
    Spouse - Karl (Micka).
  - Mr. Brinkmann.
  - Karl Friedrich Wilhelm Brinkmann.
    Spouse - Ernestine Hermine (Hildebrandt) Brinkmann.

Source: Brinkman Family Tree

The Liborius Friedrich Brinkmann Family

Liborius Friedrich Brinkmann, b. c. 1802, d. c. 1864

Introduction
Liborius Friedrich Brinkmann was born around 1802 in Germany, based on the baptism record of May 16, 1802, from Winzenburg, Niedersachsen, Germany. No birth or death records have been found for Liborius, who is believed to have died in Germany in the late 1800s. He is this author's *third-great-grandfather*. Liborius married Henriette (Lange) Brinkmann in 1826. This marriage's record revealed that Liborius's father was Johann Friedrich Wilhelm Brinkmann. Liborius and Henriette had three children, (1) Marie Sophie Henriette Brinkmann, (2) Hanna Luise Charlotte Brinkmann, and (3) Christian Karl Brinkmann.

Note: Liborius and Henriette are also mentioned in several other of the Wetteborn Parish records, and in the marriage record of their son Christian Karl Brinkmann.

Original Search for Records, Nienburg, Germany
In 2011, German genealogist Dr. Sylvia Moehle [14] did one of the first German searches for members of the earliest known Brinkmann family members. Moehle began her research by looking for records cited in the written Brinkman family history for Karl Von Brinkenhausen; Karl Von Brinkmann; Alwin August Adolf Brinkmann; and Karl Wilhelm Hermann Heinrich Brinkmann. Moehle's research yielded a German birth and baptism record for Alwin August Adolf Brinkmann and his brother Karl Wilhelm Hermann Heinrich Brinkmann. No records were found in this search for Karl Von Brinkenhausen or Karl Von Brinkmann. However, these German Brinkmann records were ground breaking and built the foundation for this Brinkmann family line.

Birth, Baptism, & Death Records Search
In 2012, German genealogist Gabriele Fricke did a search in the Evangelical Lutheran Church, Wetteborn Parish for birth or death records for Liborius Friedrich Brinkmann. None were found but an 1826 marriage record was found for Liborius Friedrich Brinkmann and his bride Henriette (Lange or Langen) Brinkmann. In 2013, another search in the Wetteborn and Einbeck Parish was conducted by German genealogist Jens Kaufmann who also did not find any birth, baptism, or death records for Liborius in the Wetteborn or Einbeck Parish. Kaufmann also did not find any records for Henriette, and no confirmation records were found for Liborius's known children. It is believed that, in 1832, Liborius moved his family to an unknown location in Germany.

Baptism Record, Winzenburg, Germany - 1802
In 2014, German genealogist Jens Kaufmann did a search at the Catholic Dioceses Church Archive, Winzenburg Parish, in Hildesheim, Germany for records of Johann Friedrich Wilhelm Brinkmann and his son Liborius Friedrich Brinkmann. A baptism record was found for Liborius dated May 16, 1802. It is believed that the pastor Liborius Pieper, who performed this baptism, was very close to Johann's family and as such Johann named his son Liborius. The baptism record contains the following:

- Baptism Record -
Name - Liborius Friedrich Brinkmann.
Birth Date and Location - May 16, 1802, Winzenburg Catholic Parish Church, Winzenburg, Germany.
Parents - Johann Wilhelm Brinkmann and Maria Sophia (Gundelach) Brinkmann.
Statement - Legitimate son of Johann Wilhelm Brinkmann and of his wife Maria Sophia (Gundelach) Brinkmann, residing at the old Glass Factory; baptized by the pastor Liborius Pieper; godfather was

Friedrich Ruhländer but since he was a Protestant, Ferdinand Flügge had to put his hand onto the boy as a veritable godfather.

Source: Catholic Dioceses Church Archive of Hildesheim, Germany, Winzenburg Catholic Church Parish Book-1802, Volume: (1781), Page: (324).

Marriage Record, Wetteborn Parish, Wetteborn, Germany, 1826

In 2013, German genealogist Gabriele Fricke did a search in the Evangelical Lutheran Church, Wetteborn Parish for records of Liborius Friedrich Brinkmann. A February 19, 1826, marriage record was found for Liborius and his bride Henriette (Lange-Langen) Brinkmann. The marriage record contains the following:

- Marriage Record -

Groom - Friedrich Brinkmann [Liborius Friedrich Brinkmann].

Bride - Henriette (Langen), [Henriette (Lange) Brinkmann].

Date, Place of Marriage, and Pastor's Name - February 19, 1826, Wetteborn Lutheran Parish Church, Niedersachsen, Germany, Pastor: J.H. Brunke.

Source - Evangelical Lutheran Church Archive of Hannover, Germany, Wetteborn Church Parish Book-1826, Page: (300), Register No: (1).

Occupation & Residence, Glassmaking Master

Liborius's 1826 marriage record cites his occupation as a *Schmelzmeister* (master smelter responsible for the melting of glass in the furnaces) at the Westerberger Glass Factory. This was a master-level glass trade and quite an accomplishment for Liborius. It is believed that his community held him and his family in high regard. In 1826, Liborius moved to another glass factory in Osterwald, a Community District within the Municipality of Salzhemmendorf, Germany. Osterwald is home to the famous Lauensteiner Glass Factory, where fine crystal glassware was made for the Royal Hannover Court from 1701 to 1824. Osterwald had several other glass factories until its demise in 1931. Osterwald is where Liborius's daughter Marie Sophia Henriette Brinkmann died in 1828 (at 1-1/2 years old). Liborius continued to work in Osterwald when his second daughter, Hanna Luise Charlotte Brinkmann, was born in 1829. In 1832, he returned to work at the Westerberger Glass Factory in Westerberg, Germany where he worked as a *Schürer* or *Schürmeister* (keeper of the fire in the glass melting furnace) and where his first son, Christian Karl Brinkmann, was born in 1832. Liborius also worked as a *Glasmacher* (blowing hot glass into mold forms) at a glass factory in Ziegenhagen, Germany around 1832. Liborius is cited in Christian Karl Brinkmann's 1864 marriage record as working as a *Schürmeister* (keeper of the fire in the glass melting furnace) at the Westerberger Glass Factory. He was the godfather for his grandson, Friedrich Ernest August Brinkmann, born in 1865 when Liborius was living in Ziegenhagen, Germany. It is not known exactly where Liborius moved his family to after 1832, or where he later worked in his glassmaking trade.

Death Record Search, Wetteborn Parish, Germany

In 2013, German Genealogist Jens Kaufmann did another full search in the Evangelical Lutheran Church, Wetteborn Parish for any death record for Liborius Friedrich Brinkmann. No death record was found.

Summary

It is not known where Liborius Friedrich Brinkmann and his line of the Brinkmann family lived before moving to Westerberg, Germany around 1826. No death records have been located for Liborius or his wife Henriette in the Wetteborn Parish. It is also unknown where Liborius and his family moved to after his son, Christian Karl Brinkmann, was born in 1832. Liborius was only about 30 years old in 1832, and is believed to have moved to another glassworks factory somewhere in Germany.

Note: Liborius's father was a glass trader in Winzenburg, Germany, which is a short distance from Westerberg, Germany.

Henriette (Lange-Langen) Brinkmann, b. c. 1793, d. c. 1870

Introduction
Henriette (Lange-Langen) Brinkmann is believed to have been born about 1793 (based on her age of 33, as cited in her marriage record) and died about 1870 in Germany. Henriette is this author's *third-great-grandmother*. No birth or death records for Henriette were located during searches in the Wetteborn Parish. We do know that Henriette married Liborius Friedrich Brinkmann in 1826, in Wetteborn, Germany. She and Liborius had three children, (1) Marie Sophia Henriette Brinkmann, (2) Hanna Luise Charlotte Brinkmann, and (3) Christian Karl Brinkmann.

Note: Henriette and Liborius are mentioned several times in the Wetteborn Parish church records, and in the marriage certificate for their son, Christian Karl Brinkmann.

Parents' Records, Westerberger Glass Factory, Wetteborn Parish, Germany
Henriette's parents are listed on her 1826 marriage record as Johann Heinrich Lange and Rosina Lange (Langen).

Henriette's Father, Johann Heinrich Lange
Johann Heinrich Lange was born about 1755 (based on his death record from 1817). Johann's birth date and year of marriage to Rosina Lange are unknown. Johann died on March 4, 1817, in the Westerberger Glass Factory near Winzenburg, Germany. He is cited as the spouse of Rosina Lange on his death record from 1817 and in Rosina's death record from 1826. As of 2014, Johann's birth, baptism, marriage, and parents' records have not been located. His death record contains the following:

-Death Record-

Type of Record - Death.
Date of Death - 4 March 1817 at 9 o'clock in the morning.
Name - Johann Heinrich Lange, *Wagoner* (wagon driver) at the Factory, 62 years and 10 months, died from weakness and tumor.
Deceased Left Behind - He left behind a widow and four children of age, and one child under age (*Henriette Lange*).
Burial - On 6 March 1817, in the Wetteborn Parish Church Cemetery.
Source - Evangelical Lutheran Church-Wetteborn Parish Death Record, 1817, Page: (119), No: (4).

Henriette's Mother, Rosina Lange
Rosina Lange (unknown maiden surname) died May 26, 1826, at the age of 68 from "breast disease." Rosina is cited as the widow of the deceased *wagoner* (driver of horse-driven carriages) Johann Heinrich Lange, who lived at the Westerberg Glass Factory near Winzenburg, Germany. Rosina's death record contains the following:

-Death Record-

Type of Record - Death.
Date of Death - 26 May 1826, at 10:00 in the evening.
Name - *Rosina Langen*, widow of the deceased *Wagoner Johann Heinrich Lange* from the factory near Winzenburg, died at age 68 years and 10 months from breast disease.
Deceased Left Behind - She left behind 5 children of age.
Burial - On 30 May 1826 in the Wetteborn Parish Church Cemetery.

Source - Evangelical Lutheran Church-Wetteborn Parish Death Record, 1826, Page: (153), No: (11).

Search for Birth & Death Records, Wetteborn Parish, Germany

In 2012, German genealogist Jens Kaufmann did a search in the Evangelical Lutheran Church, Wetteborn Parish for Henriette (Lange-Langen) Brinkmann's birth or death records. No birth or death record was located.

Note: Spelling of German Surnames, Lange & Langen

German documents spell Henriette's surname as both Lange and Langen. Variations in the spelling of surnames is common. In Germany, the dialects have been so different in the past few hundred years that some priests wrote surnames as they heard them. In Lower Saxony, the largest variations of German surnames appear to be influenced by whether (or not) the genitive (possessive) "s" is added to the end of the surname. For genealogical records it is, I think, acceptable to either use the most common spelling found in records, or to use the spelling found in a surname signature on a document of record. Either way, it is important to note in one's records which surname spellings have been found, and which spelling will be used in the main body of any genealogy tree. In this case, this written Brinkmann family history uses the spelling Lange because it is the most common spelling in German records.

Birth Record of Henriette's Illegitimate Son, Westerberger Glass Factory, 1822

In 2013, German genealogist Jens Thomas Kaufmann[15] went back and examined all the previous citations from the Wetteborn Parish Church records to double check for accuracy, and to obtain copies of records that had been omitted in previous searches. Kaufmann also discovered new records, including an illegitimate son of Henriette (Lange), Heinrich Ferdinand Lange, who was born on June 5, 1822, four years before Henriette's 1826 marriage to Ferdinand Brinkmann. The birth and baptism record contain the following:

-Birth & Baptism Record-

Type of Record - Birth & Baptism.
Date of Birth - June 5, 1822, at four 4 o'clock in the afternoon.
Child's First Names - Heinrich Ferdinand Lange.
Whether Legitimate or Illegitimate - Illegitimate.
Father's First & Last Name & Occupation - The father of the child was Friedrich Achilles living in Lamspringe.
Mother's First & Last Name - Henrietta Langen.
Parent's Place of Residence - The Glass Factory (Westerberger Glass Factory) is the mother's place of residence.
Day of Baptism - The child was baptized on June 9, 1822.
Pastor's Name - J.H. Brunken.
Godparents' - J.H. Topp.
Source - Evangelical Lutheran Church-Wetteborn Parish Church Book 1822, Page: (55), No: (22).

Marriage Record, Wetteborn Parish, Germany, 1826

In 2013, German genealogist Jens Kaufmann did a search in the Wetteborn Parish for Brinkmann records. A February 19, 1826, marriage record was found for Liborius Friedrich Brinkmann and Henriette (Lange) Brinkmann. The marriage record contains the following:

-Marriage Record-

Type of Record - Marriage.
Date - February 19, 1826.

Location - Evangelical Lutheran Church, Wetteborn Parish, Landwehr, Hildesheim, Niedersachsen (Lower Saxony), Germany.
Grooms Name - Friedrich Brinkmann [Liborius Friedrich Brinkmann].
Name & Residence of Father of Groom - The son of Wilhelm Brinkmann [Johann Friedrich Wilhelm Brinkmann], the glass trader at the glass factory near Winzenburg, Germany.
Age of the Groom - 23 years old. Has gotten fathers consent. Has not been married before.
First & Last Name of Bride - Henriette Langen (Lange) Brinkmann.
Name and occupation of the Brides Father - Daughter of Heinrich Langen, the deceased *Wagoner* of the Fuhrmann Glass Factory.
Age of the Bride - 33 years old. Has gotten mothers consent. Has not been married before.
Permission Received From Brides Parents - Permission received from the living mother (name illegible-not thought to have been at the wedding and died in March of 1826).
Source - Evangelical Lutheran Church-Wetteborn Parish Church Book, 1826, Page: (300), No: (1).

Note: Liborius was 23 when he married Henriette, who was 33 years old. His father Johann Friedrich Wilhelm Brinkmann was alive at the time of the marriage and was working at the Winzenburg Glass Factory. Liborius's mother, Marie Sophia (Gundelach) Brinkmann, is not listed on the marriage record and assumed to be deceased. Henriette lost her father, Heinrich Langen, yet her mother was believed to be alive and approved the marriage. Henriette's mothers maiden surname is not legible on this marriage record.

Marriage Record, Wetteborn Parish, Wetteborn, Germany, 1826
In 2013, a search of the Wetteborn Lutheran Parish Church Books provided a February 19, 1826, marriage record for Wilhelm Brinkmann and Henriette (Lange) Brinkmann. This marriage record contains the following:

- Marriage Record -
Groom - Friedrich Brinkmann [Liborius Friedrich Brinkmann].
Bride - Henriette (Langen) [Henriette (Lange) Brinkmann].
Date, Place of Marriage, and Pastor's Name - February 19, 1826, Wetteborn Lutheran Parish Church, Niedersachsen, Germany, Pastor: J.H. Brunke.
Source - Evangelical Lutheran Church Archive of Hannover, Germany, Wetteborn Church Parish Book-1826, Page: (300), Register Number: (1).

Death Record Search, Wetteborn Parish
In 2013, German genealogist Jens Thomas Kaufmann did a search at the Wetteborn Parish for a death record for Henriette (Lange) Brinkmann. No death record was found. It is believed that in 1832 Liborius moved his family to an unknown location in Germany.

Children of Liborius Friedrich Brinkmann & Henriette (Lange) Brinkmann

---

1. Maria Sofia Henriette Brinkmann, b. 1826, d. 1828

Introduction
Maria Sofia Henriette Brinkmann was the first child of Liborius Friedrich Brinkmann and Henriette (Langen) Brinkmann. Maria was born in 1826, in the Westerberger Glass Factory, in Landkreis, Hildesheim, Niedersachsen, Germany.

Birth & Baptism Record, Westerberger Glass Factory, Germany, 1826
Maria Sofia Henriette Brinkmann was born November 7, 1826, in the Westerberger Glass Factory, in Landkreis, Hildesheim, Niedersachsen, Germany. Maria was born nine months and seven days after Liborius and Marie married. Maria was baptized on November 12, 1826, in the Evangelical Lutheran Church, Wetteborn Parish. Her birth and baptism record contains the following:

-Birth & Baptism Record-

Type of Record - Birth & Baptism.
Date of Birth - November 7, 1826, at four 1 o'clock at night.
Child's First Names - Maria Sophia Henriette.
Whether Legitimate or Illegitimate - Born legitimate.
Father's First & Last Name & Occupation - Friedrich Brinkmann [Liborius Friedrich Brinkmann] *Schmelzmeister* (glass melting master).
Mother's First & Last Name - Henrietta Langen.
Parent's Place of Residence - The Glass Factory (Westerberger Glass Factory) is the parents place of residence.
Day of Baptism - The child was baptized on November 12, 1826.
Pastor's Name - Pastor J.H. Brunken.
Godparents' - Maria Sophia Langen, and Henriette Brinkmann.
Source - Evangelical Lutheran Church-Wetteborn Parish Church Book, 1826, Page: (74), No: (43).

Death Record, Osterwald Glass Factory, Germany, 1828
According to written Brinkmann family history, Maria married an American named Mr. Weber, and that they later moved to America. This story is not true, because we now know that Maria died on April 19, 1828, at the Osterwald Glass Factory in the village of Osterwald, Germany at the age of 1-1/2 years old. Her death record contains the following:

-Death Record-

Type of Record - Death.
Date of Death - April 19, 1828.
Place of death - Osterwald Glass Factory, Osterwald, Niedersachsen (Lower Saxony), Germany.
House Name - Brinkmann, of Osterwald, a child.
Person's Who Died & Were Buried - Henriette Maria Brinkmann, daughter of the *Schürer* (keeper of the fire) Friedrich Brinkmann at the Glass Factory in Osterwald (Germany) and of his wife Henriette (Lange) Brinkmann, Died of tuberculosis or lung disease, age 1-1/2 years.
Burial - On April 21, 1828, at the Hemmendorf Parish (Osterwald, Germany).
Source - Evangelical Lutheran Church-Hemmendorf Parish Church Book, 1828, Page: (802), No: (11).

---

2. Hanna Luise Charlotte Brinkmann, b. 1829, d. Unknown

Introduction
Hanna Luise Charlotte Brinkmann was the second daughter of Liborius Friedrich Brinkmann and Henriette (Lange) Brinkmann. Hanna who was born in 1829, in the Osterwald Glass Factory, in Salzhemmendorf, Hameln-Pyrmont, Niedersachsen, Germany. Osterwald was the site of several glass factories and where Friedrich Brinkmann worked as a *Schürer* (keeper of the fire). Hanna may have been the daughter who later married a Mr. Weber and immigrated to America (as cited above in the written Brinkmann family history).

Birth & Baptism Record, Osterwald, Germany, 1829

Hanna Luise Charlotte Brinkmann was born December 7, 1829, in the Osterwald Glass Factory, in Salzhemmendorf, Hameln-Pyrmont, Niedersachsen, Germany. Hanna was baptized on December 13, 1829, at the Hemmendorf Church Parish. The birth record contains the following:

-Birth & Baptism Record-

Type of Record - Birth & Baptism.

Date of Birth - December 7, 1829.

Child's First Names - Hanna Luise Charlotte Brinkmann was born on December 7, 1829, and baptized on December 13, 1829, of the same month.

Parents - Friedrich Brinkmann [Liborius Friedrich Brinkmann] *"Schürer"* (keeper of the fire) in Osterwald, and Henriette (Lange) Brinkmann.

Baptism - December 13, 1829, at the Hemmendorf Church Parish (Osterwald, Germany).

Godparents' - 1. Conrad Hone's wife, 2. Elias Hirschberg's wife, 3. Ludewig Kiss's wife, 4. George Hune's wife, 5. Just Hone's wife, and 6. Thomas Meyer's wife.

Source - Evangelical Lutheran Church-Wetteborn Parish Church Book, 1829, Page: (322), No: (41).

Confirmation, Marriage, and Death Record Search

No confirmation, marriage, or death records have been located for Hanna Luise Charlotte Brinkmann.

---

3. Christian Karl Brinkmann, b. 1832, d. c. 1906
(See Christian Karl Brinkmann Family History Section for further details.)

- End of Section -

Gallery

Liborius Friedrich Brinkmann

Osterwald Glassworks Factory, Osterwald, Germany, c. 1840
Liborius Friedrich Brinkmann worked here as "keeper of the fire" from 1828-1829

Antique glass wine carafes from the Osterwald Glassworks, Germany, c. 1800s

Drinking glass from the Osterwald Glassworks, Germany, c. 1800s
Source: Wikimedia Commons-Contributor: Ulrich Mayring

Hemmendorf Church Parish, Salzhemmendorf-Hemmendorf, Germany
Church parish where Maria Sophia Henriette Brinkmann was buried in 1828
Source: Wikimedia Commons-Contributor: Torbenbrinker

3. Maji — Maria Elisabetha filia legitima Arnoldi Zehren, et Joanna Maria Rübner, conjugum: baptizabat Liborius Pieper, parochus proprius; levabat Maria Elisabetha Müller, nata Dreyer, sed quia aug. conf. addicta erat, Ferdinandus Flügge ut verus patrinus puellam manum inponere debuit. — Zehren

6. Maji — Friderica Antonetta filia legitima Godefridi Hauffel, et Henrietta Stander, conjugum: baptizabat Liborius Pieper, p. prop.; levabat honesta virgo Maria Stander, soror puerpera, sed quia a. c. addicta, Ferdinandus Flügge manum puellae imponere debuit. — Hauffel

16. Maji — Liborius Fridericus filius legitimus Joannis Wilhelmi Brinkmann, et Maria Sophia Hundelach, conjugum, habitantium in officina vitriaria veleri: baptizabat Liborius Pieper, p. p.; levabat Fridericus Ruhlander, sed quia a. c. addictus erat, Ferdinandus Flügge et verus patrinus manum pueris imponere debuit. — Brinkma[nn]

22. Maji — Fridericus filius legitimus Petri Regenhard et Maria Theresia Peters, conjugum, habitantium in Klumpe: baptizabat Lib. Pieper, parochus propr.; levabat D. Godefridus Arens, Superior silvarum winzenburgensium praefectus. — Regenhard

Birth/Baptism record, Liborius Friedrich Brinkmann
Baptized: May 16, 1802, Winzenburg Catholic Church, Winzenburg, Germany
Source: Winzenburg Catholic Church Baptism Book

Birth record, Maria Sophia Henriette (Lange) Brinkmann
Born: November 7, 1826, Westerberger Glass Factory, Germany
Baptized: November 12, 1826, Wetteborn Church Parish, Germany
Source: Evangelical Lutheran Church, Wetteborn Parish Church Records

Marriage record, Friedrich Brinkmann & Maria Sophia Henriette (Lange) Brinkmann
Married: February 19, 1826, Wetteborn Church Parish, German.
Source: Evangelical Lutheran Church, Wetteborn Parish Church Records

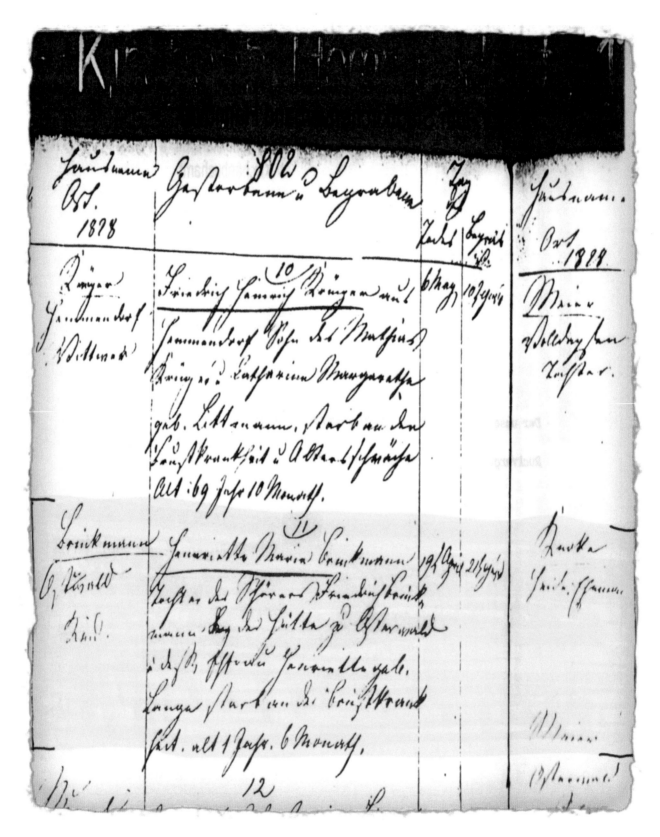

Death record, Maria Sophia Henriette (Lange) Brinkmann
Died: April 19, 1828, Osterwald, Germany
Buried: April 21, 1828, Hemmendorf Church Parish Cemetery, Germany
Source: Evangelical Lutheran Church, Hemmendorf Parish Church Records

Descendants of Christian Karl Brinkmann

Christian Karl Brinkmann.
& *Spouse* - Marie Elisabeth (Merker) Brinkmann.

- **Friedrich Ernst August Brinkmann.**
  Spouse - Edith (Erman) Brinkmann.
  - Walter Brinkmann.
  - Marie Brinkmann.
  - Paul Brinkmann.
- **Louise Auguste Sophie Brinkmann.**
  Spouse - Karl (Micka).
  - Hermine Micka.
  - Marie Micka.
  - Elvina Micka.
  - Frieda Micka.
  - Paul Micka.
  - Elizabeth Micka.
  - Henry Micka.
  - Rose Micka.
  - Paula Micka.
- **Mr. Brinkmann.**
- **Karl Friedrich Wilhelm Brinkmann.**
  Spouse - Ernestine Hermine (Hildebrandt) Brinkmann.
  - **Adolf Carl Christian Brinkmann.**
    Spouse - Margarethe Marie Martha (Graf) Brinkmann.
  - **Alwin August Adolf Brinkmann.**
    Spouse - Lillian Maria (Jarosch) Brinkmann.
  - **Hugo Frank Brinkmann.**
    Spouse - Gertrude (Proschaska) Brinkmann.
  - **Frieda Brinkmann.**
  - **Karl Wilhelm Hermann Heinrich Brinkmann.**
    Spouse - Marquerite Cadaf (Johnson) Brinkmann.
  - **Elsie Louise Brinkmann.**
    Spouse - George Herman (Mertig).

Source: Brinkman Family Tree

The Christian Karl Brinkmann Family

Christian Karl Brinkmann, b. 1832, d. c. 1906

Christian Karl Brinkmann with his two grandsons. c.1905.
Center: Christian Karl Brinkmann. Lower left to right: Adolf Carl Christian Brinkmann and his younger brother Alwin August Adolf Brinkmann. Nienburg, Germany. Source: Brinkmann Family Photo Collection

Introduction

Christian Karl Brinkmann was the third child of Liborius Friedrich Brinkmann and Henriette (Lange) Brinkmann. Christian was born in 1832 in the Westerberger Glass Factory, in Landkreis, Hildesheim, Niedersachsen, Germany. Christian is this author's *second-great-grandfather*. Christian married Marie Elisabeth (Merker) Brinkmann in 1864, and they had four children (1) Friedrich Ernst August Brinkmann, (2) Louise Auguste Sophie Brinkmann, (3) Mr. Brinkmann, and (4) Karl Friedrich Wilhelm Brinkmann. Christian died about 1906 while living with his son, Karl Friedrich Wilhelm Brinkmann. No death or burial record has been located for Christian.

Written Brinkman Family History, Claim of Nobility

Elsie Louise (Brinkman) Mertig was the *great-great-granddaughter* of Laborious Friedrich Brinkmann. Elsie wrote in her family history that Christian Karl Brinkmann married Marie Elisabeth (Merker) Brinkmann in 1863 and that they had three children (1) Friedrich Ernst August Brinkmann, (2) Louise Auguste Sophie Brinkmann, and (3) Karl Friedrich Wilhelm Brinkmann. Christian and Marie were both born in Germany and lived in Nienburg/Weser, Germany. Elsie's written history states that Christian's father Liborius Friedrich Brinkmann transferred their nobility title of Von Brinkenhausen to a German Army officer around 1837 for some form of compensation so that Liborius could feed his farm laborers and his family during the German wars and famine. As a result, "Christian Karl Von Brinkenhausen's" name changed when he was eight years old to "Christian Karl Brinkmann." This alleged title transfer is said to have occurred while the Von Brinkenhausen family was living on a large estate in Germany. The Von Brinkmann's had been well off financially in the early 1800s, before the wars in Europe and Germany took a toll on their fortune. Elsie also wrote that Christian and his son, Karl Friedrich Wilhelm Brinkmann were both skilled *Glasmachers* (glassmakers) by trade in Germany.

Note: Glassmaking trades are not commonly associated with the descendants of German nobility. Most glassmakers were called "servants" (laborers) of the glass factory in which they worked. However, there was a class of glassmakers that were artisans that made only extremely valuable crystal and glass works of art. These artisans enjoyed great social esteem. As to the claims of nobility, further detailed research needs to be completed to verify whether any of these nobility stories are true. It is common for immigrants to boast unsupported claims of nobility. As of 2014, no evidence of Brinkmann nobility has been documented.

Birth & Baptism, Westerberg, Germany, 1872

In 2011, German researcher Dr. Henrik Weingarten did a search at the State Archives of Bückeburg, Germany, where the church records for the Sülbeck Parish are kept on microfilm in the main Bückeburg archive library. A birth and baptism record was found for Karl Frederick Wilhelm Brinkmann, son of Christian Karl Brinkmann. The record cites Karl Frederick's father, Christian Karl Brinkmann, as being born in Westerberg, Germany. The birth and baptism record contains the following:

-Birth & Baptism Record-

Record Type - Birth & Baptism.
Born Date & Time - June 5, 1872, six o'clock in the evening.
Location - Schierbach Glass Factory, Sülbeck Parish, City of Nienstädt, District of Stadthagen, Niedersachsen (Lower Saxony), Germany.
Birth Name - Karl Friedrich Wilhelm Brinkmann.
Child Number - Fourth Child, third son, first marriage.
Baptized - June 23, 1872, Sülbeck Parish Church.
Parents Residence - Schierbach Glass Factory, Germany.
Father's Name - Christian Carl (Karl) Brinkmann.
Father's Place of Birth - Westerberg, Germany.
Occupation - Glass blower.
Mothers Name - Marie Elisabeth (Merker) Brinkmann, from Ziegenhagen, Germany.
Religion - Reformed Evangelical Lutheran.
Source - Evangelical Lutheran Church-Sülbeck Parish Church Book, 1872, Page: (29), No: (42).

Geographic Search for Westerberg, Germany

A geographic search revealed that two locations in Germany named Westerberg. The first is a township in the larger city of Osnabrück, in Niedersachsen, Germany; referred to as Westerberg, Osnabrück, Germany. The second is a village located near Freden, between Winzenburg and Wetteborn in the Municipality of Landwehr, in the District of Hildesheim, Niedersachsen, in the area once known as the Kingdom of Hanover. The latter is the location where many Brinkmanns lived and worked.

Records Search, Protestant Church Parish of Sülbeck, Germany

In 2011, a search was conducted by the Protestant Church Parish of Sülbeck.[16] The parish of Sülbeck has two office locations: one is in the town of Sülbeck, Germany, and the other is in the town of Nienstädt, Germany. The questions asked were if either of their parish's records mentioned a street named Schierbach, or if there was a town near their parish with the name of Schierbach? Schierbach was the name of a glass factory in the written Brinkmann family history.

Note: The parish churches responded saying they did not know any town or street with the name of Schierbach. However, they did say that the City of Nienstädt, Germany had a historic glass factory named Schierbach and that we should contact the Municipal Office in Nienstädt for further information. At first, this seemed like a dead end. Then, it turned into an incredible find. The Schierbach Glass Factory was discovered shortly after and would prove to hold many Brinkmann stories.

Geographic Name Search, Schierbach, Germany, 1872

In 2011, this author did a search for any German place names of Schierbach. The search for Schierbach began after receiving a birth and baptism record for Christian Karl Brinkmann's son, Karl Friedrich Wilhelm Brinkmann, which listed Schierbach, Germany as Karl's place of birth. At first the search for Schierbach (Schier-Bach) was unsuccessful; the parish name in the above birth certificate was listed Sülbeck, a Lutheran Church Parish in the town of Nienstädt, Germany. A letter was sent to the Mayor of Nienstädt, Rolf Hamening[17] requesting information on the name Schierbach. Mayor Hamening graciously responded, stating that there was once a large and prosperous *glassworks* (glass factory) in the Sülbeck Parish of Nienstädt, Germany.

The Schierbach Glass Factory operated for over 70 years, from 1840 until 1910. It was founded by Herr's Thiemann, Rump, and Bensemann. In 1848, it began producing glass bottles, but only had the right to produce glass bottles in the district of Schaumburg-Lippe. In 1860, the glass factory expanded its territory and added a second facility. The glass factory then bought additional land, located at Kolonat Nr. 12, in Nienstädt, and built more houses for the workers. The Schierbach Glass Factory was then bought by Herr's Rump and Riensch and employed 100 workers. There is a well known street in Nienstädt, called *Schierbach Straße* (Schierbach Road), which is next to two other streets known as *Hüttenstraßein*, and *Hüttenweg*, and are all in the municipality of Nienstädt. As of 2014, the current use of this site is unknown.

In 2011, another research request letter was sent to the Mayor of Nienstädt, Germany requesting further information on the Schierbach Glass Factory. Mayor Hamening returned a detailed copy of an old land survey map of the historic Schierbach Glass Factory. This document was drafted before the factory was built (around 1840). The drawing shows several lodging houses (built during the same period) for the glass factory's workers. One of the original street names on this map is Schierbach, which can still be found today. It is now known that this was where Karl Friedrich Wilhelm Brinkmann was born, and where his parents, Christian Karl Brinkmann and Marie Elisabeth (Merker) Brinkmann, were living and working in 1872.

Note: Christian Karl Brinkmann and his family spent seven years at the Schierbach Glass Factory. There, all four of their children were raised in factory housing on the glass factory site. In the future, it would be interesting to visit the site and photograph it. Working conditions in all the German glass factories at the time were neither safe nor healthy working environments. One might even make some general comparisons of the German glass blowers' culture to that of the American railroad and mining industries during the American Industrial Revolution. Some glass factory workers in Germany were referred to as "servants." Only a few (at progressive glass factories) received housing, schools for their children, food, and medical attention (all provided at no cost by the owners of the glass factory). Glass industry workers were very dependent on the factory owners for their survival. When any worker disobeyed the owners' wishes he could find himself (and his entire family) expelled from their housing, and their children's schools. This occurred all over Germany from the late 1800s through the early 1900s (when glass workers formed unions and went on strike for better wages and working conditions). Many of the workers suffered from respiratory illnesses caused from breathing in the silica dust from the sand and from the fumes generated by the furnaces used to melt the silica into molten glass. This was dangerous labor-intensive work, and one can only assume that there were frequent injuries. On the other hand, many workers and their families enjoyed a reasonable lifestyle, compared to other townspeople, who had no "company store" to provide for them.

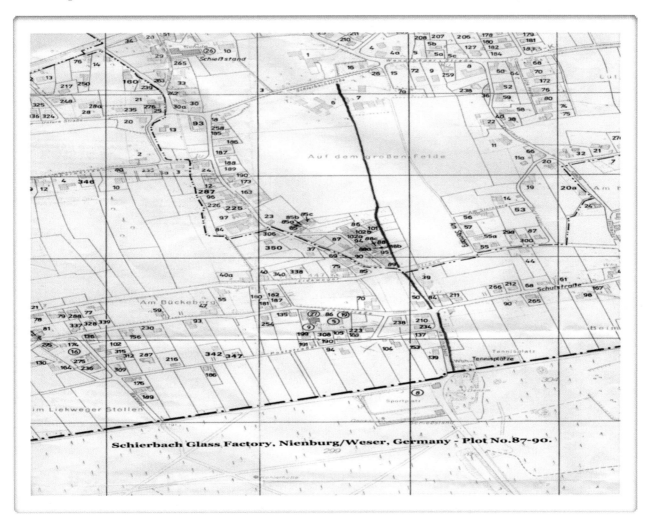

Schierbach Glass Factory plot map, Nienstädt, Germany, c. 1800s
Source: Mayor's Office, City of Nienstädt, Germany

Records Search, Birth Place Location, Wendthrohe, Germany

In 2012, a search was requested at the main Central Evangelical Lutheran Church Archive in Hamburg, Germany [18] for any records of a place called Wendthrohe, Germany, cited in the written Brinkmann family history as a location where Karl Friedrich Wilhelm Brinkmann may have lived and worked. It was thought to be near Hamburg, Germany.

Note: A response email stated that there was no place called Wendthrohe, Germany. Furthermore, the archive does not do searches on request. One must hire someone to go to the archive's library to search through the records. Although this was not initially a very successful search, this national archive would turn out to be a depository of many Evangelical Lutheran Church Parish records in Germany, and is mentioned in later record searches conducted by other researchers in Germany.

Records Search, Municipal Archive, Nienburg/Weser, Germany
In 2011, German researcher Reinhard Balschun did a search at the Nienburg Municipal Archive Depository in the City of Nienburg/Weser, Germany for any birth, death, or municipal registration records for Brinkmann family members. His response letter listed the following:

-Letter Response-
Letter Date - February 2012.
From - Municipal Archive Nienburg/Weser, Germany.
Response - Dear Mr. Brinkman, I searched the municipal archive records for Christian Carl Brinkmann by his surname spelling (Brinkmann) and did not find any records. We only have paper records concerning the registers of birth, marriage and death. Maybe Christian Carl Brinkmann died in another place in the surroundings of Nienburg. Greetings from Nienburg, Reinhard Balschun.

Note: No new records were found in this search, and no death record was found for Christian Karl Brinkmann from the period ten years before or ten years after 1906, Christian Karl Brinkmann supposed year of death, as stated within the written Brinkman family history. It is not clear why no records were found in Nienburg/Weser. However, another search at this location did find a genealogy treasure trove that produced a German Civil Registration Card form for Karl Frederich Wilhelm Brinkmann's family including: birth certificates for Ernestine Hermine (Hildebrandt) Brinkmann, Adolf Carl Christian Brinkmann, and Alwin August Adolf Brinkmann; a marriage certificate for Karl Carl Friedrich Wilhelm Brinkmann and his wife Ernestine Hermine (Hildebrandt) Brinkmann; and a death certificate for Christian Karl Brinkmann's wife, Marie Elisabeth (Merker) Brinkmann. For details of these records, see their corresponding Brinkmann history sections.

Records Search, Archives of the Church of Kurhessen, Waldek, Germany
In 2012, a search request was sent to the Osnabrück Evangelical Lutheran Church Parish Archives for any records related to Christian Karl Brinkmann. No records were forwarded to us, and our search request was referred to the Evangelical Lutheran Church District Office of Kurhessen - Waldek, [19] Germany.

Note: This is the Central Church Office that processes all Osnabrück Parish archive record requests. No records for Christian Karl Brinkmann were found between the years of 1825 and 1935. It is believed that Christian Karl Brinkmann may not have lived in this Westerberg town, or he may have belonged to the Reformed Evangelical Lutheran Church, whose area churches kept separate records.

Record Search, Reformed Lutheran Church of Osnabrück, Germany
In 2012, a search request was sent to the Reformed Lutheran Church, Osnabrück Parish Office [20] for any records related to Christian Karl Brinkmann.

Note: Their response stated that no records for Christian Karl Brinkmann were found. The parish was first established in 1892. Written Brinkmann family history for Christian Karl Brinkmann lists him as being born in 1829 (63 years before the formation of the parish). It is now assumed that this Westerberg, Osnabrück, Germany location is not where Christian Karl Brinkmann was born.

Record Search, Genealogy.net - Kingdom of Hanover, Message Board
In 2012, internet contact was made with the Kingdom of Hannover-German Genealogy Research website [21] and a posting was made asking the site's members if they had any family tree records that include Christian Karl Brinkmann or Marie Elisabeth (Merker) Brinkmann. This search asked for any records from the city of Westerberg, Germany (previously located in the old Kingdom of Hannover). A subsequent search was posted for any records related to Liborius Friedrich Brinkmann and his wife Henriette (Lange) Brinkmann.

Note: The above inquiries appeared on the sites message board and several other postings were made with no success. As of 2014, no positive Brinkmann family connections have been received on this site, and this research is ongoing.

Records Search, Genealogy.net - Lower Saxony, Message Board

In 2012, internet contact was made with the Lower-Saxony, German Genealogy Research website[22] and a posting was made asking the members if they had any family tree records for Christian Karl Brinkmann and Marie Elisabeth (Merker) Brinkmann. This search asked for any records from the city of Westerberg (previously located in Lower Saxony). A subsequent request was made for any records related to Liborius Friedrich Brinkmann and his wife Henriette (Lange) Brinkmann.

Note: The above inquiries appeared on the message board and several other postings were made later with no success. As of 2014, no positive Brinkmann family connections have been received, and this research is ongoing.

Record Search, Evangelical Lutheran Church Parish, Wetteborn, Germany

In 2012, contact was made with German genealogy researcher Gabriele Fricke.[23] Fricke believed that a search for Christian Karl Brinkmann's birth records should be undertaken in an area where an old glass factory was located, known as *Westerberger Glashütte* (Westerberg Glass Factory) in the District of Hildesheim, in Niedersachsen, Germany. The Westerberger *Glashütte* (glassworks) was founded in 1744 and operated for many years. According to Fricke, skilled glass workers often passed their trade down to their sons. Westerberg is not thought to have been an official village, or town in the 1700s, but rather served only to house glass workers from the Westerberger Glass Factory. This Westerberg Glass Factory is just down the road from the villages of the Evangelical Lutheran Church's Wetteborn Parish and the town of Ohlenrode. Fricke searched the Evangelical Lutheran Church Archives in Hannover, Germany[24] and the Evangelical Lutheran Church, Wetteborn Parish[25] (whose parish records go back to the year 1656). Several significant Brinkmann family records were found in this search for a Christian Karl Brinkmann, and other Brinkmann family members (see corresponding Brinkmann History Sections for further details).

Note: The Wetteborn Parish was a significant discovery for Brinkmann family member records, home locations, and previously unknown Brinkmann family members' names. This source will continue to be cited in future searches and records.

Birth & Baptism, Westerberger, Wetteborn Parish, 1832

In 2012, German researcher Gabriele Fricke did a search in the Evangelical Lutheran Church, Wetteborn Parish[26] for any records related to Christian Karl Brinkmann. A birth and baptism record for Christian Karl Brinkmann was found and contains the following:

-Birth & Baptism Record-

Record Type - Birth & Baptism.
Birth Name - Christian Carl (Karl) Brinkmann.
Birth Date - February 13, 1832.
Location of Birth - Westerberger Glass Factory, Germany.
Baptism Date & Place - February 19, 1832, Wetteborn Parish Church, Germany.
Location of Baptism - Evangelical Lutheran Protestant Church, Wetteborn Parish, Germany.
Father - Friedrich Brinkmann, *Schürer* (keeper of the fire) for the glass melting furnace at the Westerberger Glass Factory.
Mother - Henriette (Lange) Brinkmann.
Parents Residence - Westerberger Glass Factory, Wetteborn, Germany.
Godparents - Carl Kaufel, Heinrich Thon, and Friedrich Thon (all living within the Westerberger Glass Factory location).
Source - Evangelical Lutheran Church-Wetteborn Parish Church Book, 1832, Page: (7), No: (2).

Note: We now know that Christian Karl Brinkmann (and his parents) once lived in the small glassblowing factory town of Westerberg, Germany located near the Wetteborn Church Parish. The Wetteborn Parish was the main Evangelical Lutheran Church for several surrounding villages. Christian's family members worshiped at this church. His father, Laborious Friedrich Brinkmann moved his family to this location where he worked at the Westerberger Glass Factory. Christian Karl Brinkmann's birth record was a significant discovery that provided the first known dates for his birth and provided the names for his parents (these conflict with Christian's parents' names as they had been listed in the written Brinkman family history). His birth record has been verified by Christian's marriage record, which gives the details of his birth, and verifies his parents' names. This means that the written Brinkmann family history was incorrect in naming Christian's parents as Mr. Von Brinkenhausen and Louise (Mueller) Von Brinkenhausen. As such, the Brinkmann family record has been modified and corrected.

Records Search, Church Confirmation
During the 1800s church members who were baptized in the Evangelical Lutheran Church were expected to be confirmed by their church parish upon reaching the age of 14. There is no record of Christian Karl Brinkmann's confirmation at the Wetteborn Parish in 1846 (14 years after his birth in 1932). It is possible that he and his parents had moved from the Wetteborn Parish before 1846. As of 2014, the location where this Brinkmann family moved to is unknown.

Records Search, Telephone Book "Brinkmann" Name Search, Ohlenrode, Germany
In 2012, an address was found in a 2012 German public telephone directory for Hans Brinkmann living at Altfelder Bach 2, 31087 Landwehr-Ohlenrode, Germany. This is a small, rural village in the District of Landwehr, Germany. Ohlenrode is near the town of Wetteborn, Germany. The question was is Hans Brinkmann was part of this book's Brinkmann family Line?

Note: In 2012, a letter was sent to Hans Brinkmann asking him if he knew of a Christian Karl Brinkman. As of 2014, no response has been received.

Records Search, Town Website, Ohlenrode, Landwehr, Germany
In 2012, German genealogy researcher Heiko Fahbusch [27] sent this author an email with a web URL address for a local village near Wetteborn, Germany called Ohlenrode, in the District of Landwehr, Germany. [28] This site is great for viewing pictures of what rural life is like in Germany.

Note: In 2012, a letter and email were sent to this source requesting information on any current local Brinkmann family surnames. As of 2014, no response has been received.

Location Search, Schauenstein Glass Factory, Obernkirchen, Bückeberg, Germany
In 2012, a search for Brinkmann surnames around Obernkirchen, Germany was suggested by a person in Germany who responded to a board posting in Hannover. The posting mentioned that a popular and prosperous glass factory, called *Schauenstein Glasshütte* (founded in 1873 by Mr. Heye), was located in the town of Obernkirchen, (which is also near the old Schierbach Glass Factory in Nienstädt, Germany) in the same Sülbeck Church Parish. Obernkirchen is in the District of Schaumburg, Niedersachsen, Germany. It is a small town in the shadows of Bückeberg, Germany, located in a mountain range called the "Weser Uplands." It overlooks the vast lower-lying part of the old county of Schaumburg Lippe (now the District of Schaumburg), in Niedersachsen, Germany.

Note: In the future, a comprehensive search needs to be completed at the above locations for any Brinkmann family glass factory workers. This could turn out to be another location to which the Brinkmann's moved to for work.

Records Search, Evangelical Lutheran Church, Hildesheim District, Germany
In 2012, a search was requested at the Hannover Central Archives by German researcher Gabriel Fricke for any marriage records contained in the Wetteborn Parish Church Book for Christian Karl Brinkmann and Marie Elisabeth (Merker) Brinkmann. This search was unsuccessful. Westerberg was not found to be a village, town, or parish within this church's archive records.

Note: It is uncertain why no connection was found for the above searches. Later searches of the Hannover Central Archives were very successful in finding Brinkmann family records.

Records Search, Latter Day Saints (LDS) Mormon Church, German Records

Some German LDS German record films are available in Germany at local LDS libraries, and some LDS films from other German parishes are not available in Germany (only at the LDS archives in the United States). It seems the German national archives in Hannover allowed the LDS researchers to fully circulate LDS microfilms as they wished. This is different in other German archive libraries (such as the one in Tecklenburg) where the Lotte and Wersen Parish records are not available for circulation. Once ordered, LDS films take two to four weeks to arrive at an LDS library location. There is a charge for each film ordered and for copies of any film item; copies are not always very legible, due to poor penmanship, poor films, or poor photocopies. Many German films listed on the LDS website have notations such as with Wersen: "Access in Germany limited to members of the Church of Jesus Christ of Latter-day Saints. With no circulation to LDS family history centers in Europe including: the United Kingdom, Norway, Sweden, Finland and Iceland." This was imposed by the German archives where the materials were filmed. For details, you can contact either the originating archive or the LDS libraries about why any one batch of records has not been fully released. For example, in Münster (a parish in North Rhine-Westphalia, Germany) they did not want the Mormon Germans baptizing their Catholic ancestors, so if you wanted to use their records you would have to go to Münster.

Note: This is just one more of the many hurdles one has to jump over when doing genealogy research in Germany. There is no easy solution. Just hard work.

LDS Film Record Search, Westfalen, Wersen Parish, Germany

In 2012, a search was conducted using the Latter Day Saints[29] website search engine called "The Family Tree." The following microfiche records were available for viewing:

-LDS Films to View-

Record Type - Latter Day Saints. Family Search.org German microfilms.
Name - Parish Register of Births & Baptisms.
Parish Name & Region-Westfalen, Wersen Parish, Germany. Evangelical Lutheran Church Records.
Years & Film Numbers-1655-1799 (530830), 1799-1818 (530831), 1819-1841 (530832), 1842-1896 (530833).
Summary of Search Results-Several Brinckmann and Brinkmann surname spelling entries were found with no known direct connection to this Brinkman family line. Saved for future referral if future documents are located that refers to these years, and their corresponding names.

Note: The following LDS films need to be read and translated: Nienburg municipally censuses and house lists: 1910-1920; 2267920; address books: 1932-1925, 1903, 1909, 1912, 1939, 1950; 2267916. family registers: (no date, organized by name); lists of citizens: 1685, 1806-1854, 1808-1921; 2267916.

Records Search, Museum of Nienburg, Germany

In 2012, a request was sent to the Nienburg Museum[30] for any information they had on the Schierbach Glass Factory in Nienburg, Germany. A response letter was received stating they had a book that covered the glassblowing industry in Nienburg, Germany and which specifically referred to the Schierbach Glass Factory. The book was ordered and received.

Note: In 2012, the German version of the *Glassmaking History in Nienburg, 100 Year History, 1891-1991* was received and viewed. This is a very interesting and detailed history of the glassmaking industry in Germany. Unfortunately, it is written in German and needs translation.

However, there are great photographs in this book depicting the German glass ware and showing some of the fantastic products the artisans made. Some of the history and many of the glass object featured in this publication are included in this book.

Record Search, Evangelical Lutheran Church of St. Martin, Nienburg, Germany

In 2012, an email request was sent to the Evangelical Lutheran Church of St. Martin, Nienburg, Germany [31] to find out whom to contact for a search of Brinkmann records in the Parish of Nienburg, Germany. An email response was received from St. Martin Parish (Ms. Ulrike John). The only record they found in their search was that of the death record of Marie Elisabeth (Merker) Brinkmann, in 1895. They searched for, but did not find, any birth, death, marriage, or burial records for Christian Carl Brinkmann.

Note: Marie's death record says that, at the time of her death, she was married to Christian Karl Brinkmann It is now believed that Christian was still alive when Marie died. It is now thought that after Marie died, and that Christian moved to a new unknown location in Germany and then died at that location in Germany.

History Search, Glass Blowing History Book, by Hern Klaus Kunze

In 2012, I discovered a book written about the German glassblowing trades in the early part of the 14th through early 18th Centuries. The book, by Herm Klaus Kunze. [32] is called *The Glassmaking Kinship Book*, published in June 2010. A letter was sent to Kunze requesting further information.

Note: Kunze responded stating that his research is focused on glass blowing in Germany from the 1500s until around 1800. However, he did state that the Westerberger Glass Factory was located near what is now the Village of Westerberg, between Winzenburg and Wetteborn in the Municipality of Landwehr, Hildesheim, Niedersachsen, Germany. The Catholic church books at Winzenburg, Germany and the Protestant church books at Westerberg, Germany both mention the Westerberger Glass Factory (founded in 1744). Kunze's research ended in 1829 (the year Christian Karl Brinkmann was born). However, Kunze did say that the Brinkmann surname (before 1800) was not a well-known old glass blower family name in the Werra-Weser Mountain region of Germany. After 1800, the industrial Revolution occurred and large glass factories opened and recruited nontraditional laborers to work as glassmakers. Kunze suggested working backward through the Brinkmann genealogy to trace more ancestors (if they were traditional glass blowers) and then search for their names in his book. If earlier ancestors were located, one could then use Kunze's glassmakers registry to find more about them. As of 2014, this method has not been possible since no such Brinkmann family glassmakers' names have been found within this time-period.

Kunze was also sent a copy of a letter from a Karl Kunze [written to Ernestine Hermine (Hildebrandt) Brinkmann] in 1948, after World War II ended, that stated the dire circumstances of the German economy and his Kunze family's need for American food and money. Karl Kunze's portrait is in the Brinkmann family photograph collection in his German Natzi uniform (before the end of World War II). Karl Kunze was taken prisoner of war, and later released to his family. Karl Kunze is believed to be a close relative of Ernestine Hermine (Hildebrandt) Brinkmann and her spouse Karl Friedrich Wilhelm Brinkmann. As of 2014, Mr. Hern Klaus Kunze has not responded to this question regarding the 1948 letter from Mr. Kunze (possible relative). Some Germans just do not want to reveal their family connections to the World Wars. There is no written Brinkmann family history that lists the Kunze family members by name, but there are several old photos taken in Germany that show several Kunze family members who are definitely related to the Ernestine Hermine (Hildebrandt) Brinkmann family.

Records Search, Evangelical Church of Wersen-Buren, Germany

In 2012, the Reformed Evangelical Lutheran Church of Osnabrück, Germany [33] responded to an inquiry sent to them requesting information regarding several Brinkmann family members. Their reply stated that they did not create their church parish until after Christian Karl Brinkmann was born. However, they did recommend contacting two sources: (1) Kirchenkreis Tecklenburg,

Schulstr. 7, 49525 Lengerich; and (2) Evangelische Kirchengemeinde Wersen-Büren, Tel. 0541 / 8141492; 3. Kirchengemeinde Lotte, Bergstr. 17, 49504 Lotte, Tel. 05404 / 6067.

Note: In 2012, a letter was sent to both sources asking for information regarding any Brinkmanns in their jurisdictions. As of 2014, no responses have been received. Further research needs to be completed regarding these sources.

Records Search, Evangelical Protestant Church Parish of Sülbeck Parish, Germany

In 2012, a search was again requested at the Evangelical Protestant Church Parish of Sülbeck Germany [34] for any parish church records related to Christian Karl Brinkmann and other members of the Brinkmann family. This parish office is in the parish where Christian Karl Brinkmann once worked at the Schierbach Glass Factory. This request asked for the marriage record for Christian Karl Brinkmann and Marie Elisabeth (Merker) Brinkmann. No records were forwarded, and our request was referred to the Municipality of Nienstädt (Jörn Wille-Mayors Office) who sent a response letter advising that our request should be sent to the State Archive of Bückeburg, Germany.

Note: This referral to yet another German agency, and the lack of any real information in their responses, prompted a return request to both offices asking for an explanation of why they did not look for, or find, any Brinkmann records. As of 2014, no responses have been received. It is not unusual to send requests to some sources in Germany and never get a response to that inquiry. Germans are very sensitive about what words one uses in an inquiry and are easily offended, prompting some to simply throw ones inquiry into the trash. I find this very frustrating as an American genealogist trying to navigate both the complex German record keeping systems a the German cultural sensitivities. To be fare, I am sure this feeling must be mutual.

Records Search, Municipal Archive, Nienburg/Weser, Germany

In 2012, another search was requested of the Nienburg Municipal Archive by German researcher Reinhard Balschun in the City of Nienburg/Weser, Germany for the marriage record of Christian Karl Brinkmann and Marie Elisabeth (Merker) Brinkmann (about 1863), and for the birth record for Margaret Martha Marie (Graf) Brinkman (about 1900). The following is Balschum's response:

-Letter Response-
Letter From - Nienburg/Weser Municipal Archive.
Date - July 9. 2012.
Message - I found the birth record for Margarethe Marie Martha (Graf) born on the March 26, 1900. Your marriage record request for Christian Carl Brinkmann and Marie Elisabeth (Merker) Brinkmann is not available in the Municipal Archive of Nienburg/Weser since we only have records beginning in the year 1874. Your request has been sent to the Church Archive of the Parish of Nienburg/Weser for that record.
Signed - Reinhold Balschun.

Note: This search was requested to ensure that any marriage record for Christian Karl Brinkmann and Marie were not missed in previous searches. The search also asked for the birth record of Margarethe Marie Martha (Graf) who was born in Germany, and later married Adolf Carl Christian Brinkmann in the United States.

Marriage Certificate, National Archive of Bückeburg, Germany, 1864

In 2012, a search was conducted at the Municipality of Nienstädt by German researcher Jörn Wille for any records regarding Christian Karl Brinkmann and his wife, Marie Elisabeth (Merker) Brinkmann. The office did not have any records for the dates requested and referred the search to the State Archives of Bückeburg, Germany. [35] A review of previous contacts with the State Archives of Bückeburg (which holds all microfilm records for the Evangelical Lutheran Church Parish, Sülbeck Parish) revealed that, in December 2011, a search request was submitted to the State

Archives of Bückeburg for any records related to Christian Karl Brinkmann, born about 1829 and died about 1873. These records were searched for by German researcher Dr. Hendrik Weingarten, and no records were found. However, Dr. Weingarten did find a baptism and birth record for Christian Karl Brinkmann's son, Karl Friedrich Wilhelm Brinkmann. It identified Karl Friedrich Wilhelm Brinkmann's parents' names and their places of birth. It is important to note that a specific request for the marriage record for Christian Karl Brinkmann and his wife, Marie Elisabeth (Merker) Brinkmann, was not included in the search request from 2011. In July 2012, a new search request was sent to the State Archives of Bückeburg asking for the marriage record for Christian and Marie (between 1862 and 1864). On July 21, 2012, an 1864 marriage record was received from Dr. Weingarten for Christian and Marie. This record was one of the most important finds to date. It not only verified the marriage and birth dates for Christian and Marie, but also named their respective parents. Their parents have also been identified in other newly discovered records from the Wetteborn Parish Church. This German marriage record matched the Wetteborn Parish Church records perfectly. We now know with certainty the names and locations of Christian and Marie's parents, grandparents, and great-grandparents.

Note: Marie Elisabeth (Merker) Brinkmann was 33 years old when she married Christian Karl Brinkmann who was 22 years old. They were married in the Evangelical Lutheran Church, Sülbeck Parish, Germany while Christian worked at the Schierbach Glass Factory in Nienstädt, Germany. This new marriage record was a fantastic discovery and changed everything. It provided the framework for identifying several earlier Brinkmann generations and clarified a great deal of Brinkmann genealogy.

Death Record Search, State Archives, Hamburg, Germany
In 2013, German researcher Tiger Young did a search at the State Archives of Hamburg,[36] Germany for a death record for Christian Karl Brinkmann. The written Brinkmann family history suggests that Christian may have died in Bergedorf, Germany (near Hamburg, Germany) while living with his son, Karl Friedrich Wilhelm Brinkmann. Christian is believed to have died in 1906 at the age of 77. His son, Karl Friedrich Wilhelm Brinkmann's son, Hugo Frank Brinkmann was born in Ottensen, Germany on September 22, 1900. Ottensen is also near Hamburg, Germany. The results of this search were very disappointing. Hamburg wrote back and said they do not conduct any genealogy research for family members, and advised me to contact a German genealogy company that could come into the archive and search for records. The archive representative did say that their microfiche records cover the following record types and record dates:

-Letter Response-
Hamburg State Archives Microfiche Films - Birth, Marriages, Deaths.
Births - 1874 Prussian Records, 1876-1901 German Records.
Marriages - 1874 Prussian Records, 1876-1931 German Civil Records.
Deaths - 1874 Prussian Records, 1876-1981 German Civil Records.
Source - Hamburg State Archive, 2013.

Death Record Search, Bergedorf Civil Registry, Hamburg, Germany
In 2013, a request was sent to the Bergedorf Civil Records Office [37] in Hamburg for a possible 1906 death record for Christian Carl Brinkmann (who is believed to have died in Bergedorf while living with his son Karl Friedrich Wilhelm Brinkmann). A return email message stated that, as of March 2013, the Bergedorf Civil Registry only has the following records available for physical paper record searches: (1) birth records for the last 10 years (ending in 2003), (2) death records for the last 30 years (ending in 1983), and (3) marriage records for the last 80 years (ending in 1930). All other civil registry records are on microfiche and kept at the main archive in Hamburg, Germany.

Note: It is not unusual to have email-based church archive search requests denied in Germany. Many German church archives require that one contract with a German genealogy researcher to visit the archive and search the records. This is frustrating for American genealogists. I know of no common Internet portals to any German archives. Genealogy in Germany is an industry in itself and one needs to be prepared to spend money for results.

Summary
We know that Christian Karl Brinkmann was born in 1832 in the Westerberger glass Factory, in Winzenburg, Landwehr, Hildesheim, Niedersachsen, Germany. In 1864 Christian married Marie Elisabeth (Merker) Brinkmann in the Evangelical Lutheran Church, Sülbeck Parish Church, in Nienstädt, Stadthagen, Niedersachsen, Germany. Christian worked as a *Glasmacher* (glassmaker) at the Schierbach Glass Factory. Between 1865 and 1872 Christian and Marie had four children. In 1872, Christian was still living in Nienstädt and working at the Schierbach Glass Factory as a *Glasbläser* (glass blower). In 1895, Christian was living in Nienburg when his wife Marie died. It is not known where Christian died or where he was buried.

Marie Elisabeth (Merker) Brinkmann, b. 1831, d. 1895

Introduction
Marie Elisabeth (Merker) Brinkmann was born October 16, 1831, in Ziegenhagen, Germany. Marie is this author's *second-great-grandmother*. In 1864, Marie married Christian Karl Brinkmann, and they had four children: (1) Friedrich Ernst August Brinkmann, (2) Louise Auguste Sophie Brinkmann, (3) Mr. Brinkmann, and (4) Karl Friedrich Wilhelm Brinkmann. Marie and Christian were both born in Germany and lived all their lives in various German cities (including Nienburg). Marie died April 7, 1895, in Nienburg/Weser, Germany.

Records Search, Witzenhausen, Germany
In 2012, German researcher Mr. Horst Werner did a search at the Evangelical Lutheran Church, Witzenhausen Parish Archives[38] for any records for Marie Elisabeth (Merker) Brinkmann. Marie's place of birth, Ziegenhagen, is now a part of Witzenhausen, in the District of Werra-Meißner-Kreis, Hesse, Germany. No birth or death records for Marie were found.

Note: The search then focused on the Ziegenhagen Lutheran Parish Church in Marie's birth village of Ziegenhagen, Germany.

Geographic Search, Birth Place, Ziegenhagen, Germany
The birthplace of Marie Elisabeth (Merker) Brinkmann was Ziegenhagen, Germany. Marie and her husband Christian Karl Brinkmann had a son, Karl Friedrich Wilhelm Brinkmann, born June 5, 1831, in a place called Schierbach, Germany. Karl's birth and baptism records list his mother as Marie Elisabeth (Merker) Brinkmann, from Ziegenhagen, Germany. The town of Ziegenhagen also had a large glass factory that was in operation for many years. Most glassmakers communicated with other throughout Germany and were strong mutual trade and union advocates. They often let each other know of job openings in different parts of the country and stayed in touch with each other.

Note: Glassmakers were a tight-knit group. Marie's birth record was the first German record located that established where Marie was born, where she lived, and the name of her spouse.

Birth, Ziegenhagen, Germany, 1831
In 2012, German researcher Peter Heidtmann did a search at the Evangelical Lutheran Church National Archives, Church of Kassel, Germany [39] for a birth record for Marie Elisabeth (Merker). A birth and baptism record was found for Marie in the Ziegenhagen Parish Book. Her birth and baptism record contains the following:

-Birth & Baptism Record-
Record Type - Birth & Baptism.

Child's Name - Marie Elisabeth Merker.
Date and Time of Birth - September 22, 1831, midday at twelve o'clock.
Location - Ziegenhagen Glass Factory, Germany.
Place and Date of Baptism - Evangelical Lutheran Church - Ziegenhagen, October 16, 1831.
Names and Occupation of Parents - Jacob Merker, servant in the glass factory. Jacob's second wife was Friederike (Fiege) Merker.
Source - Evangelical Lutheran Church, Ziegenhagen Parish Church Book, 1831, Page: (9), No: (16).

Note: Marie's surname in this birth record is spelled "Merker," but in the original German birth record the ending letter of "r" was crossed out with a line through it. This correction is thought to have been made at the time of entry. *Merker* and *Merke* are similarly pronounced in German. For unknown reasons, the "r" was crossed out (apparently as an effort to make a pronunciation correction). Several other German surname records spell this surname as Merker. Unless specified; otherwise, Merker is the spelling that is assumed to be correct. Marie's middle name, Elisabeth, is also spelled here as "Elisabet," and her mother, Friederike, is listed as a "second wife" of Jacob Merker (that raises the question of who Marie's mother was. [Friederike, or someone else?] The column rows in this German-scripted handwritten record read from left to right, and the last column at the right is titled "Added Comments" (but in Marie's case it is blank). This comments column often contains interesting details that were not otherwise included (such as spousal deaths, divorces, and other personal details).

Marriage Record Search, Ziegenhagen Church Parish, Germany
In 2012, German researcher Peter Heidtmann did a search of the Ziegenhagen Evangelical Lutheran Church Parish, National Archives, Church of Kassel for a marriage certificate for Marie Elisabeth (Merker) Brinkmann and Christian Karl Brinkmann. In July 2012, a response letter stated that he did not find a marriage record for Christian or Maria with a target date of 1863.

Note: Ziegenhagen is where Marie's birth record was located; it included the names of her parents. It was believed Marie might have married Christian Karl Brinkmann in her family's hometown of Ziegenhagen, but it is now assumed that they married elsewhere.

Records Search, Evangelical Reformed Church of Hannoversch, Münden, Germany
In 2012, a search was requested at the Evangelical Reformed Church of Hannoversch-Münden, Germany for a marriage record for Christian Karl Brinkmann and Marie Elisabeth (Merker) Brinkmann. An 1864 marriage proclamation was found for Christian and Marie. This proclamation was read in the public town square on October 30, 1864, and again on November 6, 1864, and recorded at the Evangelical Reformed Church of Hannoversch-Münden in their Congregation Book.[40] The Hannoversch-Münden Parish is close to the town of Ziegenhagen where Marie Elisabeth (Merker) Brinkmann was born and where her parents lived.

Note: It was believed that there might be other records within this church that could be searched. The Merker and the Brinkmann families may have worshiped there, so other birth, marriage, and death might also be located there. In July 2012, another search was requested and a response was received stating that no additional records were found.

Marriage, Sülbeck Parish, Germany, 1864
In 2012, German researcher Dr. Hendrik Weingarten did a search at the State Archive of Bückeburg, Germany [41] for the marriage record for Christian Karl Brinkmann and Marie Elisabeth (Merker) Brinkmann. A marriage record was found for Christian and Marie dated November 19, 1864, in the Evangelical Lutheran Church, Sülbeck Parish, in Nienstädt, Stadthagen, Niedersachsen, Germany. Marie was 33 years old when she married Christian, who was 32 years old. They were married in the Sülbeck Church Parish. Their marriage record contains the following:

-Marriage Record-

Record Type - Marriage.

Date of Marriage & Location - Thursday, November 19, 1864, at noon. Evangelical Lutheran Church, Sülbeck Parish, Nienstädt, Stadthagen, Niedersachsen, Germany.

Grooms Name, Origin, Occupation & Religion - Bachelor, Christian Carl Brinkmann. Born January 13,1832, Westerberg glass factory. Reformed. Schierbach Glass Factory, Glass Blower.

Confession - Legitimate oldest son of the *Schürmeister* (glass melting master) Friedrich Brinkmann and his spouse Henriette (Lange) Brinkmann, residing at the glass factory in Westerberg, Germany.

Brides Name & Origin & Religion - Virgin, Marie Elisabeth Merker. Born September 22, 1831, Ziegenhagen, Germany. Reformed. Residing in Münden, Germany.

Confession - Legitimate daughter of the *Packmeister* (master packer) Jacob Merker, residing in Ziegenhagen Glass Factory near Witzenhausen, Germany, and the deceased Friederike Ernestine Antoinette (Fiege) Merker.

Marriage Banns: 21, 22, 23, of June in Sülbeck, and 23, 24, 30, November, Münden,Germany.

Time & Place of Marriage: November 19, 1864, in the local church, Thursday at noon.

Source - Evangelical Lutheran Church, Sülbeck Parish, Church Book, 1864, No: (24).

Note: This marriage record was one of the most important findings to date. It not only verified their marriage date (and the birth dates of Christian and Marie), but it also named their parents. Christian and Marie's parents were identified in several newly discovered records at the Westerberger Glass Factory in the Wetteborn Parish Church Book records. This new marriage record was a perfect match to the Wetteborn records and names of these Brinkmann family members. Now, the names and locations of Christian and Marie's parents (including their grandparents and great-grandparents) were confirmed. The "marriage bands" referred to in this record are public announcements read aloud by the monarchs announcers who traveled from town to town proclaiming official news at the local village church or courthouse every Sunday. It is very interesting to compare the way news was delivered to the public in the 1800s compared to today.

Birth & Baptism of Children, Sülbeck Parish Journal, Germany, 1865-1872

In 2012, German researcher Gabriele Fricke did a search at the Evangelical Lutheran Church, Sülbeck Parish, Nienstädt, Stadthagen, Niedersachsen, Germany for any Brinkmann children that may have been born or baptized in the Sülbeck Parish Church. A parish record was returned listing four children of Christian Karl Brinkmann and Marie Elisabeth (Merker) Brinkmann. The parish record contains the following:

-Birth & Baptism Record-

Type of Record - Birth & Baptism.

Date - From 1865 through 1872.

Location - Evangelical Lutheran Church, Sülbeck Parish, Nienstädt, Stadthagen, Niedersachsen (Lower Saxony), Germany.

Name of Citation Record - Personal Journal for Christian Carl (Karl) Brinkmann.

Names of Children & Dates & Places of Birth & Baptism - (1) Friedrich Ernst August Brinkmann born on October 28, 1865, in Nienstädt, Germany and baptized on November 12, 1865, in the Sülbeck Parish Church, Germany; (2) Louise Auguste Sophie Brinkmann born on May 2, 1868, in Nienstädt, Germany and baptized on May 17, 1868, in the Sülbeck Parish Church, Germany; (3) Mr. Brinkman born on February 14, 1871, (died stillborn) in Schierbach Glass Factory; and (4) Karl Friedrich Wilhelm Brinkmann born on June 5, 1872, at the Schierbach Glass Factory, Germany and baptized on June 23, 1872, in the Sülbeck Parish Church, Germany.

Source - Evangelical Lutheran Church, Sülbeck Parish Personal Journal, Nienstädt, Germany.

Note: This means that Christian and Marie had four children during a seven-year period while living in either in Nienstädt or in the nearby Schierbach Glass Factory (both are located in the jurisdiction of the Evangelical Lutheran Church, Sülbeck Parish).

Death Certificate, Nienburg, Germany, 1895
In 2012, German researcher Reinhard Balschun did a search at the Nienburg/Weser Municipal Archive in Germany [42] for Brinkmann death records. A death record was located for Marie Elisabeth (Merker) Brinkmann dated April 7, 1895. Her death record contains the following:

-Death Record-

Type of Record - Death Record.
Date - April 7, 1895, at one o'clock in the afternoon.
Name & Age - Marie Elisabeth Brinkmann, 65 years old. Born in Ziegenhagen, Germany.
Place of Death - Residence at Großer Derkunberger Weg, Nr. 614, Nienburg, Germany.
Spouse of - Christian Carl (Karl) Brinkmann.
Daughter of - Deceased married couple, glass blower Jacob Merker, and Friederike (Fiege) Merker, last residence in Ziegenhagen, Germany.
Place of Registration - Nienburg Municipal Civil Registry reported by grave digger Carl Dorges.
Source - Civil Registry, Nienburg, Germany, Death Record, April 8, 1895, No: (53).

Note: This death record conflicts with the written Brinkman family history, which lists Marie's death year as 1893. Where possible, all records for Marie have been changed to reflect the verified death date of April 7, 1895. This death record also confirms Marie's surname spelling of Merker, which is the surname used in this record. The maiden name of Marie's believed mother is now known to be spelled Fiege. Marie's spouse listed in the record is Christian Karl Brinkmann, confirming both their marriage and the authenticity of the document referring to her as Marie Elisabeth (Merker) Brinkmann.

Written Brinkman Family History, Parental Record
The written Brinkman family history lists Marie's father as August Maerker and her mother as Marie Weit. The name Weit may have been the maiden name for Marie's first mother. The name August may have been the given name for Marie's father (known herein as Jacob Merker). However, Marie's baptism record and death record list her father as Jacob Merker and her mother as Friederike (Fiege) Merker (who is also cited as Jacob's "second wife").

Note: Until proven otherwise, this Brinkmann family history will show Jacob Merker as Marie's father and Friederike Ernestine Antoinette (Fiege) Merker as her mother. More research needs to be completed regarding Marie's parents and siblings, and this search is ongoing.

Written Brinkman Family History, Jacob Mertig's Family
According to the written Brinkman family history, Marie's father was Jacob Mertig (not Jacob Merker). Jacob's brother was Hans Mertig (who owned a large carriage factory that employed 120 men). Although not verified by any records, Hans is said to have been very wealthy and lived in Saxony-Dreschen, Germany. Hans had one sister, who lived in a large castle. Upon Hans's death he willed all his money to his wife, Louise. Hans and Louise had three children, (1) Louise Mertig, (2) Marie Mertig, and (3) Peakcha Mertig.

Note: No records have been located for Hans, or his extended family. It is also unclear why the surname of "Merker" was listed in the Brinkman family history as "Mertig." Further research may reveal more details, and this research is ongoing.

1. Friedrich Ernst August Brinkmann, b. 1865, d. c. 1946

Introduction

In 2012, German researcher Dr. Hendrik Weingarten did a search at the State Archive of Bückeburg, Germany for birth records of the children of Christian Karl Brinkmann in the Municipal Archives, Nienstädt, Schaumburg, Niedersachsen, Germany. A birth and baptism record was discovered for Friedrich Ernst August Brinkmann born October 28, 1865, as the "first child, first son," of Christian Karl Brinkmann and Marie Elisabeth (Merker) Brinkmann. Friedrich is this author's *great-grand-uncle*. August Brinkmann (known in this record as Friedrich Ernst August Brinkmann) married Edith (Erman) Brinkmann in Germany (between 1890 and 1894) and died in 1946 in Germany.

Birth & Baptism, Nienstädt, Germany, 1865

Friedrich Ernst August Brinkmann was born October 28, 1865, in Nienstädt. His birth and baptism records include the following:

-Birth & Baptism Record-

Record Type - Birth & Baptism.

Date & Time of Birth - October 28, 1865, 2:00 in the morning in Nienstädt, Germany.

Name & Number of the Child - Friedrich Ernst August Brinkmann. First child, first son, first marriage.

Date & Place of Baptism - November 12, 1865, Sülbeck Parish Church, Germany.

Father - Christian Carl (Karl) Brinkmann, glass blower from the Westerberger Glass Factory, Reformed.

Mother - Marie Elisabeth (Merker) Brinkmann from Ziegenhagen near Witzenhausen, Reformed.

Parents Residence - House No. 12, Nienstädt, Germany.

Witnesses - Carl Warnik, Carl Merker, Friedrich Brinkmann (all glass blowers in Ziegenhagen, Germany) and Friedrich Brinkmann (absent at the baptism).

Source - Evangelical Lutheran Church - Sülbeck Parish Church Book, 1868, Page: (169), No: (75).

Note: One of the witnesses listed in Friedrich Ernst's birth record is Friedrich Brinkmann, who is thought to be the father of Christian Karl Brinkmann. Friedrich Brinkmann is cited as residing in Ziegenhagen, Germany and working as a glass blower.

Residences, Westerberg, Germany, 1865

Friedrich's 1865 birth and baptism records list both of his parents as being Reformed Evangelicals residing in a house number 12, Nienstädt, Germany, and notes that Christian Karl Brinkmann is from the Westerberg Glass Factory in Westerberg, Germany. Friedrick's mother, Marie Elisabeth (Merker) Brinkmann, is cited as originating from Ziegenhagen, near Witzenhausen, Germany.

Marriage, Children & Death Records Search

Friedrich Ernst August Brinkmann married Edith (Erman) Brinkmann (c. 1890-1994) in Germany. They had three children: (1) Walter Brinkmann, born 1894 in Germany and died 1935 in Germany; (2) Marie Brinkmann, born 1895 in Germany and died on an unknown date; and (3) Paul Brinkmann, born 1906 in Germany and died on an unknown date.

Note: No marriage or death records have been located for Friedrich Ernst August Brinkmann or Edith (Erman) Brinkmann, and there are no records for any of their children.

Introduction

In 2012, German researcher Dr. Hendrik Weingarten did a search at the State Archives of Bückeburg, Germany by for birth records for the children of Christian Karl Brinkmann. A birth record was located for his daughter, Louise Auguste Sophie Brinkmann.

Birth & Baptism Record, Nienstädt, Germany, 1868

Louise Auguste Sophie Brinkmann was born May 2, 1868, in Nienstädt, Schaumburg, Niedersachsen, Germany. Her birth and baptism record includes the following:

-Birth & Baptism Record-

Record Type - Birth & Baptism.

Child's Name - Louise Auguste Sophie Brinkmann. Second child, first daughter, first marriage.

Date & Time of Birth - May 2, 1868, at 5:30 A.M., House 12, Schierbach Factory, Nienstädt, Germany.

Date & Place of Baptism - May 17, 1868, Sülbeck Parish Church, Germany.

Fathers Name, Occupation, Birth Place, Religion - Christian Carl (Karl) Brinkmann, glass blower from the Westerberger Glass Factory, Germany, Reformed Evangelical.

Mothers Name, Birth Place, Religion - Marie Elisabeth (Merker) Brinkmann, Ziegenhagen, Reformed.

Witnesses - Louise Warner from Ziegenhagen, Germany (not married).

Source - Evangelical Lutheran Church - Sülbeck Parish Church Book, 1868, Page: (204), No: (46).

Children, Marriage & Death Records Search

Louise married Karl Micka in Germany and that they had nine children: (1) Hermine Micka, (2) Elizabeth Micka, (3) Elvina Mick, (4) Frieda Micka, (5) Henry Micka, (6) Marie Micka, (7) Paul Micka, (8) Paula Micka, and (9) Rose Micka. No records have been located to verify any members of this family (except the 1868 birth and baptism record for Louise Auguste Sophie Brinkmann).

Note: The search for records, and other information regarding this family member is ongoing.

3. Mr. Brinkmann, b. 1871, d. 1871

Introduction

Mr. Brinkmann is not listed in the written Brinkmann family history. However, Carl Friedrich Wilhelm Brinkmann [the known fourth child of Christian Karl Brinkman and Marie Elisabeth (Merker) Brinkmann] is referred to in Karl Friedrich Wilhelm Brinkmann's German birth certificate as Christian Karl Brinkmann's "fourth child-third son," born in Germany. The written Brinkman family history record only listed two sons and one daughter as being born to Christian and his wife Marie. Mr. Brinkmann is now known to be their child and second son.

Birth & Death, Sülbeck Parish, Germany, 1871

Mr. Brinkmann's 1871 birth record citation from the Evangelical Lutheran Church, Sülbeck Parish, Germany is in a ledger called the *Personal Journal for Christian Karl Brinkman*. Unfortunately, Mr. Brinkmann was "stillborn" on February 14, 1871, and was buried February 14, 1871, in the Evangelical Lutheran Church, Sülbeck Parish Cemetery, Germany.

4. Karl Friedrich Wilhelm Brinkmann, b. 1872, d. 1948
(See the Karl Friedrich Wilhelm Brinkmann History section for further details.)

- End of Section -

Gallery

Christian Karl Brinkmann

Family portrait of Christian Karl Brinkmann and his grandsons. At left is
Adolf Carl Christian Brinkmann, at right is Alwin August Adolf Brinkmann,
Nienburg, Germany, c. 1906
Source: Brinkman Family Photo Collection

Birth & Baptism record, Christian Karl Brinkmann,
February 13, 1832, Westerberger Glass Factory, Westerberg, Germany
Source: Evangelical Lutheran Church, Wetteborn Parish Church Record

Laufende Nummer der Taufen	Geburts-Ort, Straße, Haus-Nummer, Gutsname oder Kolonats-Nummer und dergleichen	Tag und Stunde der Geburt.	Ort und Tag der Taufe.	Geschlecht und Namen des Kindes.
16.	Ziegenhagen Glashütte	Zwei und zwanzigster Octbr. Mittags um 12 Uhr	Ziegenhagen d. 26t. Octbr.	Marie Elisabet Merker
17.	Nummer:	Fünf und zwanzigster Octbr. Abends um 3 Uhr	Ziegenhagen d. 26t. Octbr.	Johann Wilhelm Muehlhause
18.	Nummer: 91	Achtzehnter Octbr. Mittags um 11 Uhr	Ziegenhagen d. 20t. Octbr.	Marie Elisabet Frieke.
1832				
19.	Nummer 41	Zwanzigster Januar Morgens um 1 Uhr	Ziegenhagen d. 22t. Januar	Wilhelm Adam Loebermann
20.	Nummer 3	Drei und zwanzigster Febr. Mittags um fünf Uhr	Ziegenhagen d. 4t. März	Anna Elisabet Buermann.
21.	Glashütte	Achter März Mittags um zwei Uhr	Glashütte d. 6t. März	Justus Krumsieg.
22.	Ziegenberg	Kein und zwanzigster Febr. Abends um halb sieben Uhr	Ziegenberg d. 25t. März	Caroline Wilhelmine Lucie Reichmann.
23.		Drei und zwanzigster März Nachts zwischen eilf und zwölf Uhr.	Ziegenhagen d. 8t. April	Anna Margaretha Buermann.

Birth record for Marie Elisabeth (Merker),
September 22, 1831, Ziegenhagen Glass Factory, Ziegenhagen, Germany
Source: Evangelical Lutheran Church, Ziegenhagen Parish, Ziegenhagen, Germany

233

№	Namen, Stand, Herkunft, Alter, Confession und Wohnort des Bräutigams	Namen, Stand, Herkunft, Alter, Confess und Wohnort der Braut.
22.	Jfr. Johann Friedrich Gottlieb Möser, ehel. [2] Sohn des † Johann Börries Meinhard Möser, Häusling zu Gnauenhausen, und der † Engel Marie Dorothee Eleonore gb. Pape — Glaser...	Jfr. Engel Sophie Caroline Lehrman, ehel. Tochter des Heinrich Wilhelm Lohmann, Häusling zu Bergstall und der † Sophie Wilhelmine zu Gotterhaide — gb. ... 21 ... Luth. — Bergstall
23.	Jfr. Ernst Wilhelm Ludwig Hartmann, Ziegelmaurermann, ehel. Sohn der Engel Marie Hartmann ... gb. ... 28 März 1835 — Luth. ...	Jfr. Friederike Auguste Caroline Vohkening, ehel. [3] des † Bürgermeisters Colons Carl Wilhelm Vohkening N. 12 in ... und der Thelippine Marie gb. Dierkmann — gb. 23 März 1841 — Luth. — ...
24.	Jfr. Christian Carl Brinkmann, Glasmacher, ehel. ältester Sohn des Glasmeisters Friedrich Brinkmann zu Glashütte Westerberg im Gnauenhausen und der Henriette gb. Lange — gb. ... in ... 13 Januar 1832 — reformiert — Steinbach	Jfr. Marie Elisabeth Merker, ehel. [3] Tochter des † ... zu Ziegenhagen ... Jacob Merker und der † Friederike Caroline Antoinette gb. Fiege — gb. ... 1832 ... — reformiert — ...
25.	Carl Friedrich Strackmeier, ..., ehel. [2] Sohn des † ... und ... Wilhelm Strackmeier zu ... und der Wilhelmine Friederike Sophie Schütte — gb. ...	Caroline Sophie Wittenbruch, ..., ehel. [3] Tochter des † Colon Friedrich Gottlieb Wittenbruch N. 36 in ... und der † Catharine

Marriage record for Christian Karl Brinkmann & Marie Elisabeth (Merker) Brinkmann,
November 18, 1864, Sülbeck Parish, Nienstädt, Germany
Source: Evangelical Lutheran Church, Sülbeck Parish, Nienstädt, Germany

Ev.- luth. Kirchengemeinde Sülbeck

Küsterweg 1,   31688 Nienstädt
Tel. 05724 - 84 44   Fax 05724 - 44 90

Personenblatt für Christian Carl Brinkmann

Friedrich Ernst August Brinkmann
geboren am 28. Oktober 1865 in Nienstädt
getauft am 12. November 1865 -Kirche Sülbeck

Louise Auguste Sophie Brinkmann
geboren am 2. Mai 1868 in Nienstädt N.12
getauft am 17. Mai 1868 -Kirche Sülbeck

--------- Brinkmann
totgeb. am 14. Februar 1871 in Schierbach (2. Sohn)

Carl Friedrich Wilhelm Brinkmann
geboren am 5. Juni 1872 in Schierbach
getauft 23. Juni 1872 Kirche Sülbeck

Children's Birth & Baptism Personal Journal Record - 1865 thru 1872.
Christian Karl Brinkmann and Marie Elisabeth (Merker) Brinkmann.
Sülbeck Parish, Nienstädt, Germany.
Source: Evangelical Lutheran Church, Sülbeck Parish, Nienstädt, Germany.

Nr. 53

Nienburg am 8 April 1895.

Vor dem unterzeichneten Standesbeamten erschien heute, der Persönlichkeit nach _____ bekannt,

der Todtengräber Carl Dörges

wohnhaft zu Nienburg

und zeigte an, daß Maria Elisabeth Brinkmann, geborene Merker, Ehefrau des Arbeiters Christian Carl Brinkmann

63 Jahre alt, lutherischer Religion, wohnhaft zu Nienburg, großer Drakenburger Weg No 614 geboren zu Ziegenhagen

Tochter der verstorbenen Eheleute Tagelöhner Jacob Merker und Friedrike geborene Fiege, zuletzt wohnhaft zu Ziegenhagen zu Nienburg in der angegebenen Wohnung

am siebenten ten April des Jahres tausend acht hundert neunzig und fünf nachmittags um ein Uhr verstorben sei. Der Anzeigende erklärte, daß er von dem Todesfall aus eigener Wissenschaft unterrichtet sei.

Vorgelesen, genehmigt und unterschrieben

Carl Dörges

Der Standesbeamte.

[signature]

H. s.

Death Record - Marie Elisabeth (Merker) Brinkmann.
April 7, 1895, Nienburg/Weser, Niedersachsen, Germany.
Source: Nienburg/Weser Municipal Civil Record.

Chapter Six

Endnote Sources

Endnote Sources

[1] **Alvin Brinkman, Jr.**
Address: S499 Kalepp Road, Wonewoc, Wisconsin. 53968.
Email: eagleeyeme@me.com .

[2] **Max Kade Institute for German-American Studies**
Address: University of Wisconsin-Madison; College of Letters & Science, 901 University Bay Drive, Madison, WI 53705.
Phone: 1-608-262-7546.
Web: http://mki.wisc.edu/ .
Contact: Kevin Kurdylo-Librarian.
Email: kkurdylo@wisc.edu .

[3] **Germans From Russia Heritage Collection**
Address: German Russian Heritage Collection; North Dakota State University, Dept. 2080, P.O. Box 6050, Fargo, ND 58108.
Phone: 1-701-231-8416.
Web Address: www.ndsu.edu/grhc .
Contact: Michael Miller.
Email: michael.miller@ndus.edu .

[4] **Society of German Genealogy in Eastern Europe**
Address: SGGEE, Box 905 Stn. M, Calgary, Alberta T2P 236, Canada.
Web: https://www.sggee.org/ .
Contact: Jerry Frank.
Email: franklyspeaking@shaw.ca .

[5] **Donald N. Miller - Author,** *Volhynia-In the Midst of Wolves*
Address: 12814 NW Bishop Road, Hillsboro, OR 97124.
Phone: 1-503-647-5858.
Email: dnmiller@whiz.to
Website: Book location; http://www.volhynia.org/index.html

[6] **Nienburg-Weser Museum, Nienburg, Germany, Author,** *A 100 Year History of Glass Factories in Nienburg, Germany, 1891-1991*
Address: Leinstraße 48 , 31 582 Nienburg, Germany.
Phone: (0 50 21) 1 24 61.
Fax: (0 50 21) 6 23 77.
Email: info@museum-nienburg.de .
Site: http://www.museum-nienburg.de/internet/ .
Contact:Mr. Karl-Ludwig Schlichter, Public Relations and Publications

[7] **Hans-Otto Schneegluth, Author,** *Glassmaking Book in Nienburg, Germany*
Address: Oberes Feld 20, 31608 Marklohe, Germany.

[8] **Catholic Diocese Church Archive of Hildesheim, Winzenburg Parish Church**
Contact: Constanze Runge, Benutzerbetreuung.
Phone: (0 51 21) 307 - 930.
Address: Pfaffenstieg 2, 31134 Hildesheim, Germany.
Email: **constanze.runge@bistum-hildesheim.de** .
Archive: **bistumsarchiv@bistum-hildesheim.de** .

[9] **Tiger C. S. Nicholaas Young - German genealogist.**
Address: Birkenalle 44, 44.1.2, 15232 Frankfurt (Oder), Germany.
Email: germantiger@gmail.com .

[10] **Evangelical Lutheran Church - Freden Parish (source for Wetteborn Parish records).**
Address: Bachstraße 8, 31084 Freden, Germany

[11] **Catholic Church Diocese Archives of Hildesheim, Germany - Bistumsarchiv Hildesheim (source for Mariä Geburt Parish Church Records in Winzenburg, Germany)**
Contact: Constanze Runge, Benutzerbetreuung
Phone: (0 51 21) 307 - 930.
Address: Pfaffenstieg 2, 31134 Hildesheim, Germany.
Email: constanze.runge@bistum-hildesheim.de .
Archive: bistumsarchiv@bistum-hildesheim.de .

[12] **Sabine Schleichert - German genealogist**
Address: Rosa-Aschenbrenner-Bogen 6, D-80797 Muenchen, FR Germany.
Phone: +49-89-14349363
Fax: +49-89-14349364
Web Address: sabine@ggrs.com .

[13] **Ancestry Family Tree website.**
Website address: http://trees.ancestry.com .

[14] **Dr. Sylvia Moehle - German genealogist**
Address: Duestere Strasse 20, 37073 Goettingen, Germany.
Phone: +49-(0)551-770 99 91.
Email: Sylvia.Moehle@t-online.de .

[15] **Jens Thomas Kaufmann - German genealogist**
Registered Genealogist.
Address: Reisweg 10, 38116 Braunschweig, Germany.
Phone: 49-531-2512735.
Website: www.kaufmann-genealogie.de .
Email: Jens-Kaufmann@t-online.de .

[16] **Protestant Church of Sülbeck Parish, Community of Nienstädt, Germany (search for Schierbach and Christian Karl Brinkmann marriage to Marie Elisabeth Merker)**
Sülbeck Parish Office II, Nienstädt, Germany.
Community of Nienstädt.
Address: Sülbeck Road 13, 31-688, Nienstädt, Germany.
Phone: 05724-913836.
Contact: General Office.
Email: samtgemeinde@sg-nienstaedt.de .
Contact: Birgit Bleidißel.
Email: info@gemeinde-niestaedt.de .

[17] **City of Nienstädt, Nienstädt Municipality, Germany (search for Schierbach Glass Factory)**
City Administration Office.
Contact: Mayor - Rolf Hamening.
Address: P.O. BOX 11 63 - 31689 Helpsen, Germany.
Mailing Address: Bahnhofstrabe 7, 31691 Helpsen, Germany.
Phone: (0 57 24) 3 98-10.
Email: samtgemeinde@sg-nienstaedt.de .
Contact: Jörn Wille (Mayors Office)-(Contact for Brinkmann family search).
Email: j.wille@sg-nienstaedt.de .

[18] **Archives of the Church of Hamburg-Ost, Hamburg, Germany (search for Wendthohe)**
Address: Hölertwiete 5, 21073 Hamburg, Germany.
Tel: +49 40 519 000-971
Fax: +49 40 519 000-970
Note: Searches must be done on site at the archive.
Contact: Gerhard Paasch.
Email: g.paasch@kirche-hamburg-ost.de
Internet: www.archiv-hamburg-ost.de

19 Evangelical Church of Kurhessen - Waldek, Germany (Westerberg, Osnabrück Parish Brinkmann search, no records found)
Email: archiv@ekkw.de .
Phone: 0541/94049-415.
Contact: Brigitte Brune, Email: Brigitte.brune@evlk.de .
Lutheran Church District Office Church Registry,
Address: Turmstr. 10-12, 49074, Osnabrück, Germany.
Phone: 0541/94049-415.

20 Reformed Lutheran Church of Osnabrück, Germany (Westerberg, Osnabrück Parish Brinkmann search, no records found)
Email: osnabrueck@reformiert.de .
Contact: Mr. Hartmann, Email: ref.gemeindebuero.os@osnanet.de.

21 Genealogy.net. Kingdom of Hanover, Germany (Genealogy message board)
Email: hannover-l@genealogy.net .
Website: http://list.genealogy.net/mm/listinfo/hannover-l .

22 Genealogy.net. Lower Saxony, Germany (Genealogy message board)
Email sachsen-l@genealogy.net .
Website:http://list.genealogy.net/mm/listinfo/sachsen-l .

23 Ms. Gabriele Fricke (German researcher)
Education Officer, Individual Communication and IT training,
Contact: Ms Gabriele Fricke (Also known as Gaby).
Address: Kleine Heide 11 c • 31515 Wunstorf, Germany.
Email: g_fricke@t-online.de .
Phone: 05031. 90 92 79.
Fax: (05 031) 90 92 59.
Mobile: (0172) 511 36 91.

24 Evangelical Lutheran Church Archive of Hannover, Landeskirchliches Archives in Hannover, Germany (Brinkmann research by Gabriele Fricke)
Note: Church Archive does not do research for records. On site research is required and all records are on microfilm in the archive library and copies must be ordered for records of interest.
Central Reading Room.
Hildeshelmer Str 165-167, D-30173, Hannover, Germany.
Phone: (0511) 9878-555.
Fax: (0511) 9878-660.
Web Site: http://www.kirche-hannover.de/kirchenbuchamt/archivbestand.html .
Web Site: http://www.evlka.de/archiv/lesestellen1.html .
Church Records and Family Search Office.
Landeskirchliches Archive
Goethestr, 27, D-30169, Hannover, Germany.
Phone: 05115/1241-983.
Fax: 0511/1241-770.
Email: archiv@evika.de .

25 Wetteborn Evangelical Lutheran Church Parish (Brinkmann name location)
Church Office of Wetteborn
Address: Mittlere Dorfstr. 831087, Wetteborn, Germany.
Open: thursday 9:00 Uhr 12:00 Uhr.
Note: It is not possible to see the original parish church books. One must make a request for a copy from microfilm records at the main archive depository.

26 Wetteborn Evangelical Lutheran Church Parish (Brinkmann location)
See original footnote.

27 Mr. Heiko Fahlbusch - German Genealogy researcher (posting response to Brinkmann)
Email: heiko@fahlbusch-online.de .

28 Village of Ohlenrode, Landwehr, Germany. (search for Brinkmann's - near Westerberger)
Email: http://www.ohlenrode-landwehr.de/kontakt.php .
Contact: Ursula Nolte,
Address: Altfelder Bach 6, 31087 Landwehr-Ohlenrode, Germany.

29 Latter Day Saints Church (LDS) website search engine (family tree site record search engine and archive library for Brinkman's search)
Site: https://www.familysearch.org/ .

30 Nienburg-Weser Museum, Nienburg, Germany (source for glass blowing history)
Address: Leinstraße 48 , 31 582 Nienburg, Germany.
Phone: (0 50 21) 1 24 61.
Fax: (0 50 21) 6 23 77.
Email: info@museum-nienburg.de .
Site: http://www.museum-nienburg.de/internet/ .
Contact:Mr. Karl-Ludwig Schlichter, Public Relations and Publications.

31 Evangelical Lutheran Church of St. Martin, Nienburg, Germany. (source for Brinkmanns)
Church Office Address: Kirchplatz 3, 31582, Nienburg, Germany.
Church Phone: 0 50 21/91 63 10.
Church Web Site: http://www.martin-nienburg.de/ .
Contact: Office Clerk-Birgit Huettmann.
Email: birgit.huettmann@evlka.de .
Church Office-St. Martin.
Email: kg.martin.nienburg@evlka.de .
Contact: Parish Register Records-Mr. John Ulrike
Email: Ulrike John <udjohn@gmx.de> . (Contact for record searches in St. Martin's Parish Archive.)

32 Herrn Klaus Kunze, Author, *Glass Blowing History*
Address: Lange Street 28, 37170 Uslar, Germany.
Email: genealogie@klauskunze.com .
Site Link: http://klauskunze.com/heikun/os/bursfelderegister.htm .
Phone: 05574-658, 0171-6211075.
Fax: 05571 6327.

33 Evangelical Reformed Church of Osnabrück, Leer, Germany (Westerberg, Osnabrück Parish Brinkmann Search)
Office Address: Church Office,Saarstraße 6, 26789 Leer, Germany.
Church Address: Bergstraße 16, 49076 Osnabrück, Germany.
Email: info@reformiert.de .
Email: osnabrueck@reformiert.de .
Phone: 0491 9198 0,
Fax: 0491 251 9198.
Site: http://reformiert.de/landeskirchenamt.html
Contact: Mr. Hartmann, Email: ref.gemeindebuero.os@osnanet.de .

34 Evangelical Lutheran Church Parish of Sülbeck, Germany (search for marriage of Christian to Marie), (Research by Gaby Fricke)
Local Parish Office.
Note: Requested Search of Parish Baptism and Marriage Book.
Contact: Pastor Hartmut Ahrens.
Email - Pastor: ahrens.family@yahoo.de .
Email - Sülbeck Parish: suelbeck@lksl.de .
Web Site: http://www.kirche-suelbeck.de/ .
Contact: Ms. Klose and Ms. Kleinsorg (Referred to by Pastor Ahrens for research information)
Phone: 05724 - 84 44.
Fax: 05724 - 44 90.

35 State Archives of Bückeburg, Germany. (search for Christian and Marie)
Archive location for the District of Schaumburg, Germany.
Contact: Deputy Director: Dr. Hendrik Weingarten.
Archive Address: Schlossplatz 2, 31675, Bückeburg, Germany.
Web Site: www.nla.niedersachsen.de, http://www.staatsarchive.niedersachsen.de/portal/live.php?navigation_id=24784&article_id=85957&_psmand=187.
Phone: (05 722) 9677-30
Fax: (05 722) 1289
E-mail: Bueckeburg@nla.niedersachsen.de .
Contact: Office Secretary - Martina Knodel.
Email: Martina.Knodel@nla.niedersachsen.de .

[36] **State Archive of Hamburg, Germany (search for Christian & Hugo Brinkmann)**
Archive location for civil records of Ottensen and Bergedorf, (Lower Saxony) Germany.
Address: Kattunbleiche 19, 22041 Hamburg, Germany.
Headquarters Phone: 040-42831-3200.
Site: http://www.hamburg.de/staatsarchiv/ .
Email: poststelle@staatsarchiv.hamburg.de .

[37] **Bergedorf Civil Registry, Hamburg, Germany (search for Christian Carl Brinkmann)**
Cival Registry for birth, death, marriage records for Bergedorf, (Lower Saxony) Germany.
Address: Registry Office, Hamburg-Bergedorf, Wentorfer Straße 30, 21029, Hamburg, Germany.
Phone: 040/42891-3139.
EMAIL: Standesamt@bergedorf.hamburg.de .
EMAIL: julia.sypli@bergedorf.hamburg.de>

[38] **Protestant Church of Witzenhausen, Germany (search for Marie Elisabeth Merker), (no records found)**
Evangelical Lutheran Church of Hesse-Cassel-Waldeck and Witzenhausen, Germany.
Address: Schutzenstr. 6, 37213 Witzenhausen, Germany.
Contact: Mrs. Urike Dean Laakmann.
Email: dekan-witzenhausen@ekkw.de .
Phone: 05542-5953.
Email: Witzenhausen.Gemeindebuero2@ekkw.de .
Witzenhausen Parish Archive Research.
Contact: Katja Frohlich.
Address: Am Brauhaus 5, 37213 Witzenhausen, 05542-910651, Witzenhausen, Germany.
Email: witzenhausen.Gemeindebuero2@ekkw.de .
Contact: Mr. Hern Horst Werner (Archive researcher).
Phone: 05542/3309
Address: Burgstr. 18, 3721, Witzenhausen, Germany.

[39] **National Archives the Church of Kassel, Kassel, Germany. (Search for Marie Merker in Ziegenhagen.)**
Contact: Mr. Peter Heidtmann.
Address: Lessingstr. 15A, 34119 Kassel, Germany.
Email: archiv@ekkw.de .
Phone: 0561/78876-0

[40] **Evangelical Reformed Congregation of Hann-Münden, Germany (search for Merker and Brinkmann families)**
Hann-Münden Congregation.
Pastor - Pastor Ernst-Ulrich Göttges.
Web Address: http://www.hann-muenden.reformiert.de/ .
Email: eugoettges@t-online.de .
Address: Wilhelmstr. 21, 34 346, Hann. Münden, Germany.
Phone: 05541 - 433
Church Location: Burgstr. 8, 34 346, Hann. Münden, Germany.

[41] **Lower Saxony (Niedersachsen) State Archives, State Archives of Bückeburg, Germany (search for Christian and Marie)**
Archive location for the District of Schaumburg, Germany.
Contact: Deputy Director: Dr. Hendrik Weingarten.
Archive Address: Schlossplatz 2, 31675, Bückeburg, Germany.
Web Site: http://www.staatsarchive.niedersachsen.de/portal/live.php?
navigation_id=24784&article_id=85957&_psmand=187 .
Phone: (05 722) 9677-30
Fax: (05 722) 1289
E-mail: Bueckeburg@nla.niedersachsen.de .
Contact: Office Secretary - Martina Knodel.
Email: Martina Knodel <bueckeburg@nla.niedersachsen.de>